# fundamentals
# of
# learning
# and
# motivation

# fundamentals
# of
# learning
# and
# motivation

---

## Frank A. Logan
University of New Mexico

WM. C. BROWN COMPANY PUBLISHERS
Dubuque, Iowa

## Fundamentals of Psychology Series

**General Editor**
Frank A. Logan
University of New Mexico

Copyright © 1969, 1970 by
Wm. C. Brown Company Publishers

ISBN 0–697–06135–3 (Cloth)
ISBN 0–697–06136–1 (Paper)

Library of Congress Catalog Card Number: 78–96325

Second Printing, 1970

Printed in the United States of America

This book is dedicated to my children, Frank and Nancy, and to those thousands of introductory students who, although largely only faces to me, have convinced me that their first exposure to psychology should make contact with the real world as they know it.

# Contents

# Foreword

There is no single, best way to introduce students to as diverse and complex a subject matter as psychology. The special needs and interests of both student and teacher help determine the course content and organization. The Fundamentals of Psychology Series is designed better to enable the approach that I have found to be most effective.

That approach is to restrict the course content to a relatively small number of topics so as to cover them in greater depth than customary. Of course, this implies that other topics are omitted or mentioned in a very cursory manner. But my conviction is that the student is richer for having explored a few topics sufficiently to begin to comprehend the concepts and to appreciate their roles in understanding behavior.

Accordingly, at the same time this series is intended for the beginning student, its goal is to lead him further into each topic than is typical of introductory texts. This very feature may make the series also valuable in more advanced courses where the teacher wants to begin with a review of the fundamentals before proceeding to more specialized content. In either event, we hope the student will find the series interesting and challenging.

Frank A. Logan

# Preface

Psychology should be studied as a living subject matter; indeed, it is the most personal and intimate subject matter in the world. Nothing is quite so close to us as our own behavior, and nothing is quite so important to us as the behavior of others. In this spirit, although the formal vocabulary, the technical details, and the objective procedures used in the experimental analysis of learning and motivation form the heart of this book, these have been introduced with liberal illustrations from the personal experiences of most Americans.

Such illustrations are never so perfect as their laboratory counterparts simply because the natural environment is never so carefully controlled. The purer scientist may therefore be somewhat offended by the liberties I have taken in trying to make these principles of behavior real. With apologies to them, I would argue that there will be time enough for the serious student to sharpen the distinctions in his later studies. (Suggested readings for this purpose are given at the end of the book.)

There is one danger in this approach about which the reader should be forewarned. This is that he will think that psychology is simple, familiar common sense. Common sense has evolved through the generations and is often good sense. But psychology, even in its present infancy, can take you far beyond common sense—and even help correct the misconceptions and fallacies that most people take for granted. The examples given in this book are intended to help give the reader a feel for the subject matter, to help him

translate it into personally meaningful contexts. But mastering the
basic principles of behavior requires serious study and thought.


   It is the style of the author to introduce a topic with relatively
simple statements asserted boldly as being true. Let the reader
beware! Many of the attempts to summarize current knowledge
about behavior as given in this book should be qualified by a
detail here, a nuance there, an exception on one side, an elabo-
ration on the other. The underlying theory suffers many difficulties
that will not be apparent in this presentation. You should know
in advance that such deception is being engaged in.
   The reason for this approach is my strong belief that the most
useful introduction to a complex topic is a coherent oversimpli-
fication. A straight line may not always be the shortest distance
between two points, but that is a good way to begin learning
geometry. In a similar vein, habits may not be entirely permanent,
but that is a proposition that captures one essential idea about
learning and generates a host of important and largely true implications.
   This book does not give a scholarly review of conflicting data,
ideas and theories. (Formal references have been omitted from
the text, but appear in the bibliography.) It is a heavily biased
and selective presentation so as to paint a consistent and integrated picture of the fundamental principles of learning and motivation. This is felt to be a proper beginning—but it is only a
beginning. Psychology is still a scientific infant, and the reader
should not be misled into thinking that we have yet achieved a
very complete understanding of behavior. On the contrary, he
should recognize both the promise and the challenge of psychology.


   Man is an animal. *Homo sapiens* is, to be sure, a unique species
with a number of unusual characteristics, most notable among
which is the ability to talk. It is therefore not surprising that a
complete understanding of the behavior of man must include principles that can be discovered only by studying man himself. There
are species-specific characteristics of all organisms: monkeys can
oppose the thumb and forefinger of their feet; birds can fly.
Understanding any species thus requires, in part, studying that
species. At the same time, however, man shares with many other
animals some basic principles of behavior that are most easily

isolated by studying simpler organisms such as rats, pigeons, and monkeys. This book is based predominantly on research involving such animals, or man in very simple laboratory situations. Only under rigorously controlled conditions of deprivation, stimulation and past history of the organism—controls usually not attainable with humans—can the basic principles be clearly revealed. The purpose of this book is to describe some of these basic principles and to illustrate the ways in which the results of research involving animals contribute to an understanding of human behavior.

At the end of each major chapter is a list of true-false items. Each is immediately followed by a brief discussion leading to the correct answer. These items will be of greatest value to the student if he thinks about the reason for the item as well as its answer *before* reading the following description. Even the student who has studied the chapter carefully may find a few of these items difficult; these are ones that attempt to approach a topic from a somewhat different angle, in order to enrich the student's understanding. Many have been included in an attempt to correct misconceptions that some students retain. They are not exhaustive of all the content of the chapter, and hence should not be relied upon exclusively for review. However, the adequacy with which the student can understand these items should provide a reasonably good indication of how effectively he has studied.

Beginning on page 205 is a glossary containing all of the technical terms defined in this book. Knowing these definitions of terms is only part of knowing their meanings. It is ultimately of greater importance to see the relationships between the terms and to recognize the situations to which they are applicable. For example, "stimulus generalization" is defined as, "the tendency to make a learned response to stimuli that are similar to the original one." But we shall see that this tendency depends importantly on the conditions of learning. Furthermore, racial discrimination will be seen as one consequence of this fundamental principle of behavior. Definitions provide a necessary but inadequate beginning. Hence, the glossary can provide a convenient refresher as the student is developing a more complete understanding.

1 January 1970                                    F. A. Logan

This book has benefited from comments on an early draft by Mrs. John M. Rhodes, Frank A. Logan III, Douglas P. Ferraro, but most especially Louis E. Price whose numerous constructive criticisms can hardly be adequately acknowledged. For fast and excellent preparation of the manuscript, I am indebted to Ilene Bradley, Elna Parks, Jannine Perkins and especially to Eleanor Orth's untiring commitment. Finally, the book could not have been written without extra tolerance at home and in the office.

# Introduction to Learning

The Psychology of Learning is the most important topic in the world. Obviously, that is a gross exaggeration: there are many important topics. Nevertheless, if we want to understand behavior and differences in behavior, the most unique and critical property of living organisms is the capacity to learn.

Language is the principal feature that sets man apart from other animals. Language, however, is learned: talking, writing, reading. In effect, we *learn* to be human. At a higher level, most of our likes, dislikes, attitudes, opinions, beliefs, prejudices, superstitions, and personality characteristics are learned. In effect, we *learn* to be individuals. Our major social dilemmas reflect learning. Mental illness, although sometimes resulting from neurological disorders, is primarily a result of learning maladaptive behaviors and the failure to learn adaptive ones. Poverty, drug-abuse, crime, over-population and even war, while determined by a variety of complex factors, reflect to some extent the learning history of the people involved. Hopefully, an understanding of learning can help contribute to an understanding of such problems.

In this book, we can only explore the most basic, fundamental principles of learning. These have been discovered mainly in the animal laboratory or by studying humans in very simple learning situations. We simply cannot here cover in depth the full range of the Psychology of Learning. Nevertheless, one should learn about learning not only as a formal laboratory science, but also with continual appreciation of the applicability of these basic principles to the everyday behavior of people. For this reason, the technical concepts and principles are freely illustrated with some familiar situations to which they might apply. In doing so, it is assumed that the principal audience is the teacher—not "teacher" in the limited sense of a person who stands before a class, but anyone who at times attempts to affect what an organism learns. In part, this means the student who is attempting to teach himself various subject matters. It also means the parent who is largely responsible for his children's learning to become mature, adjusted adults. It also means employers, ministers, politicians and many others. All of these are, in this sense, teachers.

In short, the goal of this book is to describe the fundamental principles of learning and motivation and to illustrate how these can be useful in understanding (that is, in predicting and controlling) the learning of personally important responses.

## What is Learning?

As with many concepts that are primitive or basic to a discipline, "learning," is not easy to define. The reason for this is that we can never see learning directly; we can't point at it uniquely or study it in isolation. The only thing we can actually study is behavior and we all know that behavior depends on more than learning. Learning is thus hypothetical; something inferred from observations of behavior.

Because of the limitation that we can't isolate learning directly, the most generally acceptable approximation to a definition of learning is this: LEARNING IS A RELATIVELY PERMANENT PROCESS RESULTING FROM PRACTICE AND REFLECTED IN A CHANGE IN PERFORMANCE. This definition at least captures the necessary conditions for one to say that learning has occurred. It must result from *practice*: learning requires that the organism be exposed to the situation and engage in the behavior being studied. We can modify a person's future behavior by other interventions such as surgical removal of certain parts of the body or by the administration of drugs; changes in behavior resulting from such operations do not qualify as learning because they do require practice for their effects.

Furthermore, the effect must be relatively *permanent*. Indeed, there are good reasons to believe that it is completely permanent. At least, it cannot be so temporary that it simply dissipates over a short period of time. Practicing a response may lead to reduced performance due to fatigue, or to increased performance due to improved muscle tonicity, but these are not learning because they are readily lost through rest or disuse. And finally, we infer that learning has occurred only from a *change* in performance. This may be a decrease as well as an increase, since we can learn not to respond just as we can learn to respond.

At this point, it would be valuable if we could answer the question "What is learning?" by turning to the biological bases of learning. What actually happens to the organism when he learns something? This question is being actively researched by physiological psychologists, but at present, the knowledge is too rudimentary to be of much practical value. We believe that learning reflects a real biological change. Almost certainly, the nervous system and especially the brain is involved in the process. It now appears that learning is largely biochemical; a modification of protein molecules within the brain. But until such knowledge has advanced considerably beyond its present stage, it is of greater practical value simply to accept learning as a hypothetical process and talk about it in behavioral terms.

Hence, it is when we observe that practice has produced a more-or-less permanent change in behavior that we infer that learning has occurred. The Psychology of Learning is the scientific study of those procedures that are known to produce such effects and the systematic analysis of the result of exposing organisms to them. As a prelude, it is valuable to explore in greater detail the nature of what is learned.

## What is Learned? An Association.

One difficulty with the student's understanding of a psychological description of learning is revealed in a type of question often asked by beginning students: "Is yawning learned?" Of course, various students pose the same question using other activities, ranging from stuttering to sleeping, sighing to sexing, and scratching to seeing. In essence, this type of question assumes that we can meaningfully divide behaviors into two types: learned and unlearned. This assumption is a hangover from earlier distinctions between nature and nurture. Does intelligence depend on heredity or environment, is insanity inherited or acquired, can learned characteristics be transmitted to one's children biologically?

Psychologists have learned the hard way that such questions are simply not good ones to ask. Untold time and expense has been devoted to attempts to answer such questions and the invariable result has been that, when viewed dispassionately and objectively, behaviors can *not* be placed into two separate categories: those that occur unaffected by environmental influences, and those that depend for their occurrence upon learning. The fact of the matter is that any behavior of an organism is a joint product of both hereditary and environmental influences. The only proper question to ask in this context concerns the relative contribution to that behavior of the two factors. That is, to what extent are *differences* in behavior due to genetic constitution or to experience. It is true that humans learn to talk, but it is equally true that man is the only species physically equipped for language as we know it. No amount of training will teach a rat to talk, and no human will talk a meaningful language unless taught to do so. Man thus differs from other animals in part because he is equipped for language; men also differ from each other in part because of the language they have learned. Both nature and nurture are indispensable.

Hence, one conceptual error implied by the question, "Is yawning learned?" is the notion that behaviors are either instinctive or learned. A second kind of difficulty with the question is the implication that behaviors are learned as such. The fact of the matter is that the psychologist does not mean by "learning" the actual muscular activity involved in a response. That is to say, insofar as practice is important in acquiring the ability to move the muscles of the body, such practice does not fall within the present meaning of "learning." We are aware that you probably cannot wiggle your ears, wrinkle your nose, or spread your toes unless you have deliberately and extensively practiced these movements. Learning in this sense is certainly important, but the psychology of learning assumes that the ability to perform the behavior of interest is already available.

As used here and elsewhere in psychology, learning refers to an *association* between events. To anticipate the discussion in the next section, learning can be viewed as an association between a stimulus and a response. Learning is not in a response itself; it is in the associative connection between a stimulus and a response. Symbolically, learning is in the dashed arrow: S - - → R. You learn when and where to make certain responses, and you learn to put simpler responses together into more complex integrated acts, but you do not learn the muscular movements themselves according to the principles to be described in this book.

Because this distinction is often difficult for students to grasp initially, let us consider a specific and familiar example. Suppose the earlier question had been: "Is talking learned?" Now perhaps no student would ask that question because he thinks that the answer is obviously "yes," but in the sense of the question about yawning, the answer would be "no." As we shall use the term, you do not learn to vocalize, to utter the sounds involved in talking. For reasons not encompassed by the psychology of learning, all infants babble and in the process thereof produce and practice all of the sounds utilized in their language-to-be (plus additional sounds perhaps found in other languages but not later present in their verbal behavior). Why this is so, and how practice affects their subsequent availability, are interesting questions, but not to the psychologist of learning. When he says that talking is learned, he does not mean vocalizing itself. Instead, he means the stringing together of various vocalizations into patterns (words) and the association of these words with the meanings given them by the language system. The word "cat" involves three sounds (phonemes) roughly equivalent to the letters of the word, and the ability to produce those sounds is assumed by the learning psychologist. Learning involves combining these sounds (saying the "c" is associated with saying the "a" which in turn is associated with saying the "t") and this entire chain becomes associated with a physical stimulus, namely a cat. It also becomes discriminated from other stimuli such as dogs and fur coats, and may take on various nuances as when one woman gossips about another. These associations illustrate what is meant by the term "learning."

This is not to deny the importance of stimulus familiarity and response availability. You may recognize a person without recalling any specific associations with him; this indicates *stimulus familiarity*. You may have difficulty learning to speak a foreign language because of the unusual sounds; this requires *response availability*. But the particular learning process with which we will be concerned is *associative*. Our interest is in how you respond to the individual, and when you utter the foreign word, or in general, how prevailing circumstances determine your behavior.

Accordingly, the student asking whether yawning is learned should ask a different question: is yawning a learn*able* response? Yawning may be produced by various states of fatigue and conditions of the body without such associations being acquired through practice; babies yawn without any special training. But yawning may also be a learnable response in the sense that stimuli not initially capable of producing the response can acquire the capacity to do so. For example, you may learn to yawn when others do! The bases for such associative learning and the conditions which motivate the performance of learned responses define the domain of this book.

## What is Learned? Associations among Stimuli and Responses.

Although most psychologists agree that learning can be viewed as an associative process, there is not complete agreement as to the nature of that process. The question is, "What gets associated with what?"

There are a variety of subtle differences in the ways that question has been answered, but these can roughly be grouped into two major alternatives.

One alternative is the S-R or *behaviorist* approach. According to this view, the association that is learned is between a stimulus and a response: the learning represents *an acquired tendency to respond in a particular way when confronted with a particular stimulus situation.* You learn to put on the brake of your car if the stop-light ahead turns red, you raise your hand if the teacher asks a question you think you can answer, you experience fear if called to the Dean's office. These illustrate motor, mental, and emotional responses which you learn to perform in the presence of particular external stimulus events. The behaviorist answer to the question, "What is learned?" is such associations.

The other alternative is the S-S or *cognitive* approach. According to this view, the association that is learned is between stimuli: the learning represents *an acquired tendency to expect the occurrence of particular subsequent events whenever a particular stimulus situation occurs.* In the case of the stop light, this approach holds that you did not learn blindly to apply the brake when the light changed; rather you have learned the meaning of a red light (in this context), that you have learned to expect that an accident or an arrest might result from a failure to stop; and you utilize this knowledge in deciding what to do. The cognitive answer to the question, "What is learned?" is such knowledge.

Traditionally, psychologists have adopted one or the other of these approaches and then attempted to apply it to all forms of learning. This is certainly admirable in the image of parsimony (simplicity), but it has also led to a number of controversies that have turned out to be largely fruitless. For example, after a rat has learned to run through a maze, the S-R theorist believes that he has learned a sequence of left and right turns while the S-S theorist believes that he has learned a cognitive map of the maze including the location of the goal box. The flavor of the controversy can be understood if you reflect on your own behavior in going from one place to another. If you have done so frequently, you will probably realize that you unconsciously tend to take the same path every time. The man leaving his office may head for his usual parking lot even though, that day, the lot may have been full and he had to park elsewhere. The S-R theorist emphasizes such behavior to illustrate that learning is a sequence of responses. Yet you will also realize that, if your familiar path is for some reason blocked, then you can readily chart a new path to your goal. The man, after perhaps a few moments anguish that his car has been stolen, recalls that he parked in a different lot that day and takes off in the appropriate direction. The S-S theorist emphasizes this kind of behavior to illustrate that learning involves spatial and temporal relationships in the environment. Each theorist is hard pressed to account for the behavior emphasized by the other.

For our purposes, it is not necessary to engage in the fine-grain details of such controversies. This book has been written predominantly in the language of the S-R approach. But this is not to deny the possibility and importance of associations among stimuli. For example, when you catch a glimpse of the back of a person's head, you may (correctly or incorrectly) recognize him as a friend and conjure a total image of him including his face. This is called *redintegration*, the tendency to reconstruct an entire complex stimulus upon noticing but a part of it, and illustrates associations among stimuli. Indeed, our discussion of incentive motivation will explicitly take the view that organisms learn to expect rewards and punishments for certain kinds of behavior.

The reason for adopting the S-R language throughout our discussion of the various learning situations is because it is most likely to force the student to think objectively about behavior. The layman's understanding of behavior is already largely cognitive and intuitive; you say you understand another person's behavior when it is something you yourself would do. But we must account for maladaptive behavior as well as adaptive behavior, for stupid behavior as well as intelligent behavior, for bad behavior as well as good behavior. One feature of S-R principles is that they are quite indifferent as to the type of behavior being considered. And if you understand them, S-R principles will also help you when your intuitions fail.

# 2

# The Stimulus

Everyone already knows what a stimulus is. Terms like a light, a tone, a shock, or whatever are part of the natural language as familiar stimulus events. On this basis, one could settle for the following *formal* definition: A STIMULUS IS ANY ADEQUATE CHANGE IN ENERGY FALLING UPON AN APPROPRIATE SENSORY RECEPTOR.

Such a definition is often considered sufficient to get the beginning student past the knotty problem of identifying stimuli. But on reflection, it does not go very far beyond our intuitive, everyday language. A good definition should enable the person to identify stimuli in advance, and the one given above begs the questions of what amount of change is necessary for it to be "adequate" and what sensory receptors are, in fact, "appropriate." In this context, it might be recalled that matadors waved red flags in front of bulls for many years before it was discovered that that species is color-blind! What is adequate for one organism is not necessarily adequate for another and especially in dealing with animals other than man, it would be useful to define a stimulus so that it could be determined in advance. Unfortunately, we can not yet do so, but fortunately, this inability need not preclude further experimental analysis of behavior. We can work within the confines of a *functional* definition: A STIMULUS IS ANY EVENT THAT FUNCTIONS AS SUCH IN THE PRINCIPLES OF BEHAVIOR.

This functional definition is not contradictory to the formal one given earlier; it simply says how we go about, in practice, identifying stimuli. If an event is indeed a stimulus, then it should have the effects that previous studies of behavior have shown to be properties of stimuli. If we encounter a new event and are uncertain as to whether it is, in fact, a stimulus for the organism being studied, then we have to try it out. In doing so, we use well-established principles so that, if it is a stimulus, we will find out that it is. Then, having once proven that the event is a stimulus for that organism, we may presume that it is a stimulus in any other situation which we may wish to study. Although in the beginning this procedure is somewhat circular, it is an effective bootstrap procedure that enables us to determine what events are stimuli for the organism with which we are working. Then we can study the way identified stimuli subsequently affect the behavior of that organism.

For many purposes, there are no problems. We all know that the retina of the eye is the appropriate sensory surface upon which to present changes in illumination, and we all know that the onset of a light in a dim environment is an adequate change for most organisms with normal vision. Those who work with rats also know that they are color-blind and have relatively poor vision for discriminating shapes and contours. Those who work with pigeons also know that they have excellent color vision and quite remarkable distance acuity. These facts first had to be discovered by trying them out. (Incidentally, one can often tell in advance whether a species has color vision: organisms that are themselves physically colorful have evolved color vision as one means of identifying others of the same race—or vice versa. Colorless species, nocturnal ones in particular, are typically color-blind.) Having discovered them, however, we can proceed to use that knowledge in the further analysis of behavior.

## Events that ARE Stimuli

The student is thus left pretty much to his everyday knowledge about the events that are stimuli. For the purposes of understanding the principles to be described in this book, we can stick largely to stimuli about which there is no question. But for successful application of these principles, some events that might not occur at first thought need also to be identified as stimuli. Some of the most important of these are noted in this section.

### Stimulus Trace

Although we commonly refer to events such as a light or a tone as the stimulus, it can quickly be made apparent that this external event is not the actual energy that controls learned behavior. The brain does not see light energy nor hear sound energy. When we say that the eye is the appropriate receptor for light energy, we mean that it is the organ capable of transforming light energy into the neural impulses that are transmitted to the brain and there determine our behavior.

To be effective, a stimulus has to get inside the organism in a form
that can make contact with learned associations.

We shall refer to the stimulus as it occurs within the organism as
the *stimulus trace*. Of greater importance than simply getting the stimulus inside the organism is the assumption that the stimulus trace persists for some period of time after the external energy initiating that
trace has taken place. This assumption is shown graphically in Figure 1.
That is to say, a stimulus need not be physically present in the immediate environment for there to be an active stimulus trace within the
organism that can control behavior. We assume that this stimulus trace
decays progressively with time, providing one basis for making temporal
discriminations.

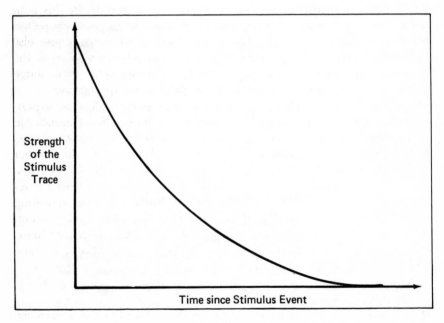

**Figure 1.** Graphic illustration of the assumption that an external
stimulus event initiates a stimulus trace within the organism that persists for some period of time during which it decays progressively.

Suppose, for example, that you were instructed to wait a minute
after a signal before beginning to respond; that you can readily do this
indicates that the stimulus trace of the signal persists within you during
that time. Perhaps a more dramatic experience would be lying half
asleep or otherwise concentrating on something else when you become

aware that the clock is striking an hour. You can typically go back into your nervous system and count the strokes that have already occurred in order to catch up and complete the count to determine what time it is. Each stroke initiated a stimulus trace which, having decayed for different lengths of time, are sufficiently distinctive to count them even though the physical energy is gone and you were not aware of the stimuli at the time of impact.

Similar properties can be shown in animal behavior. Rats are frequently trained in an apparatus containing a small bar which they can press to obtain food. But suppose they only get food when a light comes on, and then only if they wait five seconds before responding. If they press the bar too soon, the light goes out, no food is delivered, and they have to wait until the next trial when the light comes on to have another chance to get food. Rats become very proficient in this situation. With practice, they receive as many as 80% of the possible pellets of food. It is not the onset of the light that elicits the response else they would respond much sooner than five seconds. Instead, it is the trace of the light onset which, decaying over time, helps them judge when five seconds has elapsed and bar pressing is appropriate.

We do not yet know how long traces may persist. In some experimental situations, the duration appears to be only a few seconds; in other cases, the stimulus trace apparently lasts for a half-hour or more. Probably one of the determining factors is the rate at which other stimuli are occurring; a stimulus trace may last longer if it is not disturbed by subsequent input. And humans may prolong traces by reproducing them verbally, much as you do when you keep repeating to yourself a telephone number while waiting to dial it. In any event, it is important to recognize that energy changes in the world are transformed into an internal stimulus trace that may persist for some time after the event itself.

## Stimulus Decreases

When we speak of a stimulus, we generally think of the occurrence or onset of some event. A light shines, a tone sounds, or a touch is applied to the body. If you greet a passerby and he is within normal hearing range, you presume that you have provided a stimulus and may be offended if he fails to return the greeting. In general, we tend to conceive of stimuli as increases in energy.

It is important to recognize that decreases in energy are also effective stimulus events. The sun rising may increase the level of illumination and signal time to get up; but the sun setting decreases the level of illumination and equally well signals time to go to bed or engage in other appropriate night-time activities. In conversing with another person, his words are stimuli to which you respond, but his stopping talking is the cue that it is your turn to talk. The formal definition of a stimulus is stated in terms of stimulus *change* as a reminder that decreases as well as increases in energy are effective.

There is still some controversy as to whether these changes are equally effective. Certainly if the event involves the application of a very intense energy, sufficient to produce pain or discomfort, this will also contribute motivation that helps potentiate responding. There is some evidence to indicate that a comparable effect, although to a lesser degree, is true of all stimulus changes. Other evidence, however, indicates that decreases are as effective as increases. For example, human subjects have been conditioned to blink their eyes either to a small increase or to a small decrease in illumination, and there is no difference between groups of subjects trained in one or the other direction. Furthermore, when the subjects are later tested with a change in the opposite direction from that which had obtained during learning, their performance is essentially unchanged.

It thus seems likely that decreases are as effective as increases, offsets are as effective as comparable onsets—unless the change involves a state which is aversive. Important as this controversy is to the finer details of a theory of behavior, it need not detain the beginning student long. It is sufficient to recall that changes in both directions may function as stimuli in the principles of learning.

### Relationships

Organisms can respond not only to single, isolated events that fall upon an appropriate receptor; relationships among such events also qualify as stimuli. Relationships include those properties that require two or more events for their identification: being to the left of, being brighter than, being later in time, etc. Relationships are not point-at-able as a property of a single event but they nevertheless function as stimuli in the control of behavior.

One illustration of this fact is the "oddity" problem. A monkey, for example, is shown three objects, two of which are identical and the other different; a raisin is under the odd object. The objects are changed from trial to trial, and the odd object is randomly placed in any of the three possible positions. Sometimes an object is odd in one problem that, in other problems, is matched by a similar object and another one is the odd one. Monkeys solve such problems quite readily, just as have people who have played "odd man" tossing coins. Oddity is not a property of the object itself; it is a relationship to other objects that gains control over the behavior.

Although this fact is probably obvious once it is pointed out, students often forget the stimulus value of relationships when attempting to apply the principles of behavior. Or conversely, they may incorrectly assume such stimulus value when it has not been explicitly trained. You may prefer to converse with a particular person when he is in one group of people but not when he is in another group. That person may or may not detect the significance of your choice behavior.

### Context

The role of relationships as stimuli in controlling behavior can be made more specific by noting the role of contextual cues in the environment. A stimulus may occur, but it always occurs in some context. The effective stimulus is, in fact, the total stimulus complex. That is to say, if you learn to respond to a particular stimulus in a particular situation, that learning is somewhat specific to that situation.

This fact can be illustrated by a study with rats in an apparatus that involved a central startbox leading to two circular paths running around either to the left or to the right to the same goal box. The maze was shaped like a figure eight, the rat starting in the center and returning for a pellet of food. In each path, however, was a choice point exposing two doors, one black and the other white. Whichever door the rat went through, it led on to the remainder of the same path back to the goal box, but food was given in the goal box only if the rat went through (say) the black door regardless of which side of the choice point it was on. We shall see in a later chapter that this is a relatively simple discrimination problem.

Some rats were first trained to always run around the right path and others to always run around the left path. Some were trained to go through the white door, others the black door. All, however, mastered their problem in whichever location they were trained. The observation of interest was when trained rats were for the first time run in the opposite direction so that they encountered the black-white choice in a new location. Virtually none of them knew what to do! Indeed, it took almost half as many trials as required to learn the original discrimination to relearn the same discrimination in a new location. They had learned to choose (say) black in one context, but this learning only imperfectly transferred to another quite similar context.

Accordingly, when discussing a stimulus that elicits a response, it is important to recognize that the actual controlling event includes the entire situation in which that stimulus occurs. What a student learns from a lecture is partly restricted to the lecture hall itself; he will probably do more poorly if he takes an examination over the material in another room. What a student learns from studying is partly restricted to the context in which he studies; he will do more poorly on an examination over material he studied in his room because the examination is given in a regular classroom. (This is why students should be advised to arrange their study environment to be as similar as possible to the classroom environment.) The pianist may perform a piece perfectly in a practice room, but make mistakes when playing in a studio. (This is why performers should practice sometimes in the recital hall.) In short, learning always occurs in a stimulus context and is only partly controlled by the specific stimulus events that occur in that context. The same events in a different context may elicit quite different behavior.

Such a result can be deliberately trained. A dog can be conditioned to salivate when he hears a tone in one room of the laboratory, and to flex his leg when he hears the same tone in another room. Similarly, you may learn to use a knife and fork when others are dining with you but to use your fingers if eating alone. In general, the context is a stimulus and an important determinant of the response to more specific aspects of the stimulus complex.

**Feedback**

Responses produce stimuli. When you talk, you hear yourself talking; when you move your arm, you feel yourself move your arm and, if it comes in contact with something, you feel it. Stimuli produced by responses are called *feedback stimuli* because part of the consequences of those responses are fed back into the nervous system and, effectively, tell the organism what he is doing. Perhaps some responses produce very little in the way of distinctive feedback; unless profuse as in situations of sickness or anxiety, you may not be aware of salivating more-or-less continuously. But there are many instances in which feedback is vital to an understanding of behavior.

One rather dramatic illustration of the importance of feedback is the experimental situation in which auditory feedback from talking is delayed. A person talks into a microphone which records his voice on a tape recorder; his recorded voice is replayed after only a fraction of a second delay into earphones which effectively shield his ears from other sounds. He is then simply instructed to try to read some material out loud. The finding is that his reading ability is very materially affected: he reads in bursts, stutters, and talks louder and louder as if to drown out the feedback that is disturbing his performance. The fact is that we cannot normally talk without hearing ourselves talk, and if this feedback is distorted then our speech is also distorted. In well-practiced skills, we are unaware of the use of feedback; it has become automatic but its importance is inestimable. Walking, for example, requires that the person know where his feet are at each instant in order to make the next appropriate movement. People afflicted with tabes dorsalis, which involves a loss of sensory feedback from the muscles of the legs, are unable to walk, not because of lack of physical strength but because they don't know what they are doing.

It is necessary to distinguish between two effects of feedback: positive and negative. When applied to behavior, these adjectives often seem reversed. We are here talking about the *effects* of feedback and not whether those effects are pleasant or unpleasant.

*Positive feedback* refers to instances in which the effect of the feedback is to further increase the event itself. It, in effect, feeds back upon itself to produce more of the same. A simple physical example is when a microphone is placed before a loud speaker which is connected to an amplifier. In this arrangement, any noise that gets into the system is amplified and fed into the speaker; a portion of this output is fed back into the microphone which pushes it through the amplifier and out again to the speaker; this louder noise repeats the circuit getting still louder, and so on until the system has reached the limit of its capacity. The loud screech when performers inadvertently get their microphone on line with the loud speaker is the familiar result. A simple case of positive feedback in your behavior is scratching an itch; doing so increases the itch leading to more scratching, hence more itch, and so on until you are aware that it is becoming painful and try some other relief. Similarly, starting to eat peanuts or popcorn increases the tendency to continue eating. In a behavioral context, when the effect of some response leads to an increase in that very response, it is called positive feedback. Mild forms of aggression may culminate in fighting because of the positive feedback that each person's behavior produces from the other person.

*Negative feedback* refers to situations in which the effect of the feedback is to reduce the event producing the feedback. It provides a kind of error-detection-correction mechanism. A familiar example in physical science is the guided missile homing on a jet airplane. Such missiles are guided by heat from their target; whenever the feedback indicates that the missile is off target, the guidance system of the missile corrects the error and aims toward the target. In quite similar fashion, behavior is often guided by negative feedback. When you observe that your speedometer is above the speed limit, especially if you see a policeman in your rearview mirror, you decelerate your car. The speedometer tells you what you are doing, and when it is in error, you respond to correct it. At a simpler level, when you hear yourself talking too loudly, you soften your voice; when you feel yourself falling, you try to regain your balance.

The confusion that arises from these two labels is that, when applied to behavior, positive feedback is often undesirable and negative feedback is often beneficial—quite the opposite of what the terms might suggest. This confusion is compounded by an easy misinterpretation in the context of knowledge of results: being told you are right is positive feedback because it increases the tendency to repeat your response and not because the feedback is pleasant; being told you are wrong is negative feedback because it reduces the tendency to make the response and not because the feedback is unpleasant. The labels are neutral with respect to the desirability of the behavior or the pleasantness of the feedback itself. Positive feedback produces more of it and negative feedback produces less of it. In either case, one important determinant of our behavior is the feedback resulting from what we are doing.

## Events that are NOT Stimuli

The range of physical energies in nature greatly exceeds those to which our receptors are responsive. For example, our eyes can respond to light waves ranging between 360 and 750 millimicrons in length (a millimicron is one millionth of a millimeter); but "light" rays may be as short as a millionth of a millimicron and up to as long as a million miles. Similarly, our ears can hear sound waves as high as fifteen to twenty thousand cycles a second, but much higher frequencies are possible, and audible to some animals. And even within the appropriate ranges, a change in energy may be too small for us to detect it. Thus, we are not aware of everything that goes on in the world.

By and large, these limitations are not of great behavioral significance. Most sources of light produce waves within the visible spectrum, and although excessive exposure to longer or shorter waves may burn our skin or damage other organs of the body, these dangers are usually relatively minor. The student of learning must be aware of the limitations of our sensory equipment, however, since only events that arouse a receptor can serve as stimuli in controlling behavior.

### Sensory Adaptation

A stimulus is not simply an energy playing upon a receptor—it is a change in energy. If an energy change occurs and the new level persists, we gradually become unaware of the new level as an effective stimulus. This process is called *sensory adaptation.*

Familiar experiences of sensory adaptation are numerous. When you enter a dark movie theater from the daylight, you can at first see only the screen; in time, your eyes adapt and you can determine where there is an empty seat. The reverse process occurs when you leave the theater. When you jump into a swimming pool, the water may at first feel cold; in time, you adapt and may tempt others by saying that the water's fine. You are aware of the watch on your wrist for only a few moments after putting it on. In general, all of our sensory systems adapt to the continued application of energy.

Sensory adaptation is a purely physiological affair; a receptor transmits impulses to the brain whenever there is a change in energy and these diminish over time. By and large, this is an adaptive feature of such systems. If an energy change occurs and nothing is done about it by the organism, it is probably harmless or at least uncontrollable. Better, then, that the organism not be further distracted by that energy while responding to other events in his environment. This process is of interest to the student of learning because associations are formed only with effective stimuli, and persisting energies simply do not qualify after a while.

As an example with which you are familiar, consider body odor. You may be offended by a person sitting beside you and wonder how he can stand himself. Our sense of smell adapts quickly; the housewife may ask her returning husband how dinner smells because she has been in the kitchen all the time and cannot smell it. So too with persisting odors of the body. We probably over-invest in deodorants, lotions and perfumes because we know that such odors can arise and we will not ourselves be aware of them.

### Receptor-orienting Acts

Potential changes in energy may not be stimuli because the receptors are not oriented toward them. Childish superstitions notwithstanding, teachers do not have eyes in the back of their heads and light energies that do not fall upon the eyes are not stimuli. When an organism orients his receptors so as to observe energy changes of possible relevance to his behavior, we refer to *receptor-orienting acts.*

Receptor-orienting acts are most obvious in the case of vision, and some unlearned tendencies may exist. If a light flashes within our peripheral vision, we are more-or-less reflexively inclined to reorient our eyes to bring that light source into the center of the visual field for clarity. Receptor-orienting acts, however, may also be learned. We learn to glance into the other traffic lane before moving into it in order to expose ourselves to the possibility of another car already being there. An animal learning a discrimination problem in the laboratory may learn to look at that portion of the stimulus containing the relevant cues before deciding what to do. In such cases, failure to learn the receptor-orienting act results in failure to solve the problem. Many children learning to read have difficulty discriminating the letters of the alphabet because they fail to orient their eyes toward the most distinguishing features of the letters.

Receptor-orienting acts apply to all sensory modalities, although they are least important in the case of hearing. You may see a dog cock his ears better to detect a distant sound, but by and large, sound energy affects us regardless of its direction. Discriminating between tastes requires that the substances be placed on the tongue. The woman ironing may wet her finger and pat the iron to test its temperature. The cabinet maker may run his fingers along the wood to test its smoothness. An event is a stimulus only if an appropriate receptor is oriented toward it.

Receptor-orienting acts typically have no particular value in their own right. Perhaps the man orienting his eyes toward a beautiful woman receives a pleasant and stimulating experience, but in general, rewarding events are not directly dependent upon such responses. Their value, instead, is indirect. They enable us to receive potential energies in the environment which then guide us toward our goals. And in applying the principles of learning, we may have to train appropriate receptor-orienting acts, or at least we can not presume that we have actually presented a stimulus unless we are assured that the organism has his receptors oriented so as to receive them.

### Attention

Our receptors are continually being bombarded by a large number of energy changes adequate to be stimuli. Although the process is still not well understood, it is apparent to us intuitively and is increasingly being demanded by experimental data, that organisms selectively attend to certain aspects of this total stimulus complex. You may be only vaguely aware of a conversation taking place in another section of a party, but can direct your attention to that conversation if you believe something of interest to you is being said there.

There may be unlearned tendencies to attend to certain stimuli. In general, for example, size and intensity attract our attention. When looking at the evening sky, you may be attracted to the largest, brightest stars. When listening to an orchestra, you may be attracted by the loudest sounds being played. But attention is also learnable. After studying astronomy, you might be more interested in looking for constellations of stars regardless of their brightness. After studying music, you might be more interested in the counterpoint being played more softly than the melody. Attention is very much like a receptor-orienting act except that it does not necessarily involve an overt, observable response. But people can learn to attend to specific aspects of the total stimulus complex.

One kind of experimental data strongly suggestive of such a process in rats was obtained in a bar-pressing situation. In a control condition, the rats occasionally received a high-pitch tone paired at the same time with the onset of a light; on other occasions, they heard a low-pitch tone paired with the same light. Regardless of which compound stimulus occurred, bar pressing was rewarded with a pellet of food half of the time. We shall see later that animals will respond readily when a response is rewarded on only part of the trials and so in this study, the rats quickly learned to respond to both stimulus events (and not to respond in their absence when responding was never rewarded). The observation of interest was when the rats were then tested to each element of the compounds separately: the high tone, the low tone and the light. In general, they responded to each of these events when presented alone. This result was expected since, in preliminary work, the brightness of the light was adjusted so that it was more-or-less equivalent in its "attention value" to the tones.

The experimental group received the same pattern of stimulation during training: half the time high-tone-plus-light, half the time low-tone-plus-light. The reward, however, was scheduled differently. For them, responding when (say) the high-tone-plus-light occurred was rewarded while responding when the low-tone-plus-light occurred was not rewarded. Accordingly, they could and did learn a discrimination based on the pitch of the tone, responding only when the rewarded stimulus compound occurred. The important finding was that when these animals were tested with the light alone, they did not respond to it. Recognize that, from the point of view of the light, this group had the same experience as the control group; for both, half of the time that the light came on, responding was rewarded. But in the experimental group, the tone conveyed more information than the light about whether or not to respond, and the rats apparently learned to attend to the pitch of the tone and to disregard the light.

It should be apparent that the process of attention further complicates the applications of principles of learning. We may say that learning is an association of a response with a stimulus. But the stimuli that may gain the greatest control over the response are those to which the organism is oriented and, within those, the ones to which he is attending. The organism may fail to learn if he does not attend to the relevant stimuli.

## The Emotional Value of Stimuli

Stimuli vary in their emotional value to the organism: some are pleasant and some are unpleasant. We can conceptualize a continuum of attractiveness. Considering meats, for example, you might find a juicy steak extremely attractive, chicken moderately good, hamburger more or less neutral, salmon distasteful but edible, and rattlesnake meat completely unacceptable. Clearly, we like some stimulus events, are indifferent to others, and dislike still others.

When we use the word *stimulus* (S) without a modifier, it is one we believe to be neutral for the organism. Lights and sounds of various kinds generally have no unlearned emotional significance to organisms. We shall use a number of more-or-less equivalent terms for *emotionally-positive stimuli* (em+S): pleasant, satisfying, rewarding, attractive, desirable. And we shall also use several terms for *emotionally-negative stimuli* (em−S): noxious, aversive, unpleasant, undesirable. Examples of the former are food, water, erotic stimulation and the like; examples of the latter are physical blows, electric shock, and various other painful events.

In a later part, we shall discuss the procedures used to determine whether stimuli have unlearned emotional significance for the organism. We shall also show how originally neutral stimuli may acquire emotional value as a result of learning. For the time being, however, we shall rest the case on your personal familiarity with the fact that some stimulus events are desirable, some are undesirable, and that our own experiences provide a pretty good guide as to which is which.

## Stimulus Satiation

The process of sensory adaptation is a physiological one leading to reduced sensitivity to persisting stimulus energies. A somewhat similar process can occur behaviorally. *Stimulus satiation* refers to the fact that repeated exposure to a stimulus temporarily reduces its attractiveness. An emotionally positive stimulus may lose some of its attractiveness as a result of overexposure, and a neutral stimulus may become somewhat aversive if it persists. These effects are temporary but important to an understanding of the stimulus.

Although the behavior of adolescents may appear contradictory, we generally do not like to listen to the same piece of music over and over again, no matter how much we like it. Although we may flatter the cook by saying we could eat that same meal every night, we actually prefer some variety over time. We may study a landscape for a long time, but we also like an occasional change of scenery. Whatever the nature of the stimulus, we appreciate it more if we are exposed to it in moderation.

A comparable phenomenon can be demonstrated in rats. The apparatus is a T-shaped maze (see Figure 2) in which the lower stem is grey and one of the arms is white while the other is black. The rats are first placed for a while in one or the other of the arms. It makes little difference whether, during this time, food is present or not; the rat is simply exposed to that arm. The rat is then placed in the grey stem of the T and allowed to run to the choice point and turn into either arm he prefers. Virtually all rats choose the arm opposite to that to which they have been exposed. They presumably become satiated on looking at (say) the white during the exposure period and hence prefer to enter the black arm.

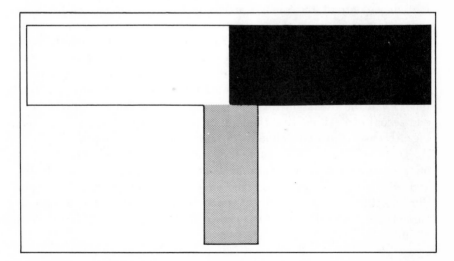

**Figure 2.** Floor plan of a T-shaped maze used to study stimulus satiation. The left arm is white and the right arm black. Both are approached from the lower gray stem.

A number of variations of this type of experiment have been con-
ducted, with the overall pattern of results consistent with the notion
that organisms *satiate* on stimuli. In everyday language, it might be
called boredom. These studies have not yet given a clear picture of the
basis for this process but we nevertheless need to recognize it in studying learning. If, for example, we were trying to train a naive rat to
turn to the right to get food in the maze in Figure 2, and he happened
to do so on the first trial, we might think that reward would make
him more likely to turn right on the second trial. If we run that trial
right away, however, he may turn left because of stimulus satiation on
the right arm of the maze.

Accordingly, not only do persisting stimuli lose their effectiveness as
stimuli as a result of physiological sensory adaptation, they also lose
their attractiveness as a result of psychological stimulus satiation. The
attention of an audience is never maintained by the drone of a mono-
logue no matter how interested the speaker may be in the subject matter. Television shows lose popularity if they repeatedly provide the
same format. Some people tire of church because they see the same
old minister standing behind the same old Bible saying essentially the
same old words—anyone would get bored no matter how religious he
might be. It is well known that children quickly tire of school. There
are certainly a number of reasons for this, but one obvious factor is
that they confront the same teachers in the same rooms at the same
time day after day.

This can happen at home. Married couples not infrequently settle
into such a routine existence together that they become bored with
each other. They arise at a regular hour, chart their path through the
day, read or watch television after dinner and retire at the appointed
time. Even the breaks in this routine, such as the Saturday-night party
and sexual expression have themselves become so routine as to be boring. Absence then may indeed make the heart grow fonder!

This is not to say that some degree of regularity and consistency in
one's environment is undersirable. Quite on the contrary, an effective
and efficient life requires that the environment be consistent and predictable. But we also become bored with the world if it is always invariant and perfectly repetitive. Hence the saying, "variety is the spice
of life."

### True-False Items: The Stimulus

1. Psychologists have not been able to define stimuli so as to identify
them in advance.

(Although we know that a stimulus must entail an adequate energy change falling upon a suitable receptor, we have no way of identifying these except by trying them out. True.)

2. The stimulus trace is hypothetical.

(Although we know that a stimulus may continue to exert control over behavior for some time after it occurs, the mechanism of this is not directly observable. Hence, the trace is hypothetical. True.)

3. Visual stimulus traces persist longer than other sensory modalities.

(There is no evidence concerning the persistence of traces as regards which modality they involve. To date, there is no reason to believe that there are significant differences among the senses. False.)

4. Turning off the lights is stimulating.

(Not only are increases in energy effective as stimuli, so are decreases. Turning off the lights thus comprises a change in energy that constitutes a stimulus event. True.)

5. You would be more likely to remember the names of your high school friends at a reunion than if you met them again individually.

(The faces of other high school friends constitute a background context to which part of your learning their names is associated. Hence, a reunion reestablishes more of the original context and facilitates memory. True.)

6. Well-learned skills, once started, run off without the need for feedback.

(During the early learning of behavior chains, we may have to consciously attend to the feedback in guiding the next response; once well learned, these become unconscious. Nevertheless, the feedback stimuli remain essential in guiding the chain toward its goal. False.)

7. Positive feedback is desirable; negative feedback undesirable.

(The adjectives positive and negative in this context have no bearing on the desirability of the feedback. Positive leads to more of the same, negative to less, regardless of whether these are adaptive. False.)

8. Since we fail to detect persisting odors but continue to see persisting lights, sensory adaptation does not apply to vision.

(Adaptation applies to all sensory modalities including vision. The reason we are unaware of this principle in vision is that the eye, apart from normal glancing around, vibrates back and forth at a rate of 50 to 60 vibrations a second, constantly exposing unadapted receptors to what we are looking at. If an image is stabilized on the retina, it disappears. False.)

9. Sticking your toe into a pool to test its temperature before diving in would illustrate a receptor-orienting act.

(Receptor-orienting acts bring the receptors into contact with stimuli. Temperature receptors are located in the skin and must be exposed to the water. True.)

10. Attention is a learnable response.

(Attention may be reflexively attracted to particular aspects of the environment, but it is also a learnable response in that we can learn to attend to particular features of the environment. True.)

11. An event must have positive or negative emotional value to be a stimulus.

(Stimuli may be arrayed in terms of their emotional value, from negative to positive. But a large number of events are emotionally-neutral yet serve as effective stimuli to which responses may be associated. False.)

12. Repetitive stimulation is undesirable; continual variety is essential.

(Although organisms become bored with repetitive stimulation, some degree of constancy and reliability is probably essential. The principle of stimulus satiation says only that some degree of variety is desirable. False.)

# 3

# The Response

The term "response" is familiar in everyday language. We say that a student responds to a teacher's question, that a friend has not yet responded to a letter, that a militant group may or may not respond to its leader's plea for order. The psychologist uses the term somewhat more broadly than customary: A RESPONSE IS ANY GLANDULAR SECRETION, MUSCULAR ACTION, OR OTHER OBJECTIVELY IDENTIFIABLE ASPECT OF THE BEHAVIOR OF AN ORGANISM.

The critical component of that definition is the requirement that a response be objectively identifiable. The importance of this can be seen in common experience. You may have been stopped by a policeman for failing to stop at a stop sign or for going through a red light and dispute with him whether you did or did not make the response in question. Children may be heard to argue, "you did!", "I didn't!", "you did!", "I didn't!" because of a failure to agree upon the response that was or was not done. And the controversy becomes even more complex when we attempt to infer the motive for a response such as whether the failure to return a greeting was a deliberate snub.

Controversies of these kinds cannot be tolerated in science. The psychologist first establishes some criterion as to how much movement is necessary for him to call it a "response," but then having objectively defined that criterion, there can be no question as to when such a response occurs. For example, to determine whether an animal made an error in running through a maze, the psychologist may place photoelectric beams in the wrong paths, and define errors as breaking those beams. Because of such contraptions, many of the experimental situations in which learning is studied in the laboratory appear to the student as contrived and artificial. Indeed they are, simply to enable the objective recording of behavior that cannot be achieved as reliably by naturalistic observation.

This poses one of the most difficult challenges to the experimental analysis of behavior: the very act of observing behavior may affect the behavior under observation. Imagine a psychologist taking a young man and his date to a drive-in movie in order to observe what really goes on in such a setting! And even in the simpler laboratory situations, problems of comparable kinds may arise. Among other things, the rat running through a maze must be removed from the goal box and his reaction to handling may affect his performance in the maze. There is no perfect solution to this dilemma. With humans, we may try to elicit their cooperation by noting that the data will be misleading unless they behave naturally or answer questions honestly. In many cases, there are objective techniques for determining whether the person did indeed cooperate. Alternatively, we may disguise the true purpose of the experiment. With animals, extensive taming and pre-adaptation to the experimental environment typically precede the actual study. Nevertheless, the serious student of behavior must always be concerned about the extent to which his presence as an observer modified the behavior that would have occurred had he not been present.

Having acknowledged this difficulty, the psychologist is relatively free to define a response any way he chooses. So long as it can be reliably observed and recorded, any bit of behavior in which he is interested may be studied. At a more sophisicated level, response definition is not as simple as it sounds. Behavior, it must be recognized, is taking place continuously over time—you are always doing something. The most fruitful way to break behavior up into measurable units is at least subject to debate. Smoking a cigarette, for example, takes place over a period of time, and theoretical scientists may disagree how best to describe such behavior. But for our purposes, it is sufficient to treat as a response any bit of behavior that we can agree upon as to whether it did or did not occur. The psychology of learning is the study of how the frequency of occurrence of such bits of behavior is modified by past experience.

## Movements and Acts

In general, there are two ways to look at behavior. When we refer to *movements,* we refer to glandular secretions or muscular actions that have no direct, physical effect upon the external environment. (Note that we are not talking about movements of the entire organism through space, only parts of the body.) You salivate, your heart beats, you may twiddle your thumbs, scratch your head, or blink your eyes. Movements may indirectly affect the behavior of another organism: when a baby cries, the mother may attend to it; when you snap your fingers, your dog may come to you. Hence, movements may provide stimuli which elicit behavior from others, but they do not have a direct physical effect on the environment.

When a response physically alters the environment or the organism's relationship to it, we refer to *acts*. When you pick up an object, push it, hit it, or throw it, you have performed an act. Although acts are certainly made up of movements, they are defined by their consequences. In everyday language, we say that the batter hit a home run, the cook burned the potatoes, the child broke the glass. In such cases, we are not so much interested in the particular movements involved in the response as we are in the effects produced by those movements. Indeed, an act may usually be accomplished in many ways. Batters may take quite different stances at the plate, use different grips on the bat, and swing with different degrees of wrist action, but it is whether and where the ball is hit that counts. So, too, in the laboratory: we may rig an apparatus so that a rat must press down on a bar to record a response, but pay no attention to whether he uses his right paw, his left paw, his teeth or his tail to effect the press.

A further distinction can be made within the concept "act." Some acts are *manipulatory;* they change some part of the environment in relation to the organism. The driver of an automobile may turn the dial of the radio, shift the gears, turn the steering wheel, and press on the brakes. In these cases, his behavior makes direct, physical contact with some object in the environment and operates upon it. Other acts are *locomotor*; they change the organism's orientation in space without affecting the environment itself. Walking, running, and jumping alter where you are in the environment.

A final distinction can be made between discrete and continuous responses. Some responses, by their very nature, are momentary, i.e., *discrete*. Other responses can be maintained for a period of time, i.e., *continuous*. In speech, for example, the explosive consonants such as "p" and "t" can at best be repeated over and over but cannot be held as can the long vowels such as "a" and "e." Similarly, a finger snap is discrete but grasping an object with your fingers is continuous. Throwing a football is discrete, carrying a football is continuous (until tackled!).

The purpose of the kinds of distinctions made in this section is to identify differences that may sometimes be important. But they are not as sharp as might be inferred. Consider, for example, the quarterback's response of "throwing a pass." This involves many movements such as tensing various muscles and looking for a receiver; but it is equally an act defined by the fact that the ball was thrown through the air. As an act, it involves manipulating the ball and perhaps potential tacklers, but the passer probably locomotes across the field in the process. The moment of releasing the ball is discrete, but the entire act takes place over a period of time. To unravel these complexities would take us far beyond the scope of this book (which, as usual, means that I do not fully understand all of the implications of these distinctions) and, for the most part, we shall simply refer to a response regardless of how it would be classified. However, the perceptive reader will note, for example, that the different types of learning situations that we shall discuss typically employ different types of responses in their experimental analysis.

## Behaviors that ARE Learnable Responses

We do not need to consider the question of whether there are behaviors that are not responses. By definition, any activity that can be reliably observed qualifies as a response. However, we may ask whether a particular response is learnable. This is asking whether a selected response can be more-or-less permanently modified, or associated with originally ineffective stimuli as a result of past experiences.

Controversy exists concerning the learnability of some responses. For example, when you are exposed to a sudden increase in the level of illumination, your eye responds by contraction of the pupil. Can this response be brought under voluntary control or at least learned in association with other stimuli that precede the light change? A more refined question is whether a response can be learned using all of the different types of learning situations. For example, we know that your heart can learn to respond by accelerating to a neutral stimulus that has regularly preceded an aversive stimulus, but one may question whether you can learn to accelerate your heartbeat if you are rewarded for doing so. One extreme illustration of this controversy concerns the production of antibodies. We know that your body responds to the presence of a virus by producing antibodies; were this a learnable response, the simplest cure for the common cold would be to train people to start producing antibodies before the virus has a chance to multiply!

This controversy is of considerable theoretical significance and is mentioned to caution the student that some responses may not be learnable. Some of the failures to date may result simply from faulty techniques; Neal Miller has recently shown that the secretions of internal organs are learnable if proper reward procedures are employed. Bluntly, your liver can learn. Nevertheless, there may be limitations on the applicability of the principles of learning; but we do not yet know the ground rules that would rigorously identify responses that are not learnable. For all practical purposes, the student will at worst rarely be in error if he adopts the hypothesis that *all observable responses are learnable and obey all of the principles of learning*. In this section, we will identify some types of learnable responses in order to enlarge your understanding of that concept.

### Not-Responding as a Response

In our discussion of the stimulus, we noted that our typical image of a stimulus is the onset of some event but that offsets were also important. A comparable reminder needs to be made with respect to responses. In short, *stopping or simply not making a response qualify as learnable responses*.

In making that assertion, we could engage in a quarrel over definitions. Since an organism is continuously behaving, one could say that not making one response is logically equivalent to making some other response. When a lost person stops calling for help because relief is now in sight, he turns to other behaviors appropriate to his rescue. When a boy does not call a girl for a date, he is doing something else (perhaps calling another). In the laboratory, a rat that does not run through the maze is doing something else such as exploring the start box, grooming, or sleeping. Nevertheless, it is convenient and informative to think of not-responding as a learnable response even though this may be accomplished by learning to do something else.

We shall encounter this notion most explicitly in the contexts of extinction and punishment. We learn not to do things for which we are punished even though we would like to do them, and we learn not to do things for which we are not rewarded even though we are freely permitted to do them. There are a variety of experimental demonstrations of these facts, but one study can be mentioned here as illustrative.

Suppose an individual rat is placed in a box that is quite barren except for a bar that could be pressed. For this and all such responses, we can determine an operant level. The *operant level* is simply the rate at which a freely-available response occurs if the consequences of that response are neutral (neither rewarding nor punishing). Your hands are not involved when you are reading a book that is lying in your lap except when needed to turn a page; during the rest of the time, your hands may be clasped, playing with each other, making minute gestures, or whatever, even though nothing is accomplished by these responses. So, too, a rat will occasionally press a bar in a box during his meanderings.

The essence of the study is simply to program delivery of food to the rat periodically provided he has not pressed the bar within the preceding minute. The occasional, perhaps accidental bar presses that constitute the operant level are largely eliminated by this procedure. The rat is rewarded for keeping his paws off the bar, and he learns to do so. Looked at another way, he is punished for pressing the bar by not getting the scheduled food delivery. But any way we look at it, this type of study demonstrates that not-responding may be viewed as a learnable response.

### Behavior Chains

Most of the responses that we have identified as acts are actually sequences of movements strung together to accomplish a goal. When this is explicitly recognized we refer to a *behavior chain*. A student doing his homework must go to his desk or the library, locate the appropriate book, read it and take notes, and then, hopefully, study those notes and think about them. This is a long and complex behavior chain. A simpler one is throwing a baseball: the pitcher winds up, cocks his arm, and lets fly. Most conspicuous is talking, where sequences of sounds and words are uttered in a pattern necessary to convey an idea to a listener.

Behavior chains are important because, once fully integrated, they then tend to run off as a single response. When you learn to type, for example, the early responses of typing letter by letter become hooked together into larger units: the word "reinforcement" may become so well integrated that it is difficult not to make a mistake in typing "reinforcing." (Similar errors happen in reading.) This integration is accomplished through feedback; the stimuli of early responses in the chain elicit the later responses directly and automatically. A behavior chain constitutes a sequence of responses initiated by an external event but then run off under the control of feedback. Once integrated, behavior chains may be treated as responses.

Much of what we call learning is, in fact, the integration of little bits of behavior into longer behavior chains. Let us consider first a laboratory example. We wish to train a naive hungry rat to press a bar to obtain food. This response is a chain composed of approaching the bar, raising on the hind paws, placing the forepaws on the bar, pressing down, releasing the bar and going to the place where food has been delivered. We teach a rat to do all this by a process called *shaping*, or successive approximations. It is like the game, "you're getting warmer" and proceeds in this case something as follows. First, the rat is allowed to discover where the food is delivered and that the click of the feeder signals another pellet of food. We do this until, wherever the rat is, he runs quickly to the feeder whenever he hears the click. Next, we wait until the rat happens to get near the bar and then deliver a pellet. This now causes him to run to the food cup but then he is likely to return to the area near the bar. Now, however, we require that he be facing the bar before a pellet is given. Once he begins to do this, we require that he stand up, later that he place a paw on the bar, and still later that he press on the bar. In sum, the elements of the desired behavior chain are progressively built into his repertoire.

Shaping responses is somewhat of an art, but several guidelines can be asserted. The first and most important is that *a behavior chain is best learned in backward fashion*—the last element of the chain should be learned first. In the bar-pressing situation, we first taught the rat to approach the food cup when he heard it click. The other two guidelines appear somewhat contradictory. On the one hand, it is important to maintain a sufficient frequency of reward to keep the organism behaving; if a standard is set for the next reward that the organism can not yet achieve, he may stop doing the things he has already learned and will have to begin again. But on the other hand, too frequent reward of a poor approximation to the desired response may cause that imperfect way of responding to become so well learned that the organism fails to continue to make progress beyond it. And hence the art is to give enough reward to keep the organism behaving but not so much at any step in the process that he becomes fixated there.

Consider, then, a father intent upon teaching his son to hit a baseball. One father spends hours pitching to his son and perhaps becoming exasperated at the lack of progress resulting from his time and effort. Another father ties a baseball to a string and hangs it from a reasonably high tree limb. The boy first learns to hit the baseball while it is motionless—the last component of the chain. This is done with the ball at different heights so he learns to aim the bat at the ball. Once progress is evident at this aspect of the task, the ball is swung from progressively further distances, and only after the boy can hit the swinging ball does the father begin throwing the ball, at first softly and then with increasing vigor.

In summary, many acts such as a rat pressing a bar or a boy hitting a baseball can be broken down into a sequence of elements that must occur in a specified order. These may be integrated into a behavior chain by shaping and then may be treated as a response for that organism.

**Response Dimensions**

There is an old saying, "It ain't what you do, it's the way what you do it," and this is true of a wide range of everyday behaviors. Speaking effectively is not simply uttering meaningful words; it is saying those words with appropriate intonation and emphasis. The quarterback must not simply pass the football; he must throw it in the right direction and with the right force to reach his intended receiver. That organisms obviously learn these things indicates that *quantitative dimensions of a response are learnable.* We shall encounter this fact more extensively in our discussion of correlated reinforcement, but one example here may be helpful.

Return to the situation of a rat pressing a bar to obtain food. The typical procedure requires only that the bar be pressed, but suppose we require a particular duration during which the bar is depressed for it to count as a response. If, for example, only responses that last between .2 and .4 seconds were rewarded, then bar presses that do not last two-tenths of a second and those that last longer than four-tenths of a second simply do not count. Rats are remarkably adept at learning this quantitative property of a bar press and can put as many as 80% of their bar presses into the requisite interval. Indeed, rats are equally capable of putting their responses into another interval, say .8 to 1.0 seconds. In similar fashion, rats can learn to press a bar with a particular force and to run at a particular speed.

Quantitative dimensions of a response are not only learnable when, as in the previous examples, successful performance demands it: they are learned in any event. This can be shown most clearly by giving humans a simple task (called paired-associates learning) in which each of several irregular patterns of lights is associated with a number. The subject's task is to learn which number goes with which pattern, as these are presented a number of times in different orders. First, a pattern appears, then the subject gives his response, and then the correct number is shown for confirmation or correction. In this situation, consider two groups that differ in only one respect. There is a brief click that occurs after the pattern is shown and the subjects are instructed to say their response at the time of the click. For one group this click occurs ¾ths of a second after the pattern and for the other group, this click occurs 2½ seconds after the pattern. In effect, one group is required to practice making their responses quickly and the other group practices responding more slowly.

After both groups have learned the associations, they can be tested with a somewhat different task. Now, they are instructed to respond to the patterns as fast as they can, each response immediately producing the next pattern. This is similar to an arithmetic speed test; see how many patterns you can name in two minutes. The important result is that the group that practiced fast can now respond significantly faster than the group that practiced slowly. One learns a speed of responding simply by practicing at that speed.

This conclusion can be extended by studying learning to learn paired-associates. Using meaningful words as stimuli and responses (e.g., the response to "wood" is "knee"), the material to be learned is presented at a fast pace for one group and at a slower pace for the other group. Every subject is exposed to a number of such lists and they gradually improve in how quickly they can learn them. Then, they are tested on new lists given at the opposite rate of presentation. The fact is that subjects cannot learn new material as well when presented at a rate different from that to which they are accustomed. In short, we learn a speed of learning.

These and other studies collectively show that we can learn quantitative dimensions of a response when required to do so, and that, even if not required to do so, we learn the dimensions the way we practice them. There are many important practical implications of the fact that response dimensions are learnable responses. As illustrative: if you practice in a slow, sloppy or ineffectual manner, you are learning to perform in a slow, sloppy or ineffectual manner!

## Response Incompatibility

When two responses cannot adequately be performed at the same time, we call them *incompatible*. You cannot simultaneously raise and lower your arm nor can you raise both feet off the ground while standing. The student cannot study and day dream, and, as the saying goes, you cannot have your cake and eat it, too. Such physical incompatibility may be only partial. For example, you can to some extent talk and eat at the same time even if it is considered impolite to do so. You will find it difficult to tap on the table with both hands but at slightly different beats that are not simple multiples of each other. Less obviously, but perhaps more importantly, you cannot at one and the same time smile while exercising an unhappy thought! Response incompatibility arises when the performance of one response partially or completely interferes with the performance of another response.

Some degree of response incompatibility may be learned. Although you can readily utter sounds with your mouth and make marks on a piece of paper with your hand, you will find it difficult repeatedly to say "black" while writing "white." A secretary cannot accurately type while listening to an irrelevant conversation, and you would find it difficult to do arithmetic if someone is saying numbers aloud in your presence. When different responses have acquired different meanings for an organism, the occurrence of one may interfere with the occurrence of the other.

We shall have occasion to refer to response incompatibility throughout this book, but especially in the context of the elimination of responses. In general, the most effective technique for modifying behavior is to replace one response with an incompatible one. Since both cannot be performed at once, the earlier response may be precluded. In addition, many difficulties in learning result from response incompatibility. A student may have difficulty because the school setting elicits anxieties that are incompatible with effective study.

## Response Satiation

We have seen that repeated presentation of the same stimulus leads to satiation or boredom with that stimulus. An analogous principle can be observed with respect to responses. Repeated performance of the same response leads to a reduced tendency to select it over other alternatives. This is called *response satiation*. As with stimulus satiation, this is a temporary state from which the organism recovers after a period of rest from that response.

You are certainly familiar with the notion of fatigue, but response satiation is more than that. Fatigue is a purely physiological process involving the muscles just as sensory adaptation is a physiological process involving the sense organs. Response satiation is a psychological effect: organisms simply become tired of doing the same thing over and over again even when the muscles are fully capable of continuing to perform that response.

Indeed, there is probably a close relationship between response satiation and stimulus satiation. We know that we become bored with external stimuli presented repeatedly. We also know that responses produce stimuli. Response satiation could thus be viewed as a special case of stimulus satiation except that the stimuli involved are response-produced. In effect, we become bored with feeling ourselves doing the same thing all the time.

The typical laboratory demonstration of response satiation involves *response alternation*. A rat might be run in a T-shaped maze but forced for a number of runs to turn to the right. If he is then given a choice, he is likely to turn left even if right-turning had been rewarded. There is no reason to believe that there is any greater muscular fatigue involved in right-turning than in left-turning, but the rat is psycho-logically satiated on the former. The greater the number of forced turns preceding an opportunity for choice, the greater the likelihood of alter-nation, and the longer the time that elapses between the forced turns and the choice opportunity, the lower the likelihood of alternation.

Response alternation is a very general phenomenon in choice situ-ations. For example, if you try to write down a list of random num-bers from zero through nine, it is easy to show that you simply cannot do so. In the first place, we all have favorite numbers and sequences of numbers. In generating a list of numbers rapidly so that you cannot deliberately avoid non-random tendencies, when you scan your list you will observe that you put down more (say) sevens than any other number and that you typically put down (say) nine after putting down a one. And you will note that you rarely repeat a number twice in succession, although, in a truly random sequence, you should repeat yourself one-tenth of the time. Organisms tend to alternate responses unless there are compelling reasons to repeat behavior.

Some psychologists have attempted to pose the question. Which is the stronger, stimulus satiation or response satiation? This probably is not a good question but it does point out that both processes are typic-ally present in most situations. If a rat is run in a T-maze in which one arm is black and the other white (Figure 2), the response of turning to the right also leads to the white stimulus. If the rat alternates on the second trial, it is difficult to know whether he is alternating his re-sponse by now turning left or alternating the stimulus by now approach-ing black. It is possible to pit the two processes against each other. If, for example, the arms are reversed before the second trial, so that now the colors are on the opposite sides from the first run, the rat can approach the different stimulus by making the same response or make the different response but approach the same stimulus. In this particular context, rats are more likely to alternate the stimulus than the response and it is thus possible that stimulus satiation is the more basic process. However, we might also presume that if the stimuli were more similar and the responses more different, the opposite result would obtain.

In any event, there is a psychological process of response satiation which leads to alternation of behavior when repetition is not demanded. And even when repetition is desirable, we may vary our behavior simply for the sake of variety. The practical importance of this phenomenon should be apparent. Earlier we noted that students may become satiated on school because they are exposed to essentially identical stimuli; now we are saying that the teacher also becomes satiated on repeatedly making the same responses. A married person may become bored with a spouse who never varies his behavior; the spouse is equally bored with himself. The person who is bored with life is one who is obliged to keep repeating the same responses or who has developed such stereotyped habits that he repeats responses in spite of a basic tendency to alternate, or who has been punished for innovative behavior and who is now afraid to try out new responses. In short, the bored are boring.

### True-False Items: The Response

1. The most critical component of defining a response is that it be objectively identifiable.

(One may define a response in any way he chooses in order to study its determinants. The only restriction is that he be able objectively to identify its occurrence. True.)

2. The most difficult challenge to the experimental analysis of behavior is to observe it without affecting it.

(Any scientist runs the risk of changing the system he is studying simply by his own activity of observing it. This is especially true of behavior since it is sensitive to the presence of others. True.)

3. As a response, breathing would be classified as a movement.

(Actions of the organism which do not directly affect the environment are considered to be movements. Although breathing might be a response that affected something—for example, blowing out a candle—normally we can think of breathing as a movement. True.)

4. The locomotor act of jumping would be described as discrete.

(Viewed in the large, there may be a sequence of activities involved in jumping, but the actual instant of jumping is discrete since it can only occur in a particular instance and not be prolonged. True.)

5. When an organism learns to do something other than the behavior we are observing, we say he has learned the response of not-responding.

(Organisms are continually behaving, but we may effectively lump together behaviors other than the one in which we are interested into a category of not-responding. True.)

6. The rate at which you cross and re-cross your legs while sitting in a lecture would constitute that response's operant level.

(Crossing one's legs is a freely available response which occurs at some rate even without explicit reinforcement for doing so. This rate is the operant level. True.)

7. A behavior chain becomes integrated by the use of feedback.

(Each bit of behavior is always followed by another bit of behavior. It is when a sequence of these become integrated so that early ones tend to lead specifically to later ones that a chain is formed. It is integrated by feedback. True.)

8. When you reward a child for doing better than usual, even though his response is still imperfect, you are engaging in shaping.

(Training a response is often best accomplished by rewarding successive approximations, progressively raising the standards as performance improves. Appropriately, this is called shaping. True.)

9. The order in which a behavior chain should be shaped is backward.

(It is not always possible to get to the end of a behavior chain without going through earlier components. When possible, however, learning is facilitated if the terminal components are learned first and earlier components are added progressively. True.)

10. If you practice writing slowly, you are learning to write slowly.

(Practice does not necessarily make perfect. Indeed, practice can be detrimental if done in an imperfect manner simply because one learns what one practices. True.)

11. Reading a book and closing your eyes are incompatible responses.

(Responses are incompatible which cannot be performed simultaneously. Sometimes one can shift back and forth between incompatible responses without too much impairment of either, but one cannot read with his eyes closed. True.)

12. Your tendency to alternate illustrates response satiation.

(We are endowed with two diametrically opposed principles: habit as a tendency to repeat responses, and satiation as a tendency to alternate. The former, however, is permanent while the latter is transitory so that in combination they maintain adjustment to a stable environment while insuring some exploration for better responses. True.)

# 4

# The Anticipatory Response

By all odds, the most basic, pervasive, and important principle of learning is that of the anticipatory response. If you want to improve your understanding of behavior, no other single principle can remotely compete with the universality of the anticipatory response. As with most principles of great general significance, the principle of the antici- patory response[1] is stated with deceptive simplicity: WHENEVER A STIMULUS MORE-OR-LESS REGULARLY PRECEDES A RE- SPONSE IN TIME, THAT STIMULUS WILL COME TO ELICIT THAT RESPONSE PRIOR TO ITS REGULAR TIME OF OCCUR- RENCE.

This principle is presented schematically in Figure 3. We first read the passage of time from left to right in the figure, with the breaks in the line indicating longer periods between events. The occurrence of a stimulus somewhere in time is symbolized by "S" and the fact that a response occurs somewhat later in time is symbolized by the location of "R". The principle of the anticipatory response states that this tem- poral sequence of the stimulus followed by the response is sufficient to produce learning: the R becomes associated with the S. The *learned* association is symbolized by a dashed arrow connecting them. With re- peated occurrence, the response occurs earlier and earlier, and thus antedates its initial time of occurrence.

---

[1]The word "anticipatory" may be misleading because it suggests that the re- sponse is made voluntarily in anticipation of impending events. The principle does not assume any such conscious process; the effect is automatic. A better word might therefore be "antedating" to indicate only that the response occurs earlier in time.

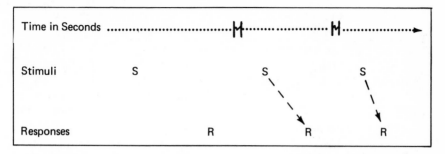

**Figure 3.** Schematic illustration of the principle of the anticipatory response. The passage of time is read from left to right, the breaks in that line representing longer intervals. Here and subsequently, environmental stimuli are represented along one line and responses along a second line. If a response occurs following a stimulus, they become associated as represented by the dashed arrow. This association moves the response forward so that it occurs sooner after the stimulus.

## Examples of Anticipatory Responses

There are several particularly important instances of this type of learning. Although these will be described somewhat differently, you should remember and recognize that the fundamental principle of the anticipatory response remains the same regardless of the particular circumstances under which it can be observed. Arrange conditions so a response occurs after a stimulus and they will become associated.

### Classical Conditioning

The most well documented and familiar form of the anticipatory response occurs in classical conditioning. We shall present this aspect in the original context in which its importance was first suggested, namely, the work of Ivan Pavlov.

Pavlov earned a Nobel prize for his studies of the digestive process. In doing so, he first developed a technique for recording the salivation of dogs. This involved a small tube inserted through the dog's cheek, and attached to one of the salivary glands. (Those who are concerned about the welfare of the dog should realize that there are many salivary glands and that no serious impairment of normal functioning was produced by this minor operation.) Pavlov wanted to determine the way salivation contributed to digestion, and in that context, the fact that the dogs soon began to salivate when they saw the experimenter and *before* they got fed was a disturbing nuisance. It then became an object of deliberate study and occupied the major remaining portion of Pavlov's life.

The paradigm (experimental procedure) for Pavlovian classical conditioning is shown in Figure 4. The Unconditioned Stimulus (hereafter symbolized as the US) could be any stimulus that reflexively produces some response of interest. In studying salivation, Pavlov typically used for the US food powder placed in the dog's mouth. He also sometimes used a mild acid. In either case, the dog naturally salivates when these stimuli occur and the response of salivation to a US is called the Unconditioned Response (UR). The US-UR relationship shown in Figure 4 is by a solid arrow to indicate that this is an unlearned connection.

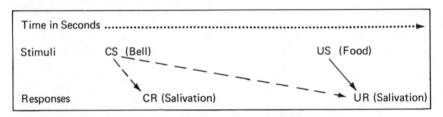

**Figure 4.** The procedure of classical conditioning. Again reading time from left to right, first a CS occurs followed in time by a US. The US reflexively elicits a UR as indicated by the solid arrow. Because of the principle of the anticipatory response, the CS becomes associated with the UR, as indicated by the dashed arrow, and moves forward in time. When the response begins to occur *before* the US, it is called a CR.

Any event to which the dog is responsive is a possible Conditioned Stimulus (CS). The typical CS is one which is initially neutral with respect to the response in question; this is based on the argument that if the response then does occur later to the CS, we can be sure that it is a learned association. Pavlov used stimuli such as a bell, a light, a tone, or the beat of a metronome as a CS. The critical feature of the experimental procedure in classical conditioning is that the selected CS is presented some short period of time before the US.

If this procedure is followed a number of times, then the CS does become associated with the response so that the dog begins to salivate when the CS occurs and before the US occurs. When the response occurs to the CS, it is now called a Conditioned Response (CR), and since this is a learned association, it is shown by a dashed arrow in Figure 4. Note that learning is an association between a stimulus and a response, in this case, the association between the CS and the CR.

Pavlov's procedure is often referred to as classical *appetitive* conditioning because the US was an emotionally-positive stimulus that elicited the consummatory response of eating. Most of the related research done in this country has involved classical *defense* conditioning because the US has been a somewhat aversive event that reflexively elicits some UR. Consider electric shock, for example. If applied to the cheek, shock elicits an eyeblink. If applied to the finger-tip, shock elicits finger-withdrawal. And if applied to the arm, shock elicits minute sweating in the palm of the hand (technically called the galvanic skin response). Each of these responses has been classically conditioned to a wide variety of stimuli in human subjects.

The student may comment that if a signal precedes an electric shock to (say) the finger tip, of course the person will withdraw his finger before the shock. But there are two ways to show that this anticipatory response principle does not represent simply a voluntary defense response. One way is to attach the shock electrodes to the finger tip itself so that the shock cannot be avoided by anticipatory responses. Even so, the human will start to withdraw his finger before the shock. The second approach is simply to instruct the human to attempt voluntarily not to make an anticipatory response. Yet even the fully informed subject voluntarily trying to restrain himself cannot do so. The tendency to make anticipatory responses in the classical conditioning situation is automatic.

### Temporal Conditioning

An event may occur regularly in time without being preceded by another stimulus. Pavlov demonstrated that this form of regularity was learnable in a laboratory conditioning situation. In *temporal conditioning,* the US occurs at regularly scheduled intervals without any explicit CS. Specifically, for example, food powder might be delivered into a dog's mouth at five-minute intervals. This procedure is shown graphically in Figure 5 which also illustrates the result that, with experience, the dog begins to anticipate the food delivery by salivating just before its occurrence.

To understand the phenomenon of temporal conditioning, recall the earlier introduction of the concept of a stimulus trace. Briefly, it is assumed that an external source of energy change is transformed into impulses within the nervous system, and that these persist for some time after the event although decaying progressively in strength. Returning to Figure 5, note that each US *is* indeed regularly preceded by another stimulus, namely, the previous occurrence of the US. That is to say, the US not only elicits the UR, but it also initiates a stimulus trace which presumably persists over the five-minute interval, still being

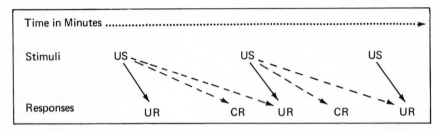

**Figure 5.** The procedure for temporal conditioning. A US occurs at regular intervals of time, each eliciting a UR. Since each US regularly precedes the next US, it serves effectively as a conditioned stimulus so as to elicit a CR prior to the occurrence of the US.

somewhat distinctive just before the next food delivery in order to elicit anticipatory salivation.

The fact of temporal conditioning has had important implications for the design of laboratory research on the conditioning process. Even when a CS is provided before the US, if the trials are repeated at perfectly regular intervals of time, we cannot be sure whether in fact the explicit CS is producing the response or whether the response is simply a result of temporal conditioning. For this reason, trials are normally presented at irregular intervals or at sufficiently long intervals to enable the trace of the earlier trial to have dissipated.

Temporal conditioning also occurs in the natural environment. Normally, humans have clocks to help them time regular events such as the rising of the sun or the eruption of Old Faithful, but even in their absence we are capable of relying on a kind of biological clock within us. For example, if we retire regularly at about the same time, we typically find that we begin to yawn and become drowsy at about that time even without looking at a clock.

Temporal conditioning *can* also lead to maladaptive forms of behavior. An excellent laboratory illustration involves monkeys placed in a small chamber for an hour or so a day. The monkeys are restrained in their chairs by a chain hanging from the ceiling and attached to their collars. The monkeys are given an unavoidable electric shock at regular intervals, say once every minute; when shock occurs, the monkeys tend to yank at their chain as if aggressing against it in their plight. The response of chain-pulling is, effectively, an unconditioned response to the shock even though it actually does not affect the duration or the intensity of the shock.

True to the fact of temporal conditioning, chain-pulling begins to occur shortly before the next scheduled shock and to persist through the shock. The situation is then changed so that shocks will no longer be given if the monkey does not pull the chain, but he will be shocked if he does. Chain-pulling is thus actually punished by shock, but the monkey continues over a period of months pulling on the chain every minute and producing the aversive electric shock. By temporal conditioning, he first becomes trapped into pulling the chain in anticipation of shock and thereafter does not learn that simply leaving the chain alone would solve his dilemma.

By and large, however, temporal conditioning is adaptive. Whenever events occur regularly in the environment, time (or better, biological processes changing over time—the stimulus trace) is a sufficient stimulus to enable us to learn that regularity and begin to respond prior to the occurrence of the event.

### Higher-Order Conditioning

In the pure form of classical conditioning, the unconditioned response is reflexively elicited by the unconditioned stimulus. The dog naturally salivates to food and you naturally blink your eye to a puff of air or withdraw your finger from an electric shock. The procedure of classical conditioning may also be used where, in the position of the unconditioned stimulus is a stimulus to which a response has previously been conditioned. This is called *higher-order conditioning*.

For example, Pavlov trained dogs first to salivate to a tone by presenting the tone before the delivery of food. Once salivation had been conditioned to the tone, he then presented a light before the tone, now omitting the food. Since the dog salivated to the tone, the response became conditioned to the light. This is called higher-order conditioning not because any new principles or more complex concepts are involved, but simply because the learning is based upon a conditioned association rather than an unconditioned one.

The procedure as described cannot continue very far or last for very long. This is because, in the absence of the food, the dog soon stops salivating to the tone (the original CS) and then also to the light. That procedure is necessary to demonstrate the phenomenon of higher-order conditioning, but we can presume that it also occurs in situations where a sequence of stimuli precede a US. If, for example, a light precedes a tone which in turn precedes food, the salivation first becomes conditioned to the tone, and then while that is maintained by the subsequent food, the response becomes further conditioned to the light. You may think of it as "higher-order" because the CS is further removed from the controlling US, and its capacity to elicit the CR depends on intermediate stimuli to bridge the gap in time.

There are many examples of higher-order conditioning in everyday life but perhaps the simplest and most common involves the use of language. A child first learns, for example, that the word "good" is followed by pleasant events and hence responds to the word with emotionally-positive reactions. He may then be taught new responses or new events are good just by calling them that; the emotions conditioned to words can be transferred to other stimuli by higher-order conditioning. It thus provides another example of the anticipatory response principle.

### Anticipatory Instrumental Responses

Although classical conditioning provides the most well-documented example of anticipatory responding, the principle of the anticipatory response is of still wider generality than we have illustrated thus far. Any set of environmental circumstances that arrange for a response to occur shortly following a stimulus will lead to an association and a tendency for the response to move forward in time on future occasions of that stimulus. This can be seen in the context of instrumental conditioning where the response is made because it is rewarded.

Figure 6 describes this effect. If one stimulus more-or-less regularly precedes a second stimulus to which the organism has learned an instrumental response, the response will tend to occur earlier in the future.

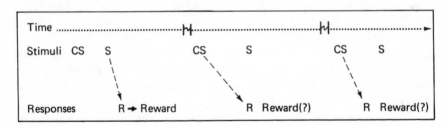

**Figure 6.** Schematic representation of anticipatory instrumental response. The second stimulus (S) does not elicit a response reflexively as in classical conditioning; rather the response is instrumental in obtaining reward. Nevertheless, a CS which regularly precedes such a stimulus will become associated with that response and tend to elicit it earlier in time.

The reason for the question marks concerning reward on those later occasions is to reflect the fact that the anticipatory response may be an error and result in denial or delay of the reward. Indeed, anticipatory instrumental responding is most conspicuous when responding too soon is wrong.

Consider, for example, the following laboratory study. We arrange a maze in which the correct path requires a rat to make seven consecutive left turns followed by a final right turn into the goalbox. After considerable training, the rat has no difficulty over the first few turns each trial but then, as he gets closer and closer to the critical last turn, his tendency to turn right increases and he is likely to make an error. The analysis of the situation is as follows: The stimuli of the seventh choice point regularly precede the stimuli of the eighth choice point, and to the latter the rat has learned to turn right to get food. This right-turning response thus tends to become anticipatory and to occur at the seventh choice point even though it is an error. This anticipatory tendency is weaker at the sixth choice point, still weaker at the fifth, and so on.

What this type of study illustrates is the fact that, in any behavior chain leading to a goal, the responses that occur late in the chain tend to occur in anticipatory fashion earlier in the chain. If these responses are incompatible with the responses actually required further from the goal, then the anticipatory response tendency will lead to poorer performance. In the maze example, turning right too soon was an error and caused a delay in obtaining the food.

Perhaps this context is a good one in which to illustrate the generality of the principle of the anticipatory response in everyday human behavior. Let us draw illustrations from various sporting activities. The racer may jump the gun, the hunter may flinch before pulling the trigger, the batter may swing before the ball gets to the plate. To elaborate on the last example, the ball leaving the pitcher's hand is a stimulus which regularly precedes the ball over the plate, and learning to swing to the latter leads to an anticipatory tendency to swing to the former. (Most little league coaches know that a feigned fast ball is the easiest way to get a novice to make a strike.) A golfer has difficulty keeping his head down because he looks up after he hits the ball to see where it is going, and this response tends to occur to the stimuli arising during earlier portions of his swing. The fisherman may jerk his line at the first nibble before a fish has a chance to take the hook. In countless instances, the skilled sportsman is the one who has learned to inhibit the natural tendency to make anticipatory responses. And that they still occur is dramatic proof that the principle applies to everyday human behavior.

Anticipatory responses are not always errors but awareness of them may be of practical value. The person who has attended many cocktail parties has had the exuberation produced by alcohol conditioned to a glass containing a drink; wise hosts serve a drink before making introductions because the newly-arrived guest will begin to act as if he's already been drinking. Similarly, the drug addict may relax simply to the insertion of the needle even if it does not contain the drug. A child may begin to cry before he is spanked; you may become anxious simply opening a telegram; a speaker may omit part of his lines. Students tend to prepare to leave a classroom shortly before class is technically over because of the anticipatory tendency to finish listening before the lecturer finishes talking. Everyone should spend several days consciously looking for instances of anticipatory responding in his everyday behavior such as removing the keys to his car while he is still several blocks away from it. We shall also encounter a great many more examples in the remainder of this book.

## Facts of Conditioning

The preceding section contained the basic contexts in which the principle of the anticipatory response can be observed to occur. Let us return to the particular instance of classical conditioning and illustrate some of the more detailed facts concerning this phenomenon.

### Course of Conditioning

Thus far, we have stated simply that the pairing of two stimuli results in the response originally associated only with the second stimulus becoming associated with the first stimulus. Or more generally, whenever a response occurs in time, it becomes associated with any stimuli which regularly precede it. At this point, we should be more specific about the course of conditioning over repeated occurrences of such sequenced events.

An idealized representation of the course of conditioning is presented in Figure 7. Along the baseline is plotted the number of times that the stimuli have been paired. Along the ordinate, or y-axis, is plotted some measure of the strength of the conditioned response, such as its amplitude or frequency. What the graph shows is that, with repeated pairings, the tendency to make the CR increases gradually and steadily until it reaches an upper limit (the asymptote) at which it levels off and continues at that strength. *Conditioning is thus cumulative, each trial building upon the strength already gained through previous experiences.*

You will note that Figure 7 does not contain any actual numbers to indicate either the number of trials or the strength of the CR. The reason for this omission is that the precise course of conditioning depends upon a number of details of the experimental arrangement. Although one can generally describe the learning of a CR as following the course depicted in the figure, there are variables that affect both the rate of learning and the final level that is attained as a result of pairing a CS with a US.

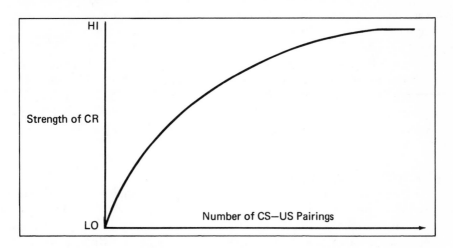

**Figure 7.** Illustration of the course of conditioning. Some measure of the strength of the CR, such as the number of drops of saliva recorded before food is delivered, increases over repeated pairings of the CS and US.

Let us consider a few of these factors to indicate the variety of more specific information available about classical conditioning. First, conditioning tends to proceed faster and reach a higher final level the more intense the stimuli, both CS and US. The stronger the stimulus preceding the US, the more likely it is to acquire the capacity to produce the conditioned response, and the stronger the unconditioned stimulus, the stronger the response that it produces and that becomes anticipatory. Hence, *the measure of the strength of conditioning depends upon the intensity values of the CS and the US.*

A second important variable concerns the distribution of trials, that is to say, the frequency over time with which the CS and the US are experienced. As has been found in most forms of learning, *distributed practice produces fastest learning.* When trials are highly massed, so that they follow each other very quickly, the number of such experiences necessary for conditioning to reach its limit is greater than when the occurrences are distributed more widely over time.

There are a number of more specialized factors that affect conditioning of which one of recent discovery may be mentioned as illustrative. In the conditioning of the human eyeblink, let us use as conditioned stimuli the presentation of a printed word flashed on a screen in front of the subject. As a CS, the word "blue" is better if it is presented in blue letters than if it is presented in red letters! Or vice versa. The incongruity of seeing a word which means one color experience presented in a contradictory color reduces its effectiveness as a stimulus.

Accordingly, the course of conditioning varies with a number of specific details of the situation, a large number of which have been experimentally identified and studied. For our purposes, however, the principal fact of interest is that conditioning is a cumulative affair so that even under the optimal conditions, it usually takes at least several trials before maximal conditioning has been achieved.

### Inter-Stimulus Interval

One variable that affects conditioning is of special interest and importance, namely the time separating the CS and the US. Thus far, we have simply described the procedure as one in which one stimulus precedes another, but the temporal arrangement of these stimuli is important in determining the eventual level of conditioning.

A large number of studies has been run to investigate the effect of this factor, and the overall pattern of results suggests a picture such as depicted in Figure 8. Here we are talking about the limit or eventual level of conditioning after a large number of trials as it is determined by the inter-stimulus interval between the CS and US. There are several things to note from inspection of this figure.

First, *there is an optimal inter-stimulus interval,* on the order of one or a very few seconds. That is to say, conditioning will achieve the highest final level if the CS precedes the US by a short interval of time in that range, with either longer or shorter intervals producing less effective conditioning. There is also an upper limit to the length of the inter-stimulus interval at which effective conditioning can be obtained. The actual value of this upper limit is not yet fully understood: for some responses of some organisms, if the US follows the CS by more than several seconds, conditioning cannot be obtained. In other cases, separations up to five minutes or more have been found to be effective. Since the details of this have not yet been fully worked out, the best we can conclude at this time is simply that conditioning is less effective when there is a separation of more than a few seconds between the CS and the US, and that if the inter-stimulus interval becomes too long, conditioning will not occur.

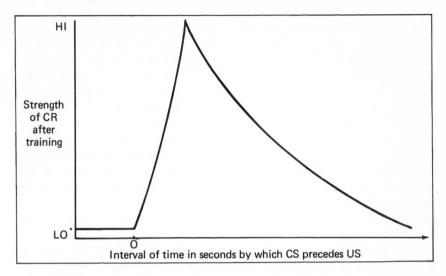

**Figure 8.** The effect of the inter-stimulus interval upon the limit of classical conditioning. Maximal conditioning occurs if the CS precedes the US by one or a very few seconds.

Turning to the shorter values, we can also note that conditioning is less effective. Notice particularly that if the inter-stimulus interval is zero (meaning that the CS and the US occur simultaneously), there is *no* conditioning. Furthermore, there is no conditioning if the US should precede the CS, that is, the stimuli are presented in backward order from the usual order. In short, conditioning only occurs if the CS precedes the US by some period of time, it will be maximal if that separation is very brief, and will be progressively poorer the longer the inter-stimulus interval is beyond that point.

We shall encounter applications of this fact in various later contexts but to anticipate one, consider the parent who wishes a child to learn not to make some response as a result of punishment. The mechanism of punishment that we shall describe involves the conditioning of the emotional responses produced by punishment to the response in question. This is an instance of classical conditioning, and the fact that conditioning is optimal at very brief separations of the CS and the US implies that punishment will be more effective if it is applied very quickly after the response which is being punished. If punishment is applied too long after the crime, punishment will be much less effective simply because the fundamental process of classical conditioning can not operate effectively.

## Latency of the CR

The latency of a response is the time following the presentation of a stimulus before the occurrence of the response. In the context of classical conditioning, latency is the time after the CS is presented before the CR begins to occur. Thus far, we have simply stated that the CR becomes anticipatory and begins to occur before the US and hence to the CS. The question now is, when in fact does the CR tend to occur?

The answer to this depends upon the inter-stimulus interval. The latency of the CR can first be observed to decrease progressively over the early trials of conditioning—it becomes anticipatory and occurs earlier and earlier. At an intermediate stage of conditioning, the CR may occur almost immediately upon the occurrence of the CS. With continued practice, however, the CR gradually moves back until it is occurring just before the scheduled time for the US. For example, if the CS-US interval is one second, then a well-established CR will be seen to occur about three-quarters of a second after the CS and hence but a quarter of a second before the US. If the CS-US interval is longer, say three seconds, then the well-established CR will be seen to occur about two and one-half seconds after the CS, in this case then, about one-half second before the US. In short, *the latency of the CR adjusts to the CS-US interval so that the CR begins to occur just slightly before the US*. It may precede the US by slightly longer when the interval is longer (which you can reasonably think of as related to the accuracy of time estimation, becoming somewhat poorer the longer the interval), and very well established CR's may actually occur almost coincidentally with the onset of the US.

With continuous responses, the CR may begin rather longer before the US and then increase in strength progressively as the US approaches. For example, when you are forewarned of an impending scene of which you are afraid, such as a performance before a group of people, you may at first begin to experience only a moderate degree of fear. This fear builds up over time, however, as the performance draws near and reaches a maximal level as you walk upon the stage. The conditioned response tends not to occur until almost time for the US but once started, it builds up progressively as that time approaches.

## Generalization

When a response has been conditioned to a particular stimulus, we find that somewhat similar stimuli tend also to elicit that response. This tendency is greater the more similar the new stimulus is to the original CS. These facts are depicted, again in idealized form, in Figure 9.

Along the vertical axis is plotted some measure of the strength of the CR. The baseline represents the difference between the original CS (the one initially paired with the US) and some other stimulus similar to it. The strength of the original CR is represented above zero and observe that, as other stimuli are increasingly different, the strength of

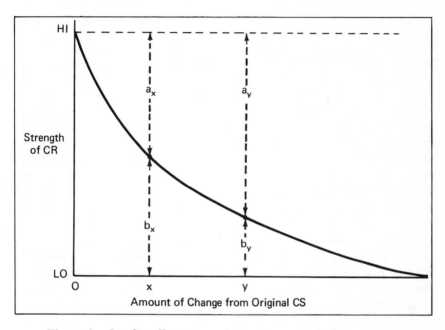

**Figure 9.** Graphic illustration of stimulus generalization. Response strength is first built up to the original CS, as shown above the zero point. This produces some generalized response strength to similar stimuli, as shown by the height of the solid curve above the baseline (e.g., generalized response to x, shown by the dashed arrow, $b_x$, is greater than that to y, shown by $b_y$). This also means that there is a loss in response strength resulting from changing the stimulus, as shown by the difference between the generalized response strength and that to the original CS (e.g., the generalization decrement to x, shown by dashed arrow, $a_x$, is less than that to y, shown by $a_y$).

the CR decreases. In the laboratory, for example, we might condition a response to a tone of 1000 cycles/second; thereafter, a tone of 2000 cycles/second would also elicit a response although weaker than the response to the original 1000 cycle tone; a tone of 4000 cycles would also elicit the response, but at a still weaker level. And so on progressively. To take an everyday example, a child who is bitten by a dog associates fear with that dog. However, similar dogs will also elicit fear, and more so the more similar they are to the dog that bit him. If this happens early before the development of language, he may even be afraid of fur coats or the teddy bear he used to like to take to bed. These represent generalizations of the fear response first conditioned to a particular dog but also elicited by other reasonably similar stimuli.

Some of the more important phenomena concerning generalization will be described in a later chapter. But here we should recognize one confusing aspect of the way psychologists speak about generalization. On some occasions, we wish to stress the fact that a new stimulus will also elicit a conditioned response. The examples given above illustrate this sense of the concept: the child is afraid of a fur coat because he was bitten by a dog. In this case, we speak of a *generalized response*. On other occasions, however, we are more interested in the fact that a change in the situation leads to a weakening of the response. For example, you might train a child how to "behave" in front of "company" and then be distressed because a new person is not treated properly. In this case, there is a lower response than we would like to have observed, and we speak of a *stimulus generalization decrement*. The principle is the same in either case—a similar stimulus elicits a somewhat weaker response than originally trained—but we sometimes refer to the fact that a response does occur to a different stimulus and sometimes to the fact that that response is not as strong as to the original stimulus.

It is worth while reflecting a moment on the biological significance of the principle of stimulus generalization. By-and-large, similar stimuli are best responded to in similar ways. Having learned how to respond to one teacher, employer, date or friend, somewhat similar responses are typically appropriate to similar people. Were it not for this principle, we would have to relearn how to behave every time there was a slight change in the situation. Accordingly, it is an enormously important property of learned associations that they generalize to similar stimuli. On occasion, however, they are not appropriate. Not all teachers are, in fact, alike, nor are all employers, nor dates nor friends. The topic of discrimination learning arises simply because generalized tendencies to respond are not always adaptive.

In any event, one of the most fundamental principles of learned behavior is that of stimulus generalization. Learning to respond to one stimulus imparts a tendency to respond similarly to similar stimuli—and more so the more similar the stimuli.

## External Inhibition

Perhaps the best way to introduce the topic of external inhibition is in the context in which it was first discovered. Following his initial discovery of classical conditioning, Pavlov explained the procedure to his assistants and sent them off to their different rooms to condition salivation in a dog. In time, one would come to Pavlov enthusiastically saying that he had also done it. So Pavlov would return with him to the room where the dog was and the assistant would proudly present the CS to the dog—who then failed to salivate! Only after this experience had occurred a number of times did Pavlov realize the trouble: the dog had learned to salivate without Pavlov present; when he was in the room, the situation was different and the conditioned response did not occur.

The principle of *external inhibition* is that, if something unusual or unexpected occurs before or during the presentation of a CS, the CR is weaker or fails to occur. In the laboratory there are many similar examples. If a heavy truck happens to pass by shortly before the presentation of a CS, the CR will be reduced. If an electric failure happens to cause the lights to flicker unexpectedly, the next trial will be affected. A familiar example of external inhibition can be seen if you have become conditioned to going to sleep at a particular time each night. If there is an unusual news event developing, or a severe storm, or anything out of the ordinary, you may look at your watch and discover that it is several hours past your normal bedtime before you realize that you are sleepy.

The principles necessary to understand external inhibition have already been introduced. First, context is part of the stimulus to which a response is learned; second, we have said that the generalized response is weaker to a changed stimulus than to the original one. External inhibition is a reflection of both of these principles: an unusual event changes the context hence changing the stimulus situation leading to a lower response strength. In short, external inhibition is a special case of stimulus generalization decrement.

## Experimental Extinction

In the laboratory, when the conditions are changed so that a CS that initially preceded a US is now presented alone, we refer to *experimental extinction*. Specifically, for example, a bell might regularly precede the delivery of food for a number of trials and thereafter, food is omitted and the bell simply presented to see how long the dog will continue to salivate to it. The results of such a procedure are shown in Figure 10.

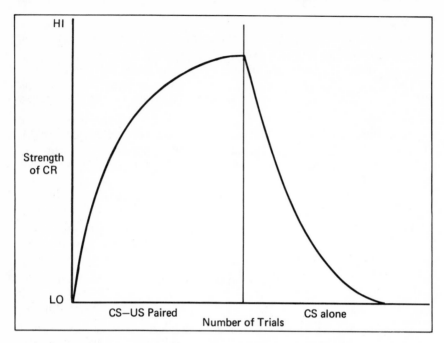

**Figure 10.** Graphic illustration of experimental extinction. In the left portion is reproduced the course of conditioning resulting from pairing a CS with a US. When the CS is then presented alone for a number of trials, the CR grows progressively weaker.

There is reproduced the original acquisition curve showing the increase in the conditioned response when the CS and US are repeatedly paired. To the right of the vertical line is shown the results of then presenting the CS alone without the US. What happens is simply a gradual decrease in the strength of the conditioned response over repeated presentations of the CS alone.

Continued occurrence of the CR to the CS is thus dependent upon the continued presentation of the US following the CS. If the conditions change, the organism gradually learns this fact and eventually stops responding. When this happens, we say that the CR is extinguished. This phenomenon will be discussed in detail in a later chapter.

There is also a related fact: If an interval of time is allowed to elapse after the experimental extinction of a CR, it will regain some of the strength lost. This is called *spontaneous recovery*. In effect, extinction is partly temporary. The conceptual significance of this fact will be discussed in the next chapter.

## Summary

Although there are many more detailed facts of conditioning, the most important ones for the beginning student are those that have been described. They may be summarized as follows:

1. Pairing a CS with a US leads to a gradually increasing strength of a CR to the CS.
2. This strength reaches an upper limit with repeated trials, which limit is greater for more intense stimuli.
3. The rate of conditioning is faster when trials are distributed over time.
4. The effectiveness of pairing a CS with a US is greatest if the US follows the CS by a few seconds. There is no conditioning if the stimuli are presented at the same time or in the reverse order, and there is poorer conditioning if the US occurs very long after the CS.
5. The conditioned response, after extended training, tends to occur shortly before the US. The longer the CS-US interval, the longer the latency before the CR occurs after the onset of the CS.
6. Responses conditioned to one stimulus generalize to similar stimuli, but less so the greater the change from the original CS.
7. The occurrence of an unusual event just before or during the occurrence of a CS leads to external inhibition producing a weaker CR.
8. Presenting the CS alone after a CR has been established results in experimental extinction, a progressive weakening of the CR.
9. An extinguished CR spontaneously recovers some strength over time.

## What a Difference a Second Makes

One way to illustrate the importance of the principle of the anticipatory response and some of the related facts is to use as CS and US two stimuli of which one is emotionally positive (such as food) and the other of which is emotionally negative (such as electric shock). Let us see what happens depending on the order of these two stimuli.

Consider first an environment in which an organism occasionally receives an electric shock which signals that he can go to a food bin and get some food. In this order, the shock is the CS and food is the US, and the emotionally positive responses to the latter become conditioned to the former. Unless it is very intense, the shock loses its aversive properties; the organism accepts the shock calmly and eagerly goes for his food. Perhaps he would prefer that a tone or a light signalled food, but he lives quite satisfactorily in such an environment.

Let us now reverse the order by the space of a single second. If in the first case food was delivered one-half second after the shock, let us now arrange an environment in which food is freely available, but one-half second after the organism takes a bite of food, an electric shock is delivered. In this order, the emotionally negative responses elicited by the shock become conditioned to the food and the organism rarely eats. He lives in a continual state of conflict and behaves poorly. His life, in effect, is miserable.

Viewed from a distance, these two environments are identical: the same amount of food and the same number of shocks could be obtained in both. But the organism's response to them is markedly different; the second event comes to dominate the situation. This is because the emotional responses to it become conditioned to the first stimulus and change its affective value. Shock can become pleasant, food can become aversive. In this light you might reflect upon the following alternative parental statements: "If we play a game first, then you'll have to do your chores" versus "If you finish your chores, then we'll play a game."

### True-False Items: The Anticipatory Response

1. The anticipatory response represents a conscious response in anticipation of an impending event.

(It is true that in many situations, humans learn that a stimulus signals an impending event and plan and prepare for it. However, the principle of the anticipatory response does not presume any such conscious processes. The tendency to respond ahead of time is automatic. False.)

2. In classical conditioning, the conditioned stimulus is the one that already produces the response and the unconditioned stimulus is the one that does not produce the response before conditioning.

(This description is reversed, even though it may sound alright. Think of the term "conditioned" meaning "learned in this situation." The association between the CS and CR is the one conditioned in the situation; the association between the US and UR is reflexive and unlearned. False.)

3. A US may function as a CS.

(A stimulus may elicit a response reflexively and hence be a US; it nevertheless initiates a stimulus trace that can come to elicit other responses if another US regularly follows it. This is illustrated explicitly in the case of temporal conditioning, where the US food not only elicits salivation when eating but also subsequent salivation antedating the next food delivery. True.)

4. Higher-order conditioning refers to higher mental processes such as thinking and problem solving.

(In higher-order conditioning a previously conditioned CS-CR association is used to condition the response to other stimuli. It does not require any new processes or principles. False.)

5. The principle of the anticipatory response may lead to maladaptive behavior.

(Sometimes, making a response early means that it was made too soon resulting in denial or delay of a reward. The principle applies in any event, but it may lead to errors. True.)

6. Conditioning is accomplished by a single pairing of a US with a CS.

(There are extreme situations in which full conditioning may be accomplished in a single experience; you might have to survive but one plane wreck to be intensely afraid of flying even though the probability of a repeat event is very remote. Under typical conditions both in the laboratory and in everyday life, at least several experiences are necessary to produce a strong CR. False.)

7. Best conditioning is obtained by presenting the CS and US at the same time.

(Simultaneous presentation of the two stimuli leads to no conditioning. Only if the US follows the CS, preferably by a short interval of time, does a CR develop. False.)

8. The CR does not occur immediately upon the occurrence of the CS.

(The CR tends to occur immediately preceding the US. If there is a reasonable interval of time between the CS and the US, there will be a reasonable interval of time after the CS before the CR occurs. True.)

9. The greater the change from an original CS, the less the generalized response and the greater the generalization decrement.

(A weaker response occurs if the stimulus is changed. We can describe this in terms of the amount of response that does occur [the generalized response strength] or in terms of the amount of response strength lost as a result of the change [the generalization decrement]. These are, however, opposite sides of the same coin . . . the more that remains, the less that is lost. True.)

10. External inhibition is produced if the subject is told not to respond.

(A person may, to some extent, voluntarily suppress a CR although he cannot do so perfectly. However, external inhibition is no more voluntary than conditioning itself; adding an unusual stimulus changes the total situation and leads to a weaker CR. False.)

11. Prolonged presentations of the CS and US result in experimental extinction.

(As long as the US is continued in classical conditioning, the CR persists. The CR grows weaker during experimental extinction by the omission of the US. False.)

12. In classical conditioning, it's what comes second that counts.

(The response that becomes conditioned is the one elicited by the second stimulus; if a response is also elicited by the first stimulus, it will not become conditioned because the CS has to precede the US. Hence, it is whatever is produced by the second stimulus that determines what is learned. True.)

# 5

# A Scientific Theory
# of Classical Conditioning

Scientists are rarely content simply to describe the outcome of their experiments in empirical terms. In addition, they are inclined to speculate about the underlying reasons for the results that were obtained. We have already informally introduced some of the theoretical ideas relevant to an understanding of classical conditioning; this chapter elaborates that theory more formally and explicitly.

It should be repeated here that this particular theory is not universally accepted. Its most fundamental assumption, that learning is an S-R association, is questioned by cognitive theorists, and some adherents to the stimulus-response approach have proposed alternative assumptions. It should also be acknowledged that some psychologists grant the ultimate value of scientific theory, but argue that the amount of empirical evidence now available concerning the learning process is still too rudimentary to justify theoretical speculations. Nevertheless, "learning theory" is an important aspect of the psychology of learning and the beginning student should at least be exposed to that part of contemporary psychology.

Our purpose is not to present all of the minute details of this theory, to examine all of its implications, nor to give a critical evaluation of its merits. The purpose instead is to expose the reader to the nature of theory in psychology and to illustrate how such a theory can help integrate a variety of phenomena under a reasonably small number of assumptions. This theory was originated by Pavlov and has been elaborated and formalized in this country by Clark Hull and Kenneth Spence. Although, as noted above, it is not universally accepted, it continues to serve as the major point of reference among learning theorists. Accordingly, it is appropriate for the student to be familiar with this approach.

## Habit: Classical Conditioning and Generalization

Let us briefly review several of the phenomena described in the previous chapter and introduce our first theoretical construct: Habit. The principle of classical conditioning is that, if a CS precedes a US that elicits a response, that response tends to become anticipatory and to occur prior to its regular time. We have already indicated the basic assumption of this theory as to the nature of what is learned, namely, an association between that stimulus and that response. *Habit* is the theoretical term for the internal process representing a learned association between a stimulus and a response.

Habit is a familiar term in everyday language, but the reader should carefully distinguish the present usage from the familiar one. When you naturally speak of a "habit," it is often in the context of behaviors of doubtful social value: the habitual smoker, the habitual drinker, the habitual speeder, or whatever. You are also talking specifically about a response and the fact that it occurs frequently. In one sense, the theoretical term habit is more general than that, since we will conceptualize all learned associations, desirable and undesirable, as habits. It is also narrower than commonly used, in that habit is an association between a particular stimulus and a particular response. Thus, the "smoking habit" would be conceptualized as a constellation of many habits, specifically the response of reaching for and lighting a cigarette having become associated with many stimuli such as finishing a meal, leaving a theater or classroom, feeling tense or nervous, and possibly simply internal cues based on the passage of time since one's last cigarette. The habitual smoker is, in effect, a person who has the smoking response conditioned to a wide variety of stimuli and who frequently finds himself smoking a cigarette without consciously being aware of having made that response.

It will also be recalled that the course of conditioning is a gradual, cumulative affair over repeated presentations of the CS preceding the US. Accordingly, we shall assume that habits vary in strength, and that a number of experiences are necessary to produce a habit of maximal strength. We have also noted the principle of stimulus generalization, namely, the fact that a response conditioned to one stimulus may be elicited by similar stimuli. Our theoretical account of this phenomenon is that habit generalizes to similar stimuli in proportion to the degree of similarity between the stimulus actually conditioned and any other stimulus that may be encountered.

To this point, the reader has probably observed that we have simply taken the empirical evidence and assumed a process inside the organism that mirrors the data. Nevertheless, the shift in terminology should be fully appreciated. Empirically (that is, in the actually observed data) we know that the strength of a conditioned response increases gradually over trials and that some response strength can be observed to stimuli that differ somewhat from the original CS. We are now saying that these observations are a result of the fact that pairing a CS with a US leads to the gradual development of habit strength within the organism, and that habit generalizes to similar stimuli. To this point, we have simply assumed that the observed strength of the CR gives a pretty good indication of the hypothesized strength of a stimulus-response association built up within the organism and referred to as habit.

## Postulate I. Habit

The elicitation of a response in the presence of an active stimulus trace leads to a habit association (sHr) between that stimulus and that response.

*Ia.* sHr increases progressively in strength with the number of such experiences, reaching an upper limit depending on factors such as the intensity of the CS and the US.

*Ib.* sHr generalizes to similar stimuli in proportion to their similarity to the original CS.

*Ic.* sHr is permanent.

The formality of this postulate should not obscure its basic simplicity. Recall our early discussion that any stimulus sets up a stimulus trace within the organism that dissipates over a period of time. If a US elicits a response while the trace of a CS is still present, our postulate says that an association will be formed. We are now labeling that association *habit,* and assuming that it grows in strength gradually over repeated occurrences. How strong it ultimately becomes depends upon specific details of the conditioning procedure: a large piece of food leads to a stronger anticipatory tendency to salivate than a small piece of food. And whatever the habit strength thus produced, there is some spread to similar stimuli.

The final assumption in the postulate, namely, that habit is permanent, may appear contradictory to common sense. What about forgetting? It would take us too far afield to answer that question completely, but a few examples may at least make the present assumption seem more reasonable. If you have had occasion to return home after several years' absence, you find your memory of the scene to be essentially complete and, indeed, are acutely disturbed by changes which may have occurred. If you try to skate, play jacks, or ride a bicycle after years without practice, those skills will return almost immediately. And you have probably at least heard of the remarkably detailed memories that can be obtained under hypnosis. For these and a variety of other reasons, it appears most fruitful to think of habits as being permanent and to account for the weakening of responses by other processes. One such process is described in the next section.

## Inhibition:  Extinction and Spontaneous Recovery

Consider next another empirical phenomenon introduced in the preceding chapter: experimental extinction. We noted, in effect, that the process of classical conditioning was reversible, that the CR developed over a series of trials in which a CS was followed by a US, but that the CR gradually disappeared over a subsequent series of trials when the CS was not followed by the US. The most obvious theoretical account of this fact of experimental extinction would be that habit is lost as a result of presenting the CS alone.

This is *not*, however, the assumption we shall make. If, after the experimental extinction of a conditioned response, a period of time elapses during which the CS is not presented, the CR is likely to reappear on a subsequent presentation of the CS. This is called *spontaneous recovery*. A conditioned response may be experimentally extinguished, but it will spontaneously recover some of its lost strength over a period of time during which the CS does not occur. Spontaneous recovery is not complete; the amount of recovery depends on how completely extinction was effected and upon the amount of recovery time permitted. Under typical laboratory conditions, a reasonable rule of thumb is that an extinguished CR will recover about half of the strength it had before extinction.

Before discussing the theoretical significance of this finding, let us dwell for a moment on its practical significance. Suppose, for example, that you have been thrown from a horse and as a result of the pain and indignity experienced, find that you are now afraid of that horse (and probably other horses as a result of generalization). You may feel that this fear is unwarranted and undertake to "get over it." Even without formally studying psychology, you would probably know to arrange a session in which you could ride a number of horses under conditions in which nothing aversive would be likely to happen. In effect, the horse is a CS, the fall was a US leading to conditioning of fear, and encountering the CS without that US will result in experimental extinction of that fear. What we are now saying is that your contrived session may be quite successful, so that you are riding fearlessly by the end of the day, but you will find that some of your fear will spontaneously recover. The next time you go to the stables, your fear will to some extent return.

The effort, however, was to some avail because your fear will, indeed, be less than previously, and if that recovered fear is also extinguished during your next experience riding, still less recovery will occur for the following occasion. The practical significance of spontaneous recovery is simply that an undesirable response cannot be completely extinguished in a single session; a series of extinction sessions is typically necessary, each time followed by some spontaneous recovery but progressively less.

The theoretical significance of spontaneous recovery is perhaps obvious. Were one to assume that habit was lost as a result of experimental extinction, then the organism would, in effect, be restored to his initial condition prior to conditioning and there would be nothing left on which to base recovery. More pointedly: although the organism is not responding at the end of extinction, there must be some habit left because the response will reappear after a while.

Accordingly, we can now introduce the other major construct within the theory: inhibition. Rather than assuming that extinction results from a loss of habit, we assume that it reflects the accumulation of another process which opposes the habit and suppresses performance. Inhibition must have somewhat different properties from habit in order to account for spontaneous recovery, namely, that it can, at least in part, dissipate over time. But the reason the organism does not respond after extinction is not because habit has been lost—it is because that habit is inhibited.

### Postulate II. Inhibition

The arousal of a stimulus trace to which there is a habit association in the absence of elicitation of that response by a US, leads to inhibition (sIr) which opposes habit.

IIa. sIr increases progressively in strength with the number of such experiences, reaching an upper limit depending on the sHr available to be inhibited.

IIb. sIr generalizes to similar stimuli in proportion to their similarity to the original CS, but generalization of inhibition is less extensive than generalization of habit.

IIc. sIr is, at least in part, temporary and dissipates with time; it can also be removed by subsequent elicitations of the response by presentation of the US following the CS.

This postulate says that the observed strength of a CR is not always a pure reflection of habit strength; rather, there are two opposing processes (sHr-sIr) which jointly determine performance. This second process builds up gradually each time a CR occurs and is not then followed by the US, and will continue to do so until the habit is completely inhibited. It is also assumed that sIr generalizes to similar stimuli, as does sHr, but not as much. If a different CS is presented, there is a greater loss of inhibition than of habit; some implications of this special assumption will be seen in the derivations in the subsequent sections.

Another difference between habit and inhibition is their relative permanence. Whereas we have argued that habit is permanent, inhibition is not. We know that extinguished responses can spontaneously recover; we also know that extinguished responses can be reconditioned by reintroduction of the US. Even after extinguishing your fear of horses, a single unpleasant experience can reinstate that fear full blown. If you have ever attempted to conceal your anxiety about an impending event, such as an examination, you are probably aware of the tenuous balance that can be overthrown by the slightest disturbance. Inhibition may suppress habit, but it is a much more fragile process.

### Derivation of Conditioning, External Inhibition, Extinction and Spontaneous Recovery

The application of this theory to the types of phenomena that we have thus far encountered is illustrated graphically in Figure 11. In the figure, habit is represented by plus-signs since it leads to a tendency to make the CR. Inhibition is represented by minus-signs since it represents the tendency not to make the response. Actual response strength, then, is the difference between the plus and minus signs and is graphed as a solid line in the figure.

During the original pairing of a CS with a US, we assume that habit builds up gradually: this habit is more-or-less perfectly reflected in performance. Shown midway during that stage of the study is the effect of introducing some novel event before or during a trial. The change in the situation leads to a temporary weakening of habit and reduced performance, but this is quickly restored after the novel event has passed.

During subsequent trials in which the CS is presented alone, we assume that habit continues unaffected but that inhibition is gradually accumulated to offset that habit. This is depicted by the rising curve of minus-signs and if these are subtracted from the habit at each point, the resulting solid line shows the decrease in performance during extinction. Further, we have assumed that inhibition dissipates to some

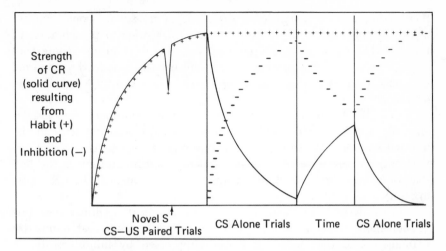

**Figure 11.** Derivation of some facts of classical conditioning from habit-inhibition theory. Habit (sHr) is indicated by plus signs and grows during trials when the CS and US are paired. Some habit would be lost by the introduction of a novel S, producing external inhibition. Inhibition (sIr) is shown by minus signs and grows on trials when the CS is presented alone; performance of the CR, as shown by the solid curve, is the difference between sHr and sIr so that experimental extinction occurs. However, sIr dissipates in part over time, leading to partial spontaneous recovery, but the recovered CR can be reextinguished by further accumulation of sIr if additional CS-alone trials are given.

extent over time so that spontaneous recovery is anticipated. Finally, re-extinction can be accomplished by again presenting the CS alone leading to the accumulation of more inhibition.

In short, this theory assumes two opposing processes, habit and inhibition. Both accumulate gradually; habit on trials with a US and inhibition on trials without a US. Both generalize to similar stimuli but habit more extensively than inhibition; habit is permanent while inhibition is more transitory. These few assumptions provide a conceptual understanding of classical conditioning itself, external inhibition, stimulus generalization, experimental extinction and spontaneous recovery. We shall not need any additional assumptions to handle some additional phenomena.

## Disinhibition

Most of the phenomena described thus far fit pretty well with intuitive expectations: experimental analysis has essentially refined them. But consider the following study: first a response is conditioned and then extinguished repeatedly so that little or no spontaneous recovery occurs. Then a novel or unusual event occurs prior to presentation of the CS. This is the same operation we described in the context of external inhibition, the presence of an unusual stimulus in the situation, but now it occurs after extinction rather than during original conditioning.

Our natural expectation would be that the conditioned response, if anything, would be still weaker than would have occurred without the unusual stimulus. What Pavlov first observed, however, is that the CR is stronger than expected. The phenomenon of *disinhibition* is the fact that an extinguished conditioned response may reappear if the CS occurs in an unusual context.

Let us again pause to reflect upon the practical significance of this phenomenon. Perhaps there is no more dramatic proof that habits are permanent and that they are simply suppressed by inhibition. If we return to the fear-of-horses example, you may have completely gotten over your fear under normal circumstances, but if something unusual or unexpected happens before you go to the stables to ride, your fear is likely to return. Notice in particular that this event need not have any particular relation to horses. If, for example, driving to the stable you have a narrow miss at an accident, you are likely to find yourself somewhat more fearful of a horse when you arrive. Even if you go to a different stable, some fear may return.

What we are saying is that a person who has once learned a conditioned response will never be the same as the person who did not learn that response in the first place, even though the former may have successfully extinguished the response. A child that is permitted to learn to fear the dark may overcome that fear as an adult, but he is not the same as an adult who never learned to fear the dark. If something happens to change the normal routine of his life, the learned-but-extinguished person will experience a return of his fear while the never-learned person can take such an event in stride. For example, the person who has unusual difficulty adjusting to the death of a loved one is perhaps the person who has normally overcome a number of fears and anxieties which are then disinhibited by this trauma.

Disinhibition can be derived from the habit-inhibition theory of classical conditioning. This derivation is shown graphically in Figure 12 (where straight lines are used for convenience of exposition). As with the discussion of stimulus generalization, we are plotting along the baseline the change from the original CS, produced in this case by a change in the context. We have to assume that habit strength is weaker to a different stimulus since that was the way we explained external inhibition. But we have also assumed that inhibition does not generalize as extensively as habit; this assumption is depicted by the minus-signs in Figure 12, decreasing more rapidly than the plus-signs as the CS is changed. Again computing performance as the difference between habit and inhibition, the solid line in Figure 12 shows the predicted level of performance. Specifically, although there is no performance of the CR at the original CS (where the base line is zero), changing the CS somewhat leads to increased performance because inhibition is decreased more than habit.

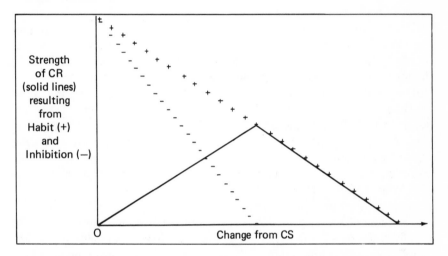

**Figure 12.** Derivation of disinhibition from habit-inhibition theory. The original CS is shown above zero on the baseline, and it is assumed that conditioning built up some habit but that subsequent extinction built up an equal amount of inhibition so that no CR would occur. If the situation is changed, however, as by the introduction of an unusual event, both habit and inhibition will suffer a generalization decrement, but inhibition more so than habit. This is reflected by the steeper row of minus signs than plus signs. Since the strength of the CR is the difference between habit and inhibition, as shown by the solid line, the CR is expected to occur if the situation is changed after experimental extinction.

Our explanation of disinhibition, therefore, is simply that a change in the situation leads to somewhat less habit, but to a greater loss of inhibition, so that the *net* tendency to make the response (habit minus inhibition) increases. The theory also predicts that the amount of disinhibition will depend upon the amount of change that occurs; the CR will be stronger with moderate changes than with very small ones, but will get weaker again with very extensive changes. Although we cannot put exact numbers along the baseline of Figure 12, this general pattern of results is consistent with our knowledge of disinhibition.

## Differential Classical Conditioning

The value of a theory is only partly illustrated by its capacity to integrate a number of known phenomena and to provide understanding of them in terms of a small number of assumptions. It is best illustrated when the theory is applied to somewhat different situations and can correctly predict what will happen.

Differential classical conditioning is a procedure involving two similar stimuli used as CS. For convenience in referring to a particular example, let us return to the Pavlovian laboratory and use a moderately high-pitched tone as one CS and a somewhat lower tone as a second CS, with dogs and food and salivation. On some occasions, the high-pitched tone is presented and is followed by the delivery of the US food. We shall call this tone CS+. On other occasions, interspersed irregularly and unpredictably with the CS+ are occasions on which the low-pitched tone is presented and *not* followed by the US food. We shall call this tone CS−. The question is, can the theory correctly predict what the results of this procedure will be?

The implications of the theory are shown graphically in Figure 13. Let us describe it sequentially. The essence of the derivation is to determine the development of habit and inhibition over trials of differential classical conditioning and to compute from those the response strength expected to the two stimuli. Our first assumption is that the elicitation of salivation by food following CS+ will lead to the progressive development of habit strength to that stimulus. This is shown by the increasing curve of large plus-signs identified as cs+Hr. Our assumption is that this habit will generalize to similar stimuli, and for purposes of illustration, let us assume that the difference in the pitches of the two tones is such that the habit generalized to CS− is about half that developed to CS+. Accordingly, habit will also accrue to CS− according to the curve of small plus-signs identified as cs-Hr. We are saying simply that the pairing of one CS with a US leads to some tendency to respond to it, and some generalized tendency to respond to similar stimuli—and plotting the growth of these tendencies over successive trials.

Next, the fact that salivation is not elicited by food following the CS− implies that inhibition will be developed to that stimulus. Since inhibition can only begin to accumulate when there is habit available to inhibit, the growth of sIr is more gradual. An approximation to the expected growth of inhibition to CS− is shown by the curve of small minus-signs identified as cs-Ir. This inhibition will, in turn, generalize toward the CS+, but this generalization is less than that for habit; in the graph we have assumed that about one-fourth of the inhibition accumulating at CS− generalizes to CS+ and this is graphed by the large minus-signs identified as cs+Ir. Basically, we are assuming that once the CR begins to occur to the wrong stimulus as a result of generalization, it begins to be inhibited and some of this inhibition will generalize back to the correct stimulus.

The expected response strength of each stimulus can now be computed by simply subtracting, at each point, its sIr from its sHr. This has been done for the two stimuli separately, that to the CS+ shown by the wide solid line and that to the CS− by the narrow solid line. The theory predicts that the CR will grow progressively to CS+ although not getting to quite as high a level as if no CS− were included (because of generalization of inhibition) and that the CR will at first increase but then decrease to CS− (at first as a result of generali-

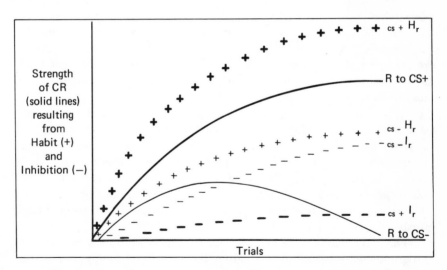

**Figure 13.** Derivation of differential classical conditioning from habit-inhibition theory. CS+ is followed by the US, leading to habit as shown by the large plus-signs; this habit generalizes to CS− as shown by the small plus-signs. CS− is not followed by the US, leading to inhibition shown by the small minus-signs; this inhibition generalizes to CS+ as shown by the large minus-signs. Subtracting habit from inhibition to each stimulus leads to expected performance, the wide solid curve to CS+ and the narrow solid curve to CS−.

zation of habit from CS+ and then as a result of inhibition built up to it).

The solid curves in Figure 13 represent, in somewhat idealized form, the types of experimental data obtained in studies of differential classical conditioning. They also represent, of course, adaptive behavior. If you find that one horse is "spooky" and likely to buck while another similar looking horse is calm and manageable, it is appropriate to differentiate between them so as to fear the one and not the other. While we can not pursue them here, the theory has a large number of additional implications, some of which seem contrary to our everyday expectations but which have nevertheless been confirmed by careful experimental analysis. Indeed, very much the same theory has been applied to other types of learning situations such as will be discussed in the following chapters. It is this generality that has kept habit-inhibition theory attractive.

### Experimental Neurosis

One use of the procedure of differential classical conditioning is to determine how fine a discrimination an animal is capable of. With humans, of course, we can simply ask whether two tones sound alike or different, but with animals, we need to develop some nonverbal response by which they can communicate to the experimenter. Clearly, if an animal can learn to respond differentially to two stimuli, he can discriminate between them.

In an effort to obtain such information, Pavlov would first employ differential conditioning with stimuli that were quite dissimilar, say, a very high-pitched tone versus a very low-pitched tone. He would then make them progressively more similar in an attempt to find out where the discrimination broke down indicating that the animal could no longer respond differentially. Interestingly enough, he found that when the stimuli became very similar, not only did the discrimination break down, so did the dog!

The dog would show obvious signs of fear and anxiety about the experimental situation, so that rather than standing quietly in the stock and salivating when appropriate, he would resist the situation. This behavior carried over to his total behavior. He would huddle in a corner of his living cage, cower at the sight of his familiar handler, refuse to eat regularly, and overreact to the slightest sound or distraction. Pavlov called this result an *experimental neurosis* because of its apparent similarity to many human neurotic behaviors, and he usually had to send the dog away from the laboratory for a rest cure of tender care in the country.

Perhaps this extrapolation to human neuroses is exaggerated, but there is mounting evidence that many maladjustments do, in fact, result from a person being confronted with very difficult decisions in which there are strong tendencies to make a response (habit) and strong tendencies not to make the response (inhibition). Not infrequently, the latter tendency is a result of punishment rather than simply failure of reinforcement, but the conflict between strong tendencies certainly is a conspicuous part of the misery that results in neurotic behavior. While the story of human neuroses is undoubtedly more complicated, research with animals would strongly suggest the following dictum: if you are concerned with the general well-being of another person, avoid forcing him to confront severe conflict between habits and inhibition. If a child is strongly tempted to engage in some behavior as a result of pressure from his peers, but is strongly inhibited by threats of parental displeasure, the seeds of neuroses may have been planted.

The concepts of habit and inhibition, as developed here, are certainly rudimentary and at best suggestive. Nevertheless, the range of phenomena to which they apply strongly suggest that some such mechanism is a useful way to conceptualize learning. Performance is a two-way street: traffic flows in one direction to produce responding and in the opposite direction to resist responding. In some form or other, at least this image derived from habit-inhibition theory has many important and largely-true implications for the understanding of behavior.

### True-False Items: A Scientific Theory of Classical Conditioning

1. The value of a theory resides primarily in how well it correctly describes what is really going on inside the subject.

(The value of a scientific theory resides in how correctly it describes data; in this case, behavior. It is not necessary that there really be a "habit" and an "inhibition" localized in the person for the theory to be of value. False.)

2. Habit refers to excessive indulgence in a behavior so that it becomes socially undesirable.

(Although the term is often used in this manner in everyday language, here habit refers to an association between a stimulus and a response. False.)

3. Good habits spontaneously recover more than bad habits.

(The principle of spontaneous recovery is quite indifferent as to the desirability of an extinguished response. False.)

4. Inhibition refers to an inability to behave naturally because of fear and anxiety.

(Again in everyday language, we often speak of an "inhibited" person as one who seems overly fearful or anxious. However, here inhibition refers to the process resulting from nonreinforcement and opposing habit. False.)

5. The fact that reconditioning following extinction proceeds faster than original conditioning implies that habits are quickly regained.

(Extinguished responses are, indeed, regained rapidly. Recall, however, that habit is not lost during extinction; rather, inhibition is built up. Hence, reconditioning involves the removal of inhibition and this fact indicates that inhibition is removed more quickly than habit is gained. False.)

6. If you want to overcome a habit "once and for all," it is best not to include any unusual experiences in the context of that habit.

(Even if you repeatedly extinguish a response in a single context, it will be subject to disinhibition if any unusual experiences happen. Better, then, to include some unusual experiences during the extinction process so they will no longer be unusual and produce disinhibition. False.)

7. Disinhibition indicates that extinguished habits fail to generalize.

(When a conditioned response is extinguished, the result is inhibition of the habit. When the situation changes, both processes suffer a generalization decrement, but habit generalizes more than inhibition producing a net increase in response tendency. False.)

8. From the theory, we would predict that conditioning would occur as rapidly if some times the US is omitted or if it is given every time the CS occurs.

(Each time the US is omitted, habit fails to increase and there is also an increase in inhibition. Both of these effects would mean that the CR would gain strength more slowly if only part of the trials include the US. False.)

9. From the theory, we would expect that external inhibition would result from an unusual event no matter how long it occurred before the next trial.

(External inhibition would result only if an unusual event occurred soon enough before a trial that the trace of that event still persisted so as to change the context. False.)

10. From the theory, we would predict that generalization would be less if the CS changed from trial to trial during conditioning.

(Although varying the CS from trial to trial would lead to slower learning, the wider the variety of stimuli to which the CR has become conditioned, the wider the range of generalization that would be expected. False.)

11. From the theory, we would predict that differential conditioning could not occur if both stimuli were first followed by the US after which only one of them is followed by the US.

(If both stimuli are followed by the US, both will gain equally in habit strength. Nevertheless, if subsequently the US is omitted following one of them, inhibition would begin to accrue to it and lead to differential responding to the two stimuli. False.)

12. If we are to prevent mental illness, we must avoid inhibitions.

(Conflict arises only when a strong inhibition opposes a strong habit. If a response is completely inhibited, as following extinction, no experimental neurosis is found. Inhibition of undesirable responses is adaptive. False.)

# 6

# Positive Reinforcement

Mankind certainly did not wait for the advent of scientific psychology to discover the principle of positive reinforcement. From the time man began to domesticate animals (including his children), he surely recognized that the behavior of organisms can be brought under control by the administration of rewards. Accordingly, although it is still difficult to provide a completely adequate statement of the principle of positive reinforcement, the reader is already familiar with the fact that WHENEVER A RESPONSE IS CLOSELY FOLLOWED IN TIME BY A REWARD, THE TENDENCY FOR THAT RESPONSE TO OCCUR IN THE FUTURE IS INCREASED ACCORDING TO THE AMOUNT, DELAY, AND QUALITY OF THE REWARD.

Again the reader should not be misled by the apparent simplicity of this principle. In later sections of this chapter, we shall explore some of the details surrounding its application. First, however, let us discount two popular misconceptions about the principle of positive reinforcement.

*The reward does not have to be an effect of, that is, produced by, the response in order for it to be effective.* The law simply states that the temporal contiguity of a reward with a response is sufficient to increase the likelihood of that response. This fact was demonstrated most clearly in a study done by B. F. Skinner.

He first placed a pigeon in an apparatus containing a food hopper that could be exposed to the pigeon automatically. He set the apparatus so that the food hopper was exposed periodically, say, for three seconds every thirty seconds. Note that the pigeon had nothing whatsoever to do except eat the food when it was available. Nevertheless, Skinner observed that the pigeon began increasingly to engage in some type of behavior such as strutting around the cage with its neck stretched upward. Skinner could not predict *what* the pigeon would learn to do, and in fact, the same pigeon might change behaviors occasionally. But *that* the pigeon would learn something was predictable from the principle of positive reinforcement.

The reasoning is as follows. When the reward is delivered, the pigeon is of necessity doing something. If, for example, he was exploring the top of the box when a reward came, then he is more likely to resume that type of behavior after the reward. This means he is likely to be doing the same thing the next time a reward is given, and so on, progressively. The pigeon, in effect, becomes trapped into making a response as if it produced the reward when, in fact, the reward was completely independent of his behavior.

Skinner called this superstitious behavior in the pigeon because it appears to be similar to one basis for the learning of human superstitions. With the emphasis of modern science on discovering the true causes of events, we are no longer prone to mass superstitions such as sacrificial rites to the gods, rain dances, and witch doctors. But we are still subject to the principle of positive reinforcement and when something good happens to us (and similarly when something bad happens), we tend to search our recent behaviors for what we did to deserve it. Although perhaps somewhat ashamed to admit it, almost all of us have our private superstitions. A very common example is the tendency to avoid saying what a nice day it is for the picnic lest observing the fact should cause it to rain.

The second disclaimer concerning the principle of positive reinforcement is that the person does not need to recognize a causal effect of his response in producing the reward. The principle says that the effect of rewards is automatic and the organism does not need to "see" the relationship. Although the area called "learning without awareness" is still somewhat controversial, the weight of the evidence favors the present interpretation. All of us, for example, have various mannerisms of which we are unaware (and which we might wish to change were we aware of) that have been learned because of their effects.

One way to illustrate this fact experimentally is to ask college students simply to say words at random under the guise of a study of vocabulary frequency. The experimenter writes the words down as they are said and casually mutters "un-huh" when the subject happens to say a plural noun. Social agreement is a kind of reward for humans, and the subjects increasingly give plural nouns without being consciously aware of doing so.

This is not to say that conscious awareness cannot affect learning. When we are aware that our behavior did not affect the reward, we can try to talk ourselves out of developing a superstition about it. And when we are conscious of our behavior producing a reward, we can rehearse that sequence of events in order to foster learning. But the important point remains: *awareness is not necessary for learning to occur.*

These qualifications are important for effective application of the principle of positive reinforcement. Consider, as one example, the parent who feeds a baby on a closely timed schedule. The baby is fed by the clock whether hungry or not. Picking the baby up provides a strong reward of contact comfort and feeding is also a reward if the baby is hungry. If, therefore, the baby is crying at the time the clock says to feed him, picking up and feeding him increases the likelihood of his crying in the future! The parent may not intend to reward such behavior and the baby may not be aware of what is going on, but the principle of positive reinforcement works relentlessly on behaviors, desirable or undesirable, intentional or adventitious.

The principle of positive reinforcement is studied experimentally in two types of situations: operant conditioning and instrumental conditioning. In *operant conditioning,* a response is freely available to the organism, at least for some period of time during which he can respond as frequently as he wants. In the laboratory, for example, a rat may be in an apparatus containing a bar that he can press at any time. Similarly, studying is a freely available response to students. In this type of situation, we will be principally concerned with how the principle of positive reinforcement determines the rate at which the response occurs over time. In *instrumental conditioning,* a response is periodically enabled by the environment so that its occurrence is restricted to discrete trials. In the laboratory, for example, a rat may be released from a start box enabling him to run through a maze, but he cannot do so except when the start door is opened. Similarly, the student periodically has the opportunity to attend a lecture. In this situation, we will be principally concerned with how the principle of positive reinforcement determines the likelihood and speed with which the organism responds when an opportunity arises. The principle is the same in both cases; only the conditions under which it is observed differ.

Before describing some of the details of these two types of conditioning, it is necessary to discuss the problem of identifying rewarding events. That is to say, how can we determine which events will, in fact, lead to an increase in the tendency to make responses which produce them?

## Events that ARE Rewarding

The principle of positive reinforcement is of wide generality and great practical significance. In applying this principle, however, one inevitably faces the problem of identifying those events that are, in fact, rewarding. We may have a pretty good intuition that food will reward a hungry organism, but we really do not know in advance what commodities constitute food for a particular species. Pigeons reject raisins while monkeys devour them eagerly even when reasonably satiated. One child may spend hours to earn praise or a good grade from a teacher while another is largely indifferent to such events. Surely it would be advantageous to be able to know in advance whether a presumed event would serve as a reward.

There is, to date, no agreed-upon solution to this objective. However, psychologists have taken several approaches which deserve some discussion.

### Functional Identification

We have already noted that the basic technique for determining whether an event is a stimulus is a functional approach: events that can be shown to function as stimuli in behavioral laws are stimuli. In practice, the most common method for making the further determination of whether a stimulus is emotionally positive is also functional. That is to say, *a reward is a stimulus that has been shown to function as a reward in the principle of positive reinforcement.*

The basic procedure is as follows: the organism is placed in a learning situation in which prior knowledge insures that the response is readily learnable when followed by known rewards. The stimulus event in question is then given following that response, and if some appropriate response measure indicates learning, the event is classified as a reward. The circularity of this procedure is reduced by the further assumption that that event will function as a reward for that and similar organisms in the learning of other responses.

One illustration of how this procedure can lead to the discovery of unexpected rewarding events can be seen in the effects of electrical stimulation of the brain. Shock can be administered through small electrodes lowered into the brain through a hole drilled into the skull of a rat. Now it is well known that electric shock applied to the paws or other exterior surface of a rat is aversive. It would thus seem reasonable to expect that a shock applied internally would also be aversive. Surprisingly, stimulation of certain regions of the brain (notably the septum) are actually rewarding rather than aversive.

Rats quickly learn to press a bar to produce brain stimulation. The detailed results are somewhat different from those found using hunger and food. For example, the rat may require several preliminary brain shocks to "prime" his behavior before he begins to respond himself each day. But the power of this reward is apparently considerable. If the rat is left alone with two bars, one of which produces food and the other of which produces brain stimulation, he may need to be rescued from the situation after a day or so since he is likely to starve to death because of his preference for brain stimulation.

The full impact of this discovery has by no means yet been felt. Our understanding of the underlying biological mechanisms of reward will undoubtedly be significantly advanced by further experimental analysis of this effect. In the meantime, we can say that electrical stimulation of appropriate regions of the brain qualify as rewards simply because they have been shown experimentally to have that property. We accept as rewards events that function as rewards.

### The Drive-Reduction Hypothesis

To date, the most influential hypothesis concerning the critical property of an event for it to qualify as a reward was first formalized and integrated into a general behavior theory by Clark Hull. The *drive-reduction hypothesis* asserts that rewarding events are ones that result in a reduction in some prevailing drive of the organism.

The popularity of this hypothesis stems in part from its wide generality. Most of the stimuli actually used as rewards can readily be seen to fall under this rule. Eating food reduces hunger, drinking water reduces thirst, copulating reduces the goading of sex. More important, however, is the biological significance of such a rule. As we shall see, most, if not all, primary drives are based upon survival needs of the organism: we must eat to live. Imagine an organism that was not rewarded (in the sense of learning responses) by the receipt of food. Each time he became hungry, he would have to engage in more-or-less random trial-and-error behavior until he chanced to find and consume food. Such an organism would obviously be at a disadvantage in competition with an organism that could profit from his experiences and come to make his food-getting responses quickly and efficiently. The data are consistent with this compelling argument, and at least a weaker form of the drive-reduction hypothesis is true: *all events that lead to drive reduction are rewards.*

The original, stronger hypothesis, that all rewards involve drive reduction, has been questioned by a number of psychologists, but perhaps most vigorously by Fred Sheffield. His own hypothesis was that it is not drive reduction that is rewarding, but rather that it is simply making the consummatory response itself. His first attack upon the drive-reduction hypothesis involved the use of saccharine. Although this substance tastes sweet, it is not digestable and is eliminated from the body chemically unchanged. Consistent with Sheffield's notion, consuming saccharine is a fully effective reward for rats. They will press bars or run mazes in order to consume this nonnutritive substance.

The difficulty with these demonstrations was the failure to distinguish carefully between drive and need. We shall make that distinction more fully later. The important fact in this context is that hunger as a psychological drive is not the same as the biological need for food. It is possible to argue, therefore, that although saccharine is nonnutritive, it is essentially indistinguishable from sugar; in effect, the organism is tricked into reacting as if the hunger drive had been reduced. Consistent with this argument, subsequent studies have shown that prefeeding a rat with saccharine decreases the amount of nutritive food which it later consumes.

More difficult to dismiss is another series of studies by Sheffield. The event that presumably reduces the sex drive is orgasm, but is erotic stimulation short of orgasm rewarding? If so, this fact would be consistent with the hypothesis that making the consummatory response constitutes reward with eventual drive reduction being an incidental by-product of normal consummation. Sheffield might have asked this question of young, unmarried couples, since the known incidence of petting strongly suggests an affirmative answer. But he demonstrated the fact experimentally with rats. For example, he showed that male rats would learn to run through a maze to a goal box containing a receptive female rat with whom he was allowed to copulate but not sufficiently to produce ejaculation. Pleasurable stimulation appears to be rewarding even if no obvious drive reduction results from such stimulation.

Other critics of the drive-reduction hypothesis have used somewhat less direct approaches. They have shown that monkeys will repeatedly dismantle mechanical puzzles for no other reward than simply doing so; indeed, performance may be worse if food is given for working the puzzles. Monkeys will also solve problems that enable them to look out into the laboratory, and even rats will learn responses that turn on lights or that expose them to novel situations that they can explore. These are a few of the situations in which performance changes occur in the absence of any obvious source of drive reduction.

But proponents of the drive reduction hypothesis have been tenacious in their belief, perhaps because no equally simple and compelling alternative has yet been proposed. Sex is known to be incompatible with fear, and perhaps rats are fearful in a maze and engaging in sexual stimulation provides a means of reducing fear. Similarly, monkeys may be fearful in an enclosed box. In sum, the work of Sheffield and others has placed difficult strains upon the strong form of the drive-reduction hypothesis, but it has as yet refused to die.

### Secondary Reinforcement

When we refer to *primary* reinforcement, we refer to events that function as rewards without any special training. Food to a hungry organism and water to a thirsty one are familiar primary reinforcers. But obviously, little everyday human behavior is actually controlled by such primary events. Perhaps of greater practical importance, therefore, is the concept of *secondary reinforcement*. Stimuli which are initially neutral in emotional value may acquire reinforcing properties as a result of being paired with primary rewarding events. The basic procedure is classical conditioning: the positive emotional responses elicited by a primary reward may become associated with a neutral stimulus according to the principle of the anticipatory response.

There are several laboratory demonstrations of this phenomenon. In an early one, rats were trained to press a bar to obtain food that was delivered with a distinctive click of the feeding mechanism. During extinction, some rats continued to receive the click (but no food) while the others got nothing for continuing to press the bar. The rats that received the click persisted longer in pressing, presumably because the click had regularly preceded food delivery and had acquired secondary reinforcing power which maintained the response longer than when it was omitted.

A stronger demonstration is when a new response is learned to obtain stimuli whose reinforcing value has been acquired. One way to do this is to first run rats down a short straight alley, sometimes terminating in a white goal box and sometimes in a black goal box. The white box contains food; the black box is empty. After a number of runs to each goal box, these are placed at the ends of a T-maze— now both being empty. Nevertheless, the rats develop a temporary preference for going in the direction of the white goal box which had previously contained food, thus displaying new learning of a maze to get a stimulus previously associated with food.

Still more comparable to learned rewards for human behavior are studies using token-rewards. Chimpanzees will work for grapes for a while but then become satiated and quit. One way to get around this problem is to use a vending machine that delivers grapes when a poker-chip is inserted; this pairing effectively establishes the chips as secondary reinforcers. The chimps will then work consistently to accumulate a supply of poker chips which they later can turn in for grapes.

The obvious analog of this last procedure is money; pieces of paper have little or no intrinsic value, but may acquire reinforcing value by being paired with a wide variety of rewards and pleasures. Virtually everyone has learned the value of money, although some seem more addicted to it than others. In other cases, the events that have secondary reinforcing value are more varied among people. It is true that most students accept praise and good grades from teachers as secondary reinforcers, but not all do. Most people are rewarded if you will simply listen while they talk; others require verbal approval. Some people are strongly competitive and enjoy displaying their ability and versatility; others find cooperation more satisfying. These are but a few of the countless array of events that have acquired reinforcing value for people.

The basic mechanism is always the same: *events that have been associated with rewarding experiences acquire reinforcing power*—the sight of another person, a stamp collection, news that one's favorite team won their game. We differ as to what events have acquired such secondary reinforcing effects because we differ in the learning experiences we have had. But all of the principles of classical conditioning apply to the learning of secondary reinforcement, and one way to identify rewards for an individual is to study his past history. And one way to misidentify rewards is to assume that everyone else has had the same experiences you have had and hence is rewarded by the same events you like. The flashy sports car may be a symbol of success for one young man; a patched-up heap of a car the ultimate for another.

## High-Probability Behaviors

Recently, David Premack has suggested a very useful way of identifying rewarding events. His notion is that organisms are rewarded by being permitted to engage in behaviors which they, at the moment, have a strong tendency to make. In the vernacular, organisms learn responses that enable them to do things they want to do.

Suppose we gave a hungry rat a choice between running and eating. Obviously, he would prefer to eat. This preference shows that eating is a higher probability behavior than running, and hence the typical finding that a rat can be rewarded for running by being permitted to eat. One of Premack's demonstrations reversed this relationship. He satiated rats on food while depriving them of activity. Now the rat would prefer to run rather than to eat. He then showed that rats would eat when satiated in order to be permitted to run. Parents are already familiar with this fact, since a child may be induced to eat an undesired food in order to be excused from the table and begin to play.

This approach has considerable practical utility. Find out what a person wants most to do, and then enable him to do it provided he practices the task you want him to learn. If a child wants to watch television, he might be required to clean his room first—rather than afterwards. If a student wants to play during recess, he might be required to demonstrate that he has learned his lesson before being dismissed—rather than scheduling recess time independent of his learning. If a boy wants to engage in a little necking, a girl might resist unless his dress and manner are ones of which she approves—rather than thinking that later she can correct his faults.

The high probability behavior approach to identifying rewards is not necessarily contradictory to the drive-reduction hypothesis. Presumably, when an organism wants to do something, it is because he is motivated to do so, and doing it reduces that motivation. Premack's idea is nevertheless valuable as a means of identifying rewards. One does not have to explore the underlying motives for a child wanting, for instance, to color a picture. If you ask him and he says that that is what he wants to do, then you can proceed directly to arrange conditions so that he can color a picture after he has practiced a desired task.

## Summary

The principle of postive reinforcement says that responses become more likely to occur if they are followed by rewarding events. The following two sections describe these effects in greater detail. But the first problem is to identify rewarding events. There have been a variety of attempts to solve this problem other than the ones described here, but none of those has gained wide acceptance. But we can summarize the current state of knowledge briefly. You know you have a reward if it will reduce a person's drive or if he has a high probability of making a response which you control. And if you have a stimulus which has previously been associated with known rewards, it can also serve that function. Otherwise, you know you have a reward only if you have previously found out that it is. These guidelines, although not providing a satisfactory scientific theory of reward, do provide enough information to employ the principle of positive reinforcement with great effectiveness.

## Operant Conditioning

When a response is freely available, at least for periods of time during which it may be made repeatedly, it is referred to as an operant response and the experimental analysis of it is called operant conditioning. The principal variable of interest in operant conditioning is the *schedule of reinforcement.* Specifically, the goal is to describe how performance of a response that is freely available is affected by the schedule that determines when reward is available for making that response.

Consider, for example, the response of looking in your mailbox. Under normal circumstances, you may perform this response at any time and as frequently as you wish. However, mail is usually delivered once, twice, or in some places a half-dozen times a day, and looking in your mailbox before the next delivery is never rewarded. Looking in your mailbox is controlled in part by the schedule of mail deliveries.

There are two basic types of schedules of reinforcement each of which has two basic variants. The first is when reward is scheduled according to time. The mailbox example is one illustration. Although the response may be made at any time, it actually is reinforced only at certain times determined by the environment. When the time between reinforcements is constant, it is called a *fixed interval* schedule; for example, reward might be obtainable once a minute, once an hour, once a day or on any other schedule that is regular. Everyday examples of perfectly constant intervals are uncommon, but listening for the hour chime on the radio so as to set your watch would almost qualify as a fixed-interval, one-hour schedule.

More commonly, the interval between available rewards varies. In the limiting case, this variation is random and unpredictable, and is called a *variable interval* schedule. The classic picture of a motorcycle policeman waiting behind a billboard for a speeding motorist is under control of a variable interval schedule because the opportunity to make an arrest may occur at any time.

The second basic type of schedule is based upon enumeration, i.e., the counting of responses. In the simplest possible schedule, every response is reinforced; since reward is continuously available, this schedule is referred to as *continuous reinforcement.* For example, every time you turn on the faucet, water appears. But under many circumstances, a number of responses are required to effect the reward. When this number is constant, we refer to a *fixed ratio* schedule because the ratio of the number of responses per reward is always the same. Again, perfectly constant schedules are rare, but a bridge player must deal exactly fifty-two cards in order to engage in the game.

When the number of responses required to produce reward varies from occasion to occasion, we refer to a *variable ratio* schedule. The number of swings of the axe required to chop down a tree varies from tree to tree. In ratio schedules, reward is continuously available but typically more than one response is required to obtain it.

These four basic schedules will serve to illustrate the domain of operant conditioning and an understanding of them is a prerequisite to dealing with more complex schedules. To repeat, reward may be scheduled according to time (interval schedules) or enumeration of responses (ratio schedules); in either case, the schedule may be fixed or variable.

### Fixed-Interval Schedule Behavior

The optimal behavior in a fixed interval schedule is easy enough to surmise in advance: the organism should wait precisely the length of the interval and then make a single response, receive reward and wait again. This would insure that he would receive all of the rewards that are available with the least possible effort. There are, however, two closely related reasons why organisms do not adjust this well.

The first is simply that our natural timing capacity is not perfect. All mammals contain what may be called an "internal clock," an ability to judge the passage of time presumably on the basis of rhythmic processes within the organism. But this judgment is only approximate. A person with a watch, or a rat given a comparable timing stimulus, could handle a fixed interval schedule more accurately. But in the absence of these, we can only approximate a fixed interval.

The second reason for failure to adjust optimally is the principle of the anticipatory response. If a rewarded response occurs at the end of an interval of time, this is regularly preceded by earlier temporal cues which should also tend to elicit the response before its regularly scheduled time. Even were timing perfect, there would be a tendency to begin responding before the appointed hour. For example, you may know full well that the dining room does not open until 6:00 P.M. for dinner and you may also know that it is now only 5:30 P.M., but unless there are stronger competing alternatives, you are likely to begin approaching the dining room in order to be there when it opens.

Thus comes about the typical behavior observed when an organism is studied under a fixed interval schedule of reinforcement. For a while after a reward is received, he does not respond at all. Even his imperfect clock knows that it is not yet time, and it is too far away for anticipatory responses to be very likely. As time passes and the appropriate hour approaches, the anticipatory tendency increases and the temporal cues become similar to the reinforced ones and responding begins—at first slowly and then progressively more rapidly so that he is almost certain to make a response at the time a reward is next available. The behavior is often referred to as a "fixed-interval scallop" indicating that stable performance under such a schedule exhibits first a very low rate of responding and then a continuously increasing rate as reinforcement time approaches. This behavior is shown graphically in Figure 14.

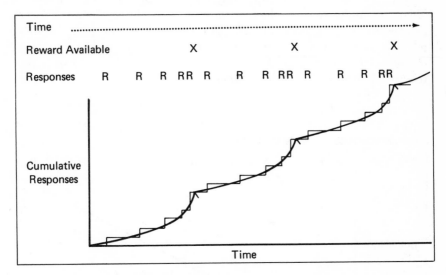

**Figure 14.** Performance under a fixed-interval schedule of reinforcement. Reward is available at regular intervals over time, indicated above by X's. Performance shows a pause after each reinforcement and then a gradually increasing frequency of responding as the next scheduled reward approaches. Separate responses are shown by R's in the figure, and these are cumulated in the lower graph to indicate the fixed-interval scallop. (In the cumulative record, each response steps the curve up a notch, and the slash mark indicates the occurrence of reward.)

This is the type of behavior that can be observed when, for example, a housewife is roasting meat scheduled to cook for an hour. If we observe her "looking in the oven" behavior, it will typically begin to occur well before the hour is up and progressively increase in frequency as the time to remove the roast approaches. It is the type of behavior that has led to the saying, "a watched pot never boils" . . . although eventually, of course, it does.

## Variable-Interval Schedule Behavior

When reward is scheduled according to a variable interval, the organism has no way of knowing when a response might be reinforced.

In the idealized case, reward might occur at any time with an overall frequency depending on the average length of interval between rewards. In this schedule, once a reward is "set up," the next response will be reinforced, and hence one way to adjust to such a schedule would be to respond at a very slow rate. Doing so, however, might delay getting some rewards that are set up soon after the last one. The behavior of organisms under such a schedule shows a kind of compromise between responding very rapidly in order to be sure to get every possible reward and responding very slowly in order not to make many more responses than necessary. The result, as shown in Figure 15, is a relatively low but steady rate of responding.

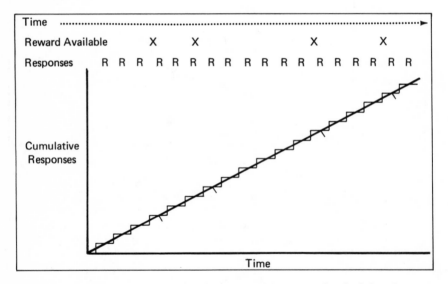

**Figure 15.** Performance under a variable interval schedule of reinforcement. Reward is available at unpredictable times. The response rate is essentially constant, reflected in a steadily increasing cumulative record.

### Fixed-Ratio Schedule Behavior

In a fixed-ratio schedule, reward is available at any time but several responses are required in order to obtain it. Accordingly, the organism is free to obtain as many rewards as he wishes and as rapidly as he can produce the requisite responses. Under these circumstances, the behavior shows two distinct features: a pause after reinforcement, and then a rapid and steady response rate until the ratio is complete.

In effect, once the chain is begun, there is no better approach than to run through the entire ratio as rapidly as possible. After obtaining the reward, however, the organism is likely to take a break before starting off again. The duration of the pause, naturally enough, depends on the length of the ratio; the longer the ratio, the longer the pause before responding begins. But once it is under way, there is an essentially uninterrupted sequence of responses. This type of behavior is illustrated graphically in Figure 16.

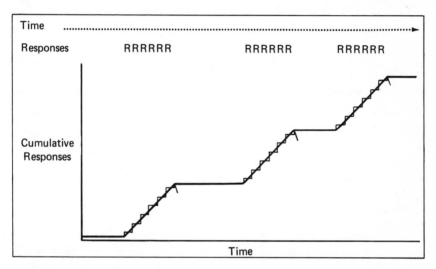

**Figure 16.** Performance under a fixed-ratio schedule of reinforcement. In this illustration, reward is always available but requires six responses to obtain it. There is a pause after each reinforcement and then a rapid run of responses sufficient to obtain another reward.

## Variable-Ratio Schedule Behavior

In a variable-ratio schedule, reward is available at any time, some number of responses is required to obtain it, and the number varies unpredictably from occasion to occasion. As with the fixed ratio, once an organism begins to respond, there is no better approach than to complete the ratio whatever it happens to be. But there should be less tendency to pause after a reward because the next ratio might be a very short one. There may be some pause after the reward, especially as the average length of the ratio gets very long, but the tendency is to respond quite rapidly and steadily. This type of behavior is graphed in Figure 17.

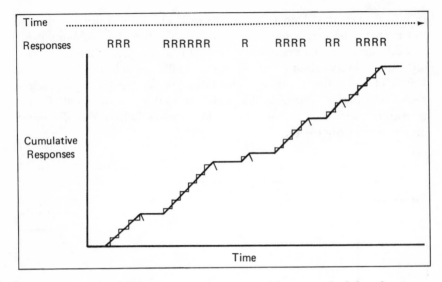

**Figure 17.** Performance under a variable-ratio schedule of reinforcement. The number of responses required to obtain reward varies from occasion to occasion. A brief pause after reward is followed by a high rate of responding until the next reward is obtained.

## Complex Schedules

An enormous number of more complex schedules can be designed by various combinations of these four basic schedules. For example, a *mixed* schedule is one in which two different schedules are combined so that sometimes one is in effect and sometimes the other is in effect. If there is some external stimulus signalling to the organism which schedule is in force, it is referred to as a *multiple* schedule. Several schedules may be running for different responses at the same time, the organism may be given a choice between alternative schedules, or they may be run in sequence so that first one and then the other must be satisfied in order to obtain reward. By-and-large, the behavior observed under these more complex schedules can be seen as some reasonable combination of the performance generated by the simple schedules which comprise them. Suppose, for example, that a fixed-interval schedule is combined with a fixed-ratio schedule so that reward is available at regular intervals but a number of responses is required to obtain it when available. This causes the organism first to wait out most of the interval as characteristic of a fixed-interval schedule, but then to respond at a high, steady rate as characteristic of a fixed-ratio schedule once he begins to respond. The behavior looks very much like that in Figure 16 except the pause after each reward is now controlled by the length of the fixed-interval schedule.

## Summary and Applications

The rate at which freely available responses occur over time is importantly controlled by the schedule according to which such responses may be rewarded. When reward is confined to regular or fixed intervals, responding tends to be confined to those intervals. When reward is confined to intervals which occur irregularly and unpredictably, responding tends to be steady but relatively slow. When reward is always available but several responses are required to get it, responding is rapid once it begins but there is a pause after each reward before starting again. This pause can be reduced or eliminated by varying the number of responses required. And various combinations of these behaviors can be obtained by various combinations of appropriate schedules.

There are two ways in which these facts are important in controlling behavior. One concerns attempting to control the behavior of another organism. It is important to schedule rewards to produce the rate of responding which you desire. For example, if a wife views "his favorite dinner" as one of the rewards a husband receives for returning home each night, preparing this dinner at regular intervals such as every Thursday night is not behaving optimally. Such a fixed-interval will lead to weaker tendencies to come home on other nights. Better the dinner be scheduled at variable intervals so as to maintain a steady rate of expectation. Similarly, the teacher who gives examinations at regular intervals and the parent who schedules presents around regular events such as birthdays and Christmas may not be exercising the type of control that would produce the optimal constancy of behavior.

The other way in which these facts can be important concerns the scheduling of one's own rewards. We are all in a position to administer some rewards to ourselves, whether it be a treat to a movie, a splurge on food or clothing, or simply some free time to daydream a while. We can thus, in part, control our own behavior by the way we schedule these rewards. This is of special value when the schedule imposed by the external world is not one that generates optimal behavior. For example, the worker should normally maintain a steady rate of production even though "pay day" puts him on a fixed interval schedule that tends to produce a pause and then an accelerating rate of responding. Even as simple a procedure as waiting to get a drink of water until after you have finished a designated task can have a large effect upon your productive capacity.

## Instrumental Conditioning

When a response is periodically enabled by some controlling event in the environment, we refer to it as an instrumental response and the experimental analysis of it as instrumental conditioning. The major variable of interest in instrumental conditioning is the *condition of reinforcement*. Specifically, we are interested in the way the strength of an instrumental response is determined by the properties of the reward such as its amount, delay, quality, or probability.

One way to focus on the difference between operant and instrumental conditioning is to return to the situation in which an experimenter is attempting to teach a rat to press a bar. From the rat's point of view, this is an operant situation in which the bar is freely available but let us now look at it from the experimenter's point of view. Although it is true that he could deliver rewards to the rat any time he wishes, the act of "rewarding a response" can occur only when that response is made by the rat. In effect, then, the experimenter's response is an instrumental one that is enabled by the behavior of the rat. In similar fashion, a parent wanting to reward good behavior in his child can only effectively give rewards when instances of good behavior are observed.

Recall that a schedule of reinforcement in operant conditioning is the program according to which reward for a response is available; this may occur either according to time or enumeration of responses. The condition of reinforcement refers to the descriptive properties of the reward itself: how big it is, how good it is, how quickly it is received. The purpose of this section is to consider those properties of the reward known to affect the tendency to make instrumental responses.

### Amount of Reward

Perhaps the most obvious property of a reward concerns its amount or quantity. The effects of amount of reward have been studied in a variety of instrumental contexts, the simplest of which is a rat running down a short straight alley toward food reward. Combining the results of these studies, we can represent the effect of this variable according to the graph in Figure 18. Two properties of this graph deserve mention: first, as intuitively expected, *performance in general increases the larger the amount of reward received*. Second, however, the curve shows "diminishing returns" in the sense that adding a unit of reward to a small value increases performance more than adding that unit to a larger reward. In the language of the economist, the "marginal utility" of reward is a decreasing function; increasing salary by ten cents an hour means more to a person with low income than to a person with higher income.

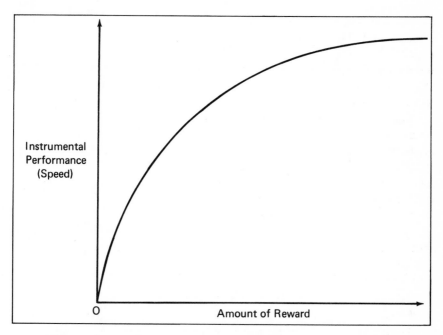

**Figure 18.** Summary of experimental findings showing that instrumental responding, as measured for example by the speed of making a response once it is enabled, is greater the larger the reward.

At this point, we can illustrate the difference between the effects of a variable such as amount of reward on instrumental as opposed to operant response. Consider a rat living in a situation in which he earns all of his water by pressing on a bar that is freely available. In this operant context, we can study the effect of giving rewards of different sizes for pressing the bar. The results of such a study are depicted in Figure 19. In terms of daily intake, the rat consumes more water the larger the drop of water he receives for bar pressing. But in terms of response output, he makes fewer responses. The presumed reason is perhaps obvious: the rat's thirst is reduced more quickly the larger the drop of water he receives for bar pressing. Hence, he needs fewer of them to maintain equilibrium and if we measure the operant response by its rate of occurrence, we would conclude that response strength is weaker the larger the reward. It is this interaction of reward with drive motivation that makes the operant situation a complicated one in which to determine the effects of conditions of reinforcement.

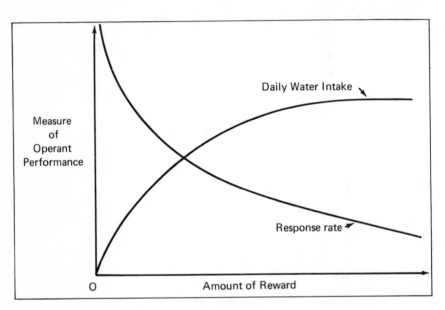

**Figure 19.** Effect of amount of reward in an operant situation in which a rat earns all of his water by pressing on a bar. As the amount of reward for bar pressing increases, so does the animal's daily water intake. However, his response rate decreases, presumably because he can obtain all the water he wants by making fewer responses.

It should be noted that a comparable complication can arise in the instrumental situation if the trials are given very frequently, because the subject's drive may also be reduced in that situation. But we can arrange to control drive by distributing the trials at widely spaced intervals in instrumental conditioning, and when we do so, we find that response strength measured in such ways as response speed is greater the larger the reward.

One additional question should be considered in this context, namely, the effect of changing to a new amount of reward after performance has stabilized on one amount. Reward can be either increased or decreased and the result is clear: *a change in the amount of reward leads to a rapid change in the level of performance in the direction appropriate to the change.* Increasing the reward leads to increased performance; decreasing the reward leads to decreased performance.

In the case of decreasing the amount of reward, a further effect has frequently been observed: performance not only decreases but temporarily drops below that which would normally be maintained by the smaller amount. This is sometimes called the "depression effect" on the assumption that the subject's response to reduced reward is emotional. An alternative label is "negative contrast" simply to indicate that the reward is reacted to as if it were smaller than it actually is. It is known from studies of human perception that, if subjects are first confronted with a series of large objects and then are asked to estimate the size of a smaller object, they will judge it to be smaller than it actually is as a result of contrast with the large objects with which they have been familiarized. Similarly, a small reward is not only smaller than that to which the subject may have been accustomed, but may temporarily appear still smaller by contrast with those larger rewards.

We can not yet state with certainty whether the opposite kind of effect occurs when the reward is increased. It has been observed in several studies and referred to as the "elation effect" or "positive contrast" since the organism not only increases performance, but reaches a temporary level above that achieved by subjects exposed only to the large reward. However, this effect is at least illusory since the majority of studies have failed to demonstrate it, and experimental rationalization of these conflicting results remains to be achieved.

In any event, performance does change rapidly following a change in the amount of reward, in a direction appropriate to the direction of change. At least in the case of reduced reward, this result is temporarily excessive, the organism dropping below the appropriate level. With continued experience, however, whether from the beginning of training or after a change, performance stabilizes at a level that is dependent upon the amount of reward, generally being larger the larger the reward but with diminishing returns.

## Delay of Reward

To this point we have talked about rewards as following immediately upon a response. It is, of course, possible for rewards to be delayed and to occur some period of time after the response in question. This condition of reinforcement has also received extensive experimental study.

It is probably not surprising to learn that *the performance of an instrumental response is poorer the longer the time of delay of reward.*

This basic fact is illustrated graphically in Figure 20, noting that the optimal condition of reinforcement involves no delay but that some performance can be maintained by rewards that occur some time after the response. This graph also shows the "diminishing returns" feature of delay of reward: the detrimental effects of an added unit of delay decreases the longer the absolute length of delay involved.

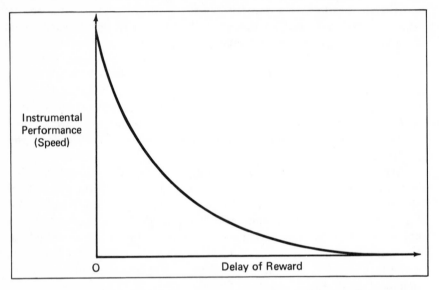

**Figure 20.** Summary of experimental findings showing that instrumental performance, as measured for example by the speed of making a response once it is enabled, is weaker the longer the time of delay of reward after the response.

It is not possible to put specific numbers along the baseline of the delay graph showing how long after a response a reward may be given and still have an effect. The order of magnitude with which we are dealing is measured in seconds; even a delayed reward must occur rather soon after the response for it to be effective at all.

One reason for the difficulty in placing actual intervals along the baseline can be seen by considering the differential effect of delayed reward in instrumental and operant contexts. In operant conditioning, the response is freely available and may be made repeatedly. Suppose, then, that a response in fact initiates a delayed reward that will occur without further responding at some later time. During that time of delay, however, the organism may engage in more of the same behavior so that the actual time of delay cannot be rigidly controlled.

Specifically, for example, a bar press may set the occasion for reward several seconds later, but the rat may continue to press the bar during that time so that reward occurs immediately following a later press. For this reason, delay can best be studied in an instrumental context where the response can be disabled during the delay interval.

But even in the instrumental situation, the organism is always doing something during a delay period after a response before reward. It now appears that *the major factor determining the detrimental effects of delayed reward is the behavior that occurs during the delay interval.* To the extent that the organism engages in responses that are incompatible with the reinforced response during the delay period, those later responses are more strongly reinforced than the intended response and hence are likely to compete with it. Conversely, to the extent that the organism engages in little overt behavior and, in effect, quietly waits for his deserved reward, the detrimental effects of delay are less.

Delayed reward is very common in everyday life and, indeed, one of the important factors distinguishing mature from immature individuals is the ability to sustain what is often called "delayed gratification." Rather than demanding immediate satisfaction for their responses, mature humans have learned to tolerate delay, especially when this increases the payoff. One common illustration is in the behavior of good students. Studying regularly throughout a course is not rewarded immediately by the teacher since exams are scheduled at intervals, but good students know that their diligence will eventually be rewarded.

There are two ways that language can help humans offset the detrimental effects of delayed reward. One of these is being told (or telling oneself) that this response will be rewarded sometime later; these words provide for immediate secondary reinforcement to help bridge the time of delay of actual reward. The second effect of language is the ability to reinstate the rewarded response verbally just before the delayed reward occurs. Thus, when a parent says, "I am giving you this reward because you behaved so well at the party," this helps to insure that the reward affects the intended response rather than those that might have more immediately preceded the reward. Neither of these effects, however, is perfect and the optimal condition of reinforcement even for humans is when reward occurs as quickly as possible after the response.

## Partial Reinforcement and the Goal Gradient

An instrumental response may not be reinforced on every occasion that it occurs. Not every time that you attend a lecture, a concert, or a movie is the experience enjoyable. Similarly, a rat may not find food at the end of a maze every time he runs there. When reward occurs on only part of the trials of an instrumental response, we refer to *partial reinforcement*. Note that we are not saying that only part of the reward is received; rather we are talking about the frequency or probability with which reward occurs or does not occur following a response.

One result of partial reinforcement is quite universally found: performance improves more gradually than if every trial is reinforced. You may think of the procedure as a combination of acquisition and extinction of the response, with the decremental effects of the nonreinforced experiences retarding the development of the incremental effects of the reinforced experiences. Accordingly, although performance can be maintained with partial reinforcement, and indeed is perhaps best maintained with partial reinforcement, original acquisition is faster with continuous reinforcement.

Before describing the performance resulting from partial reinforcement, it is necessary to introduce the concept of the *goal gradient*. Whenever reward occurs at the end of a sequence of responses, such as running through a maze, taking an examination, or writing a theme, we can look at the behavior as it changes over time during the response chain. The goal gradient refers to the changes in performance that occur as a goal is approached.

The effects of continuous and partial reinforcement on the goal gradient are depicted graphically in Figure 21. Looking first at the performance over a behavior chain when reward is received every time, we find a steady increase that continues progressively until very near the end when performance decreases somewhat. This latter effect presumably reflects the fact that the end of a response chain signals the beginning of new behavior; these other responses become anticipatory and tend to interfere with completion of the behavior chain itself.

Next, let us observe performance when the completion of the behavior chain is followed by reward only part of the time. Again, performance increases over the early portions of the chain, and as depicted, actually reaches a higher level than produced by continuous reinforcement. That is to say, at least some portions of the response may be performed with greater vigor if the response is only occasionally rewarded. As the chain continues, however, the performance produced by partial reinforcement begins to decrease sooner and more rapidly, terminating at a lower level than if reward is regularly received. In short, partial reinforcement leads organisms to start faster and run harder, which may mean with long chains that they actually complete the response sooner, but they taper off more quickly and end up at a slower speed than produced by continuous reinforcement.

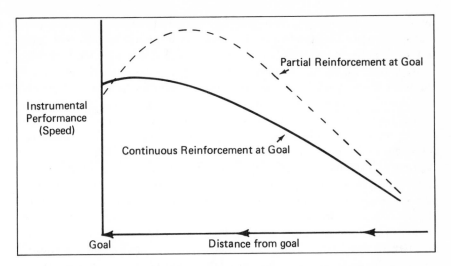

**Figure 21.** The goal gradient for continuous and partial reinforcement. The goal is approached from the right toward the vertical axis. In the case of continuous reinforcement, speed increases as the goal is approached except very near the goal where the organism must stop. In the case of partial reinforcement, speed is generally faster than with continuous reinforcement, except the organism begins to slow down sooner and ends at the goal slower than if reward occurred every time.

We can understand part of this effect from theoretical constructs already introduced: habit and inhibition. Recall our assumptions that reinforcement produces habit while nonreinforcement produces inhibition and that habit generalizes more extensively than inhibition. Accordingly, the reason that the partially-reinforced organism begins to slow down as the goal is approached and eventually reaches a lower level near the goal is the presence of inhibition resulting from occasional nonreinforcement. We may describe this analysis informally as follows: when an organism receives only occasional reward, he begins each trial optimistically as if this may be one of the times he gets reward. As he gets closer to the goal, however, the inhibition resulting from occasional nonreinforcement begins to appear, changing his attitude to one of pessimism.

You are undoubtedly familiar with this phenomenon. A student may start out on a project or paper with enthusiasm, confident that this one will lead to a good grade; as he nears the completion of his paper and then has to turn it in for grading, he becomes increasingly convinced that his paper will not be judged as good as he initially thought it would be. Similarly, an author begins each new book or article thinking he will surely have an impact, but his enthusiasm tapers off as the end is in sight. This tendency may be so strong that the inhibition near the goal actually exceeds the habit; if so, he never finishes the response. Instead, he stops short of the goal and turns to begin another response about which, now at a far distance from its goal, he can be enthusiastic. Many garages are filled with unfinished inventions!

By way of summary of the effects of partial reinforcement, several results may be reviewed. As might be expected, performance improves more gradually but nevertheless is ultimately maintained effectively by partial reinforcement. Furthermore, the performance generated by partial reinforcement may come to exceed that produced by continuous reinforcement, especially during the early portions of a behavior chain. As the goal is approached, however, the fact that there is occasional nonreinforcement produces a rapid decrease in the vigor of the response, so that it terminates at a level below that produced by continuous reward. We shall also observe in a later chapter that partial reinforcement has important effects on the persistence of a response and the generality of learning.

## The Power of Positive Control

We may have committed a crime. If you have read this chapter muttering to yourself, "I knew all that," it has been a waste of time. Perhaps it is true that if you deliberately set about to teach your dog a new trick, the facts and principles described in this chapter can only help you understand a little better why your natural techniques work reasonably well. But the power of positive control is an enormous potential, too little used and too much misused. Several examples may help convince you.

### Mail

A letter from a child away at school or in a distant land in the service is a great reward to his parents. A letter from home is equally a reward to the child, especially if he is somewhat homesick. But we are likely to schedule our lives so that letters are written and mailed with regularity, so that they arrive on a fixed-interval schedule. The parents' response of expecting a letter wanes after receiving one, but then increases progressively to a high pitch when the scheduled time arrives. Small wonder they become frantic if the letter is not there.

Or the child at school perhaps feels a little more lonely as that day dawns, stays late in bed, cuts a class and waits for his letter to arrive. At best, he is wasting a pellet of reward; at worst, he is rewarding behaviors quite the opposite of those his parents had hoped to train. Better he place the letter unopened on his desk, find a friend who did attend the class, copy his notes, do some extra study to make up and *then* devour his pellet. And the beauty is that he will not have to do this many times before he can open his mail box and read the letter immediately, knowing that it is rewarding appropriate behavior.

### Listening

Listening is a powerful reward to most people. We all have troubles and like to bend a sympathetic ear with them. The person who realizes this and has a little skill in the art of shaping can, for example, induce the stranger sitting beside him in an airplane to talk about his problems within the time it takes the plane to leave the gate and get into the air. Perhaps you do not want to listen to a stranger's problems (unless he will return the favor and listen to yours!) but sometimes it can be useful. Consider the waitress confronting what seems to her an endless flow of largely nondescript faces, grunting their way through life. If you pause but a moment to say, "Hello again, how are things today?" you will soon become recognized as a person deserving special treatment. A similar story could be told in the context of an employer's relationship with his employees.

We are more likely to misuse the reward of listening. The amateur psychologist may think he is helping people by listening to their troubles and responding sympathetically. But likely, he is rewarding the person for feeling sorry for himself! You will never be the most popular listener if you respond critically, helping the person see how he has contributed to his own misery and how he might do something about it. But you will be a respected listener when the person is really in trouble.

And don't forget yourself. If you seek out listeners who will "understand," you are contributing to your own self-pity. Indeed, even listening to yourself can be misused. In sum, every time you listen, you reward the behavior being uttered. If that be gossip, if that be vulgarity, if that be bigotry, if that be deceit—and so on—you help train those ways of thinking.

### Conclusion

The problem of identifying events that are rewarding is difficult to the theoretical scientist but it is easy in everyday life. A great many of these are social and can be used to control the attitudes and behavior of ourselves and those around us. A wife's smile and welcoming kiss rewards a husband's return home. A husband's compliment rewards a wife's efforts to be attractive and to prepare enticing meals. Sex is rewarding to oneself and one's spouse. There is, of course, money; but there are also praise, attention, and those so-called "best things in life" that are free. The goal should be to learn how to use, and how to avoid misusing, the power of positive control.

### True-False Items: Positive Reinforcement

1. A "superstition" is a response that was originally learned because it produced positive reinforcement and which persists even though it no longer does so.

(A response that no longer produces reinforcement undergoes experimental extinction. Human superstitions may have supernatural and mystical overtones, but are related to the laboratory findings that responses may be learned because they happen to occur before a reward even though they do not actually produce the reward. False.)

2. Adolescents with poor vocabularies often learn to say "you know . . ." because their listener agrees with them.

(Agreement is a form of secondary reinforcement for humans and will increase the frequency of responses even though both parties are unaware of what is going on. True.)

3. Awareness of reinforcement is unnecessary and unimportant.

(When the human is aware of whether or not a response produced a reward, he can rehearse his behavior verbally and help bring it under appropriate control. False.)

4. We determine whether grades and teacher approval are rewards for a student by functional identification.

(Whether grades and approval by a teacher are rewards depends on whether they have acquired secondary reinforcing value during the student's past history. Students differ in this regard, and one must therefore find out whether they are rewards for any particular student. True.)

5. It follows that if all drive-reductions are rewards, then all rewards are drive-reductions.

(The logic is fallacious. Most psychologists agree that all instances of drive-reduction are rewarding, but many contend that there are also other sources of reward. False.)

6. Boys really don't like to pet with girls who won't go "all the way."

(Various forms of sensory pleasures, including erotic stimulation, appear to be reinforcing even though they do not culminate in the reduction of a primary drive. False.)

7. A husband who occasionally and unexpectedly brings flowers or presents to his wife is providing her with variable-interval reinforcement.

(Assuming she is not the suspicious type, a wife accepts flowers and presents from her husband as an extra reward for her efforts. Although birthdays, Christmas, and similar occasions may occur at irregular intervals, they are predictable and hence do not generate the steady behavior characteristic of a variable-interval schedule. True.)

8. A girl who sometimes accepts and sometimes declines a boy's request for a date is placing him on a variable-ratio schedule.

(If her acceptances depend on her other opportunities, this would be more nearly an interval schedule. If, however, she varies the number of times he has to call before accepting, then it is a variable-ratio schedule that generates a high, steady rate of responding. True.)

9. A person can control his own behavior by scheduling those rewards that he himself controls.

(Rewards affect behavior with equal force whether administered by oneself or by an outside agent. Few people have learned to use the principle of positive reinforcement in the control of their own behavior. For example, a student may go to the movies before rather than after finishing his homework. True.)

10. The rate of operant responding depends on the schedule and not the condition of reinforcement.

(The condition of reinforcement is its momentary properties such as amount. Although the schedule of reinforcement is studied in the operant conditioning context, the rate of a freely available response does depend on the reinforcement condition as well as the schedule. False.)

11. It is usually best to delay rewards for a while because the person will come to want them more after a delay.

(Although there may be special circumstances in which delaying a reward makes it more valuable, typically the greatest effect on instrumental performance is obtained by giving rewards immediately. False.)

12. Organisms may perform more vigorously if they don't get a reward every time.

(If reward is too infrequent, the organism may be reluctant to complete a response lest it be nonrewarded again. Short of that point, however, occasional reward produces a higher level of overall performance than consistent reward. True.)

# 7

# Negative Reinforcement

Organisms not only attempt to maximize their contact with pleasant events, they also attempt to minimize their contact with unpleasant events. Indeed, the so-called instinct for self-preservation suggests that we will do more to avoid physical harm than to obtain physical pleasure. Some people may occasionally endure pain or take risks in the interest of personal gain, but more often than not, we behave as if we strongly dislike discomfort. Accordingly, there is also the principle of negative reinforcement: WHENEVER A RESPONSE IS CLOSELY FOLLOWED IN TIME BY THE REDUCTION IN AN AVERSIVE STATE, THE TENDENCY FOR THAT RESPONSE TO OCCUR IN THE FUTURE IS INCREASED ACCORDING TO THE DEGREE OF REDUCTION INVOLVED. Reducing, or preferably terminating, an unpleasant situation is reinforcing and makes preceding behavior more likely.

The same disclaimers made previously concerning positive reinforcement apply equally to negative reinforcement although little experimental evidence has been obtained with respect to them. Negative reinforcing events do not need to be actually produced by the response for it to be learned, nor need the person be aware of any causal connection between his behavior and the event for it to be effective. Negative reinforcement is as automatic and inescapable as positive reinforcement.

Some psychologists have used the term "negative reinforcement" as another way of saying "punishment"; the present usage is more common and appropriate. The concept of reinforcement is always one of strengthening something, and it is called negative only because it is occasioned by reducing stimulus conditions rather than presenting them. In another context, a coach might strengthen a team by removing a discordant or ineffective player, even if no replacement were available. In the present context, it is true that the basic principles of positive and negative reinforcement are very much the same although they are studied in somewhat different contexts. But there is nevertheless justification for the distinction.

In part, this is because some of the procedures described with respect to positive reinforcement are difficult or impossible to employ with respect to negative reinforcement. For example, we could say the expression, "variable interval negative reinforcement" but it is not at all clear how such a schedule could be realized. An organism would have to be left in an aversive state with a response available which would occasionally permit reduction of that state. But then the aversive state would have to be reinstated on some schedule.

Principally, the reason for distinguishing between positive and negative reinforcement concerns the other effects of those events in addition to the reinforcing effect itself. Consider two rats that have been trained to press a bar in a small box, one of which learned that response when hungry to obtain food, and the other of which learned that response to turn off a mildly painful electric shock that sometimes came on in the box. Insofar as their bar-pressing behavior is concerned, they may perform equally well. But the rat controlled by positive reinforcement (food) displays distinct eagerness when the experimenter approaches to take him from his home cage to the apparatus; the rat controlled by negative reinforcement (shock termination) may make distinct efforts such as biting the experimenter in order to stay out of the situation.

So, too, with children, some of whom learn to play the piano under the support of praise and encouragement and some of whom learn to play under threat and denial unless they practice. Both procedures may produce equally good piano players. But the child trained with positive reinforcement will approach the piano in the future voluntarily while the child trained with negative reinforcement will have to be persuaded to exhibit his talent. The next time you see an animal act, try to figure out whether the tricks were trained with praise, food, and affection or whether they were trained under threat of physical violence. Most of us intuitively prefer a performance in which we feel the performers really enjoy performing. In short, an organism's attitudes toward his environment are importantly affected by whether positive or negative reinforcement has been used to promote learning.

It may therefore seem strange, and is perhaps unfortunate, that most human behavior is under "aversive control," including punishment as discussed in a later chapter. Many churches find it easier to threaten damnation than to offer attractive inducements for moral behavior. Even the Commandments are more "thou shalt not" than "thou shall"! Our legal system, geared as it is to fines and imprisonment, capitalizes on the power of negative reinforcement. And most parents, although proclaiming about love and affection, typically control the behavior of their children by threats and punishments. Aversive control is so pervasive in our society that it may well help create in young people a negative attitude toward life.

Like it or not, behavior is importantly controlled by the principle of negative reinforcement, and its experimental analysis is therefore a proper topic for psychology. In this section, we shall review two basic procedures in which this principle is revealed: escape learning and avoidance learning.

## Events that ARE Aversive

Before doing so, it is necessary to answer the question of how aversive events are identified. By now, the reader should be prepared for an approach to this question which involves a functional definition. An *aversive event* is one the termination of which has been found to lead to an increase in the probability of responses which precede that termination. Aversive events are unpleasant, noxious, ones the organism seeks to remove. They are emotionally negative and their termination is reinforcing.

There are three properties of aversive events that will be important to the subsequent development. The first of these is that they elicit some unlearned, motor responses. If a shock is applied to the paws of a rat, he squeals and prances around the cage; if a child touches a hot stove, he reflexively withdraws his hand. Secondly, these events also elicit an internal, implicit response of fear. We shall have more to say about the nature of this response later under the topic of secondary motivation. And finally, aversive stimuli not only have emotional consequences but are stimuli in the sense that new responses can be learned to them.

## Primary Negative Reinforcement: Escape Learning

When an organism is in a primary (unlearned) aversive state and a response is required to reduce or eliminate it, we refer to *escape learning*. A wide variety of conditions are painful or unpleasant by their very nature and we dislike them instinctively. Physical blows, intense heat or cold, bright lights, loud sounds, and extreme pressures provide countless familiar examples of aversive states. Electric shock has been the most commonly used condition in the laboratory because of the ease with which it can be controlled in intensity and turned on and off. When an organism finds himself in such a state, he naturally tries to terminate it (escape from it) and will learn responses that accomplish this goal.

You have learned to put on a coat when you are cold. You may have learned to fight when attacked by another person or animal. You have learned to take an aspirin if you have a headache. You have learned a variety of techniques for reducing itches, burns, and painful objects such as a cinder in your eye. These are a few everyday illustrations of escape learning, the paradigm for which is shown in Figure 22.

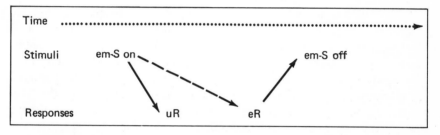

**Figure 22.** Schematic description of escape learning. An aversive event (em–S) happens, it may elicit a variety of unlearned reflexive responses (uR) but remains on until a particular escape response (eR) is made.

In escape learning, there is nothing the organism can do to prevent the onset of the aversive event. Only after it happens can he do anything about it. Normally, aversive stimuli produce vigorous responding which, in many cases, is successful in removing the painful event. When this is the case, no learning is required. It is when our natural responses to the aversive stimulus do not remove it that we are left in a motivated state, try out other responses, and learn the one that works most effectively. Hence, escape *learning* is more than simply escape; it is when a new response becomes associated with the aversive event. This is indicated by the dashed arrow in Figure 22.

When the instinctive responses to the aversive stimulus are incompatible with the escape response, they become the major impediment to escape learning. Under the high motivation induced by a painful event, the organism engages vigorously in many reflexive activities. If engaging in these reduces the likelihood that he will ever even try the response that is actually effective in escaping the pain, then it is simply unlikely that he will receive the negative reinforcement necessary for learning. A response must be made in order to be reinforced and sometimes shaping may be necessary to produce a desired escape response.

Consider, for example, trying to train a rat to stand immobile on a grid floor hot with electric shock in order to get it turned off. The rat's natural response is to jump and prance around, and maybe even roll onto his back so that his fur will insulate his skin from the painful shock. Repeatedly engaging in these behaviors simply precludes a stationary stance. Training such a response would inevitably be difficult, but might be accomplished by requiring at first only a very brief moment of immobility and then progressively lengthening the requirement as the rat began to learn.

Such difficulties with escape learning may be observed in humans. Our natural tendency when irritated by an itch is to scratch it. Only by experience and with difficulty have we learned that this response is quite incompatible with the effective treatment. When sunburned, we are tempted to take a cold bath for temporary relief, but actually a mildly uncomfortable hot bath is more likely to reduce the persisting pain. The asthmatic encounters an even more trying problem. Difficulty with breathing tends to lead to gasping and increasing anxiety, responses which are quite the opposite of those most appropriate to an asthmatic attack. He must learn to overcome these natural tendencies, to relax and breathe slowly to gain relief.

By way of summary, escape learning is based on negative reinforcement, the reduction or termination of an aversive state. When reflexive responses are inadequate, new responses will be learned, but this will be difficult if the required response is incompatible with the natural response.

## Secondary Negative Reinforcement: Avoidance Learning

Although we have not yet discussed in detail the principle of secondary motivation, the basic ideas are sufficiently familiar that a brief prelude should enable us to discuss avoidance learning. The important fact is that originally neutral stimuli may acquire learned aversive properties by being paired with events that are aversive. The fundamental procedure is that of classical conditioning: a stimulus which precedes an aversive unconditioned stimulus will itself acquire motivating properties. This is referred to as secondary not because it necessarily is weaker or of lesser importance but only because it is learned. This learned drive is often called "fear."

When we refer to *secondary negative reinforcement,* we refer to the termination of a stimulus that has acquired aversive (fear-inducing) properties as a result of past experience. The context in which this principle is studied is called *avoidance learning,* which occurs when an organism can learn a response that will prevent the occurrence of an aversive event. The paradigm for this type of learning is depicted in Figure 23.

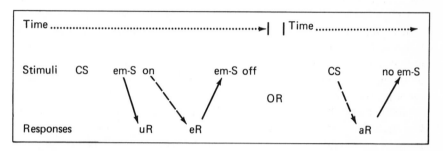

**Figure 23.** Schematic description of avoidance learning. A warning signal (CS) precedes the occurrence of an aversive event (em–S) which elicits unconditioned responses but also a learned escape response (eR). If, however, an avoidance response (aR) occurs before the em–S, it is prevented.

Basically, the difference between the escape learning and avoidance learning situations is this: in escape learning, there is nothing the organism can do to prevent the occurrence of the aversive event; the best he can do is terminate it quickly once it occurs. In avoidance learning, in contrast, if the organism responds in time, he can prevent the aversive event from happening at all. He has greater control over his environment.

Our analysis of avoidance learning assumes first that the warning signal (CS), since it precedes an aversive event (em-S), will itself acquire secondary aversive properties as a result of classical conditioning. Fear, originally elicited by the em-S becomes conditioned to the CS. When an avoidance response occurs, the CS is terminated leading to secondary negative reinforcement for making the response. In effect, avoidance responses are learned because they get the organism out of situations of which they have learned to be afraid.

Everyday examples of avoidance responses are numerous and hardly need identification. We noted that you may put on a coat to escape from being cold; you may also put on your coat before leaving the house to avoid ever getting cold. A small boy may learn to avoid being attacked by a bully by staying away from places where an encounter is likely to occur. And a girl may learn to avoid unpleasant dates or jobs by developing a headache or other type of psychosomatic sickness that excuses her from them; such an avoidance response may turn out to be more dangerous than the events being avoided.

There are a number of variants of the basic avoidance learning paradigm that have been experimentally analyzed. For example, the avoidance response is learned most rapidly if it is the same as the escape response required once the aversive event occurs. The reason for this can be seen by again referring to Figure 23. Since the CS regularly precedes the occurrence of the escape response, they will become associated and, by the principle of the anticipatory response, that response will move forward in time and occur early on later trials. Hence, the organism is likely to make the avoidance response before the em-S simply as a result of classical conditioning and hence encounter the secondary negative reinforcement. If, on the other hand, the avoidance response is quite different from the escape response, then it is less likely to occur and be learned. In interpersonal conflicts, for example, the avoidance response is typically the making of compromising actions while the escape response, if aggression does start, is to fight; people (and nations) may have difficulty learning to avoid conflict because of this incompatibility between the avoidance and escape responses.

Although we can not review all of the variants of avoidance procedures, one in particular deserves mention. This is called *nondiscriminated avoidance learning* because there is no explicit warning signal preceding the em-S; rather, the em-S simply occurs at regularly scheduled times. The procedure is analogous to that previously described as temporal conditioning except that now the US is aversive and can be avoided by anticipatory responses. Organisms can learn to avoid regularly scheduled aversive events, presumably also on the basis of the decaying trace of the preceding aversive event (or the response which prevented it from occurring). Closing the windows of your house before leaving in anticipation of the regular summer afternoon shower, seeing a doctor or dentist at regular intervals, and even winding your watch each morning may be thought of as avoidance responses performed to prevent the unsignalled aversive consequences of failing to make them.

Avoidance responses are extremely persistent. The reason for this is simply that the response removes the organism from the feared situation and hence prevents determining whether the feared event will actually occur. This is true even when the response is no longer adaptive. The boy who became afraid of the bully may continue to avoid confronting him even after they have both matured so that a fight might not occur or, if it did, the match would be more even. Laboratory studies have shown that the "enforced reality testing" procedure is not as effective as might be presumed. For example, a dog that continues to run away from a compartment in which he used to receive shock but which is now actually safe, may be forced to sit in the compartment by putting up a barrier so he can not get away. Once the barrier is removed, however, he is likely to resume avoidance responding. In effect, he learns that the situation is safe when the barrier is in place, but that is a different situation from the one in which shock occurred. Similarly, the father may lead his young son by the hand to confront the bully and thereafter say, "See, he really didn't hurt you, did he?" And this simply confirms that the boy is safe when his father is around but it hardly reduces his fear of confronting the bully alone.

## Learning NOT to Learn

We noted earlier that aversive control may not be as desirable as positive control because of the emotional consequences engendered. Organisms will learn to escape or avoid aversive situations but their enthusiasm for doing so is minimal. There is also the possibility that aversive events not only affect the organism's behavior in that situation, but also his ability to adjust to future situations.

### Helplessness

R. L. Solomon has trained dogs to make an avoidance response in a shuttle box. Two compartments are separated by a hurdle over which the dog can jump, and electric shock can be given on either side independently. The procedure is that a light comes on in the compartment in which the dog is then located, signalling an impending shock ten seconds later. If the dog jumps in time, the light goes out and no shock is given; if he fails to jump before the shock, he must then jump over the hurdle to escape it. Consistent with our earlier discussion, normal dogs readily learn not only to escape but to avoid shock by jumping during the warning light.

Solomon placed dogs in a sling and gave them a series of unavoidable and inescapable electric shocks. Although they were capable of struggling against the sling and the restraining ropes that held their paws, they could do nothing that was effective about the shock. Occasionally it occurred, ran its course and terminated. All they could do was lie in the sling and "take it."

The day after this admittedly aversive experience (actually, the shock used in these studies was not so intense as to be traumatic), the dogs were for the first time placed in the shuttle apparatus where they could avoid, or failing this, escape the shock. The critical result is that many of these dogs did not learn either response. They did not learn to jump when the light came on, and not because they failed to detect the significance of the light. They would soon begin to cower and whimper during the interval before shock arrived. More surprisingly, they did not even learn to escape from the shock; instead, they stood on the hot grids and "took it." Even if they happened occasionally to move across the barrier, or if they were pulled across by the experimenter, the resulting negative reinforcement was largely ineffectual. The next trial, they were likely to remain in the shock compartment until the experimenter, out of kindness, turned the shock off.

Apparently, if an organism is first required to endure an aversive state about which he can do nothing, he not only learns to submit to it but also to act helpless in a new situation that he can control. To extrapolate this generalization to a human situation, consider the student who finds a classroom aversive because he is doing poorly there. He may try out a variety of ways to improve his performance, but the teacher, by now having decided that he is a dunce, continues to give him the same bad grades. He may learn that he is helpless in class and give up trying, not only there but in later classes where the teacher might be more responsive to his efforts. The important practical implication is this: if one uses aversive control, it is important to be responsive to the other person's efforts to affect it. Otherwise, he may learn to be helpless.

### Elicited Aggression

One limitation of the principle of secondary negative reinforcement has been indicated by the result of putting two organisms together in the same aversive situation. N. H. Azrin and R. E. Ulrich, for example, have shown that shocking two rats at the same time in the same apparatus induces them to aggress against each other. Even though neither is responsible for their discomfort, they fight.

What is more important is that two rats might first be trained to avoid an electric shock by turning a wheel when a warning light comes on five seconds before the shock. This training is given individually until both are avoiding almost all of the threatened shocks. If, however, they are then placed together in the situation, their avoidance behavior is virtually eliminated. They may continue to escape the shock effectively once it comes on, but this is followed by aggression against each other. And finally, if they are returned to the situation individually, they are likely not to resume avoidance responding.

Essentially the same result occurs if neither rat is first trained in the avoidance response, or even if one is trained and the other is naive. The presence of another organism in an aversive situation provides a new stimulus that may interfere with adjustment. This is particularly true when a single avoidance response is required to prevent the shock for both of them; if both must respond, as by, for example, jumping over a hurdle, little impairment results. It may be said that misery loves company, but perhaps were there no company, the person would learn more effectively how to cope with his environment.

## True-False Items:   Negative Reinforcement

1. A positive reinforcer is one that strengthens responses and a negative reinforcer is one that weakens responses.

(Reinforcers always lead to strengthening; the distinction is whether the event is the onset of something pleasant or the offset of something unpleasant. These are positive and negative reinforcement respectively. False.)

2. Superstitions can be formed on the basis of negative reinforcement.

(Negative reinforcement is effective even if it is not actually produced by a response but simply follows it. Many "old-wives remedies" for sickness are superstitions based on negative reinforcement. True.)

3. The total pattern of behavior is the same following positive and negative reinforcement.

(A specified response may be controlled equally well with either source of reinforcement, but negative reinforcement requires that the organism first be placed in an aversive state. This can lead to unpleasant associations with the situation. False.)

4. Aversive events elicit responses reflexively and hence cannot be treated as stimuli to which new responses can become associated.

(Aversive events do elicit a variety of reflexive behaviors, which sometimes are adaptive in removing the source of irritation. When this is not the case, however, new responses will be learned to such events. False.)

5. Dropping out of school illustrates escape learning.

(If a student is doing poorly in school, that situation becomes aversive. Each day he leaves school, he receives negative reinforcement. Eventually, he may drop out completely. True.)

6. It is easier to learn some escape responses than others.

(It is difficult to learn an escape response that is incompatible with the responses produced reflexively by the aversive event. Hence, if several escape responses are possible, the organism is more likely to try out and learn those compatible with his reflex behavior. True.)

7. The difference between escape learning and avoidance learning is the presence of a warning signal in the latter.

(Avoidance learning does usually entail a warning signal preceding the aversive event. However, it also requires that some response is possible to prevent the occurrence of that event. Telling a boy that his father will spank him for his misbehavior when he gets home doesn't foster avoidance learning unless the boy can do something to avoid the licking. False.)

8. Termination of a warning signal constitutes secondary negative reinforcement.

(It is assumed that the warning signal takes on learned aversive properties by classical conditioning. Its termination is therefore reinforcing, and is called secondary because it is learned. True.)

9. It is easier to learn some avoidance responses than others.

(Learning to respond before an aversive event is difficult if the response required then is incompatible with the one made to the aversive event, either reflexively or as an escape response. This is because these latter tend to become anticipatory. True.)

10. Preventing the avoidance response so as to force the organism to confront the feared situation and find that it is not now dangerous is not very successful; this can be understood by reference to stimulus generalization decrement.

(The situation must inevitably be changed in order to force an organism to confront a feared stimulus. Hence, extinction does not occur in the same situation as when the avoidance response is possible. True.)

11. One can learn to "give up" in the face of aversive control.

(If an early environment is not responsive to one's efforts to control aversive events, the organism may generalize this experience and not even try in later situations where he can control such events. True.)

12. Parents may train their children to squabble with each other.

(Doing chores around the home may be viewed as avoidance responses to prevent parental displeasure. If a single chore is assigned to several children, none may do it voluntarily; after being reprimanded by the parent, the children may squabble. True.)

# 8

# Response Persistence: Extinction, Counterconditioning and Punishment

When dealing with practical problems involving learned behavior, the most important consideration is often the persistence of the response. This sword cuts with two edges: sometimes the problem is to increase persistence, and sometimes the problem is to decrease persistence. The goal in most educational contexts is not only to provide for the learning of correct responses but to insure that they will continue in the future. We can teach safe driving habits and even evaluate this learning before issuing a driver's license, but the hope is that these habits will continue when an instructor is not around to give rewards for driving carefully and, indeed, in spite of temptations from one's peers to do reckless things. The other edge of the sword is also important: we may be aware of undesirable habits that we have acquired and be distressed with their persistence in spite of our efforts to break them. Accordingly, the psychology of learning has long been concerned with the factors that affect response persistence following original learning.

The technical dependent variable studied in this context is *resistance to extinction*. This is simply a measure of the number of times a response will occur after all reinforcement for the response is stopped. The purpose of this chapter is to consider some of the factors that affect resistance to extinction and some of the procedures that may eliminate persistent responses.

## Factors Which INCREASE Response Persistence

We can subsume a large amount of experimental research under a single principle: RESISTANCE TO EXTINCTION IS GREATER THE GREATER THE VARIABILITY DURING ORIGINAL LEARNING.

Variability may involve the stimulus, the response, or the reinforcement; we shall consider each of these briefly.

## Stimulus Variability

The greater the variety of stimuli encountered during the learning of a response, the more persistent it will be. Suppose we train some rats to run in a single straight alley for food while another group of rats has the same number of rewarded learning trials but in several different alleys that vary in width, brightness, floor-texture, and the like. Then reward is removed for both groups and their speed of running is measured over a series of extinction trials. The group running in a single alley will stop running significantly sooner than the group running in several alleys.

One way to understand this phenomenon concerns the number of habits involved. An organism trained to a single stimulus does have some generalized tendency to respond to similar stimuli, but these will not be as strong as if he has actually learned to respond in various situations. Hence, stimulus variation during training produces more habits in the sense of associating the response with a variety of stimuli . . . and each of these has to be extinguished before the response is eliminated. One of the reasons undesirable responses are especially persistent is that they are often learned in a number of different contexts: the adult who does not like to go to parties has probably had unpleasant experiences in several such contexts.

## Response Variability

The larger the number of variants or ways of making a response that have been learned, the more persistent it will be. One clear experimental demonstration of this fact is to train pigeons to peck at a key that can detect the particular location on the key actually struck. We first require that the pigeons vary the location at which they strike periodically in order to receive reward. After reward is removed, such pigeons display considerably greater resistance to extinction of the pecking response than pigeons permitted to peck at a single location.

Response variability may also be understood by considering the number of habits involved. In this case, each variant of the response entails a different habit, and the more of these that have been learned originally, the more there are to persist during extinction. As each variant is partially extinguished, another is available to be tried and during that time, the first one undergoes spontaneous recovery and will recur again later.

## Reinforcement Variability

Perhaps no other phenomenon has received as much attention by experimental psychologists as the effect of variability of reinforcement on resistance to extinction. Variability may be obtained in an operant situation by the variable schedules of reinforcement; in the instrumental situation, variability may be obtained by varying the amount or delay of reward or simply giving partial reinforcement. So well established is the principle that it is labeled the *partial reinforcement effect;* responses that are only occasionally rewarded during acquisition persist longer during extinction.

Reinforcement variability may be simply a special case of stimulus and response variability. On the one hand, reward is a stimulus which is part of the context in which learning occurs, and hence variability in reward leads to more varied stimulus conditions. Furthermore, reinforcement variability often leads to greater response variability since the organism is less likely to become focused on a single way of responding. This is presumably because occasional nonreinforcement weakens each variant of the response enough so that others are tried and receive occasional reinforcement. However, the generality of the partial reinforcement effect has led to a variety of special theories to account for it.

One of these involves the concept of *frustration.* Consider first extinction following continuous reinforcement. The organism has never encountered nonreinforcement in the situation prior to extinction, and when he does so, two things are likely to happen. First, he is likely to react emotionally to frustration by making responses that are incompatible with the trained response itself; these tend to become anticipatory and interfere with smooth performance. Furthermore, he begins to anticipate frustration and the natural response then is to stop responding and avoid the situation. In short, the continuously reinforced organism stops responding rapidly because he is highly frustrated by nonreinforcement and because he has not learned how to deal effectively with it.

In contrast, the organism trained with partial reinforcement has encountered nonreinforcement during original learning. Although this should also be frustrating for him, he eventually tries again and gets rewarded for doing so. In effect, he learns to accept nonreinforcement as part of the situation and to continue to respond in spite of occasional frustration. In the vernacular, we could call this result the development of frustration tolerance. Not expecting reward every time, the organism learns to "take no for an answer;" however, expecting reward part of the time, the organism learns to "try, try again." Being accustomed to occasional nonreinforcement has, in effect, prepared him for the continuous nonreinforcement experienced during extinction.

Of special significance to this understanding is the fact that the partial reinforcement effect can generalize from one situation to another. That is to say, extinction of one response that has received continuous reinforcement will be slower if a similar response has received partial reinforcement. Learning to tolerate frustration in one situation helps doing so in other situations.

### Punishment

A final factor that leads to increased resistance to extinction is, somewhat surprisingly, punishment. The role of punishment in eliminating responses will be discussed later in this chapter. But if punishment fails to eliminate a response, it will lead to greater persistence of that response than if punishment had never been involved. This is sometimes referred to as *fixation*.

To demonstrate fixation in the laboratory, we first train rats to turn to (say) the right in a T-maze to obtain food. Enroute to the goal, electric shock punishment is given for turning in that direction, but not of sufficient intensity to prevent the rat from proceeding. After such training, the reward is placed in the left goal box. Rats that had received shock for making the right turn now take substantially longer to learn the new rewarded response than rats trained without the use of punishment.

Presumably the reason for fixation is that learning to respond even though one anticipates punishment is very similar to learning to respond even though one anticipates frustration. Learning one therefore generalizes to the other. Consistent with this interpretation, partial reinforcement also makes organisms more resistant to the interfering effects of punishment.

### Summary

Let us try to summarize these factors which increase response persistence by considering a parent who deliberately wanted to teach his child to persist in displaying a temper outburst when denied his desires. Perhaps no parent would want to do this, but consider what he would be well-advised to do. First, he would insure that denial occurred in a variety of situations and that various forms of temper displays were performed. He would not reinforce such displays regularly but would only occasionally give in to them. Further to fixate the response, he would even sometimes punish the child, but not often enough or severely enough to eliminate the response. Several years of such diligent training could produce a person who would never be able to control his temper in the future! Perhaps the reason for giving this example is obvious: how many parents actually behave in this way, unaware that they are inadvertently training a persistent, undesirable response?

## Factors Which DECREASE Response Persistence

In one sense, we have already identified some of the factors that decrease response persistence. Constancy of the learning conditions, with respect to stimuli, responses and reinforcements, coupled with the lack of aversive consequences leads to less resistance to extinction. There are, however, several other factors which lead to still less persistence.

### Amount of Reward

We have seen that large rewards lead to better performance than small rewards, when measured in terms of the vigor of the response during acquisition. The opposite, however, occurs during extinction. Extinction is faster following large rewards.

Perhaps the reason for this is also related to frustration: the person accustomed to consistent large rewards experiences greater frustration when reward is removed than the person who only expected a small reward in the first place. Accordingly, occasional large rewards may be desirable to produce a high level of responding, but if persistence of that response is of concern, consistent large rewards will actually lead to less resistance to extinction.

### Extended Training

A certain amount of training during which rewards are administered frequently may be necessary to bring the desired response to a high level of proficiency. Training may be continued beyond that point, however, with frequent reward given even after there is no further evidence of improvement. While this is certainly effective in maintaining the response during that time, the resistance to extinction is reduced by such extended training.

The reason for the loss in persistence resulting from extended training is not yet well understood. One important factor, however, relates back to response variability. During continued training with reward, the response is likely to become increasingly stereotyped so that it is performed in a single, invariant way. Accordingly, it will extinguish rapidly.

## Summary

For the purposes of this summary, let us consider a parent who wishes to train his child to be a "quitter" when he faces the occasional failures that adults invariably experience. First, he would attempt to see that the child always succeeded as he was growing up, and would give him consistent large rewards for his success. Not only might he "spoil" him in this way, but he would continue to protect him from failure well into adolescence and, insofar as possible, into young adulthood. Later, as an adult, that person's response to failure will be to quit. Again, one can reflect on the number of parents who so indulge their children in these and similar ways, quite unaware of what they are training.

# Eliminating Responses

We have asserted that habits are permanent. Without retreating from the power of that assertion, we must nevertheless realize that behavior can be modified. Even well-learned habits may be affected by later experiences. There are three basic ways this is accomplished: extinction, counterconditioning, and punishment. Each of these is briefly discussed in the remainder of this chapter.

## Extinction

We have already introduced the concept of experimental extinction in the context of classical conditioning, and there described how responses might be eliminated as a result of nonreinforcement even though the underlying habits were presumed to be left intact. The theory was that extinction results in the development of inhibition that opposes habit.

The preceding sections of this chapter have identified some of the conditions during learning that affect the resistance to extinction of a response. Not only does persistence depend on the way the response was learned but factors within the extinction experience itself also affect resistance to extinction.

First, the rate of extinction depends on the distribution of the extinction trials over time. Learning (habit) occurs more rapidly if the experiences are widely distributed over time; extinction (inhibition) occurs more rapidly if the nonreinforced experiences are massed so they occur in rapid succession. Spontaneous recovery will, of course, occur but extinction is better accomplished by a series of highly massed episodes than if individual trials are spread out over time.

A second fact is that extinction is more rapid to a somewhat different stimulus than to the original stimulus itself. Not only is the response weaker to a different stimulus, but what strength it has is lost more readily than to the actual trained stimulus. One practical application of this fact is in attempting to extinguish strong fears. It is often advisable to begin with a situation that produces only mild generalized fear and extinguish that before advancing closer to the situation in which the fear was learned. The procedure of shaping which we described with respect to training responses can equally well be applied to their elimination. In doing so, however, it is important to recall that inhibition does not generalize very broadly, so that smaller steps have to be taken in shaping extinction than in shaping acquisition.

### Counterconditioning

Considerably more effective than relying solely on nonreinforcement of a response to lead to experimental extinction is the procedure of *counterconditioning*. This is a procedure in which not only is the original response nonreinforced, but a new response, incompatible with the original response, is reinforced. In this case, not only is the old habit inhibited by extinction, but a new habit is developed that competes with the original one and tends to replace it.

Counterconditioning is now regarded as the basic mechanism of what is popularly referred to as "forgetting." You may, for example, have now forgotten a long-unused telephone number because numbers are frequently occurring in your everyday experiences in a variety of sequences and combinations. Learning new numbers tends to develop new associations that interfere with the recall of old numbers. In such an image, forgetting largely becomes a problem in retrieval: the old learnings remain as habits but are so highly overlaid by more recent habits that the individual has difficulty recovering them. This is why recognition is easier than recall; the correct answer reinstates the cues that facilitate discriminating one response from another.

In practical situations, counterconditioning is especially important in instances where a habit is strongly motivated as a principal means of obtaining satisfaction. This is because, if reinforcement of the old habit is simply denied, extinction of that response will nevertheless leave the organism without an alternative. This is all too obvious when a rat is living in a box where he has pressed on a bar for his food and now the bar is inoperative; not only is the response extinguished but so is the rat! It is less obvious in many everyday situations. A child, may, for example, misbehave as his only means of obtaining parental attention. In an attempt to eliminate misbehavior, the parent may refuse to attend to the child, but his needs for affection remain. In such a case, it is important that the parent determine the motivation for the behavior and provide an alternative, socially acceptable outlet for it. In important situations, extinction should be combined with counterconditioning. Not only is the response thus eliminated more rapidly but the underlying needs of the organism can still be satisfied.

### Punishment

Like it or not, punishment remains the most widespread practice in attempting to eliminate responses. We are punished by parents, teachers, peers, society and even ourselves in an effort to control the tendency to make responses deemed undesirable. The principle of punishment is similar to that given with respect to reinforcement: WHENEVER A RESPONSE IS CLOSELY FOLLOWED IN TIME BY AN AVERSIVE EVENT, THE TENDENCY FOR THAT RESPONSE TO OCCUR IN THE FUTURE IS DECREASED ACCORDING TO THE INTENSITY, DELAY AND QUALITY OF THE AVERSIVE EVENT. We shall see, however, that this principle must be understood in relation to the principle of the anticipatory response.

As with reinforcement, there are two types of punishment. *Negative punishment* occurs when a response is followed by the termination of a rewarding state of affairs. For example, taking food from a rat, a toy from a child, or money from an adult illustrate negative punishments. *Positive punishment* occurs when a response is followed by the onset of an aversive event. Shocking a rat, spanking a child, or insulting an adult illustrate positive punishments.

It should also be noted that the concepts of the conditions and schedules of reinforcement can equally be applied to punishment. Where the condition of reinforcement included its amount, the condition of punishment includes its intensity. Where reinforcement might be scheduled on a (say) fixed interval schedule, so, too, can punishment be scheduled. A fixed-interval schedule of punishment would mean simply that the next response to occur often a constant period of time is followed by an aversive event. Receiving bills at the end of each month is something like a fixed interval schedule of punishment for the responses of consuming the commodity for which you must now pay.

The experimental analysis of punishment has not proceeded as vigorously as has that of reinforcement, and the effects of the various possible conditions and schedules of punishment are not yet well understood. In part, this is a result of some early researches leading to the belief that punishment only suppressed behavior but did not actually

forward—a response that is compatible with the punished running response. And quite as implied by the principle of the anticipatory response, such a punishment does not eliminate the instrumental response but actually facilitates it. The rats actually run faster if they are shocked in their hind paws for running than if no punishment is given; the rats are effectively making anticipatory jumping forward responses while they are running into the shock area.

This leads to an important rule: the most effective punishment is one that "suits the crime." This is accomplished when the response produced by the punishment is incompatible with the punished response so that, when the former becomes anticipatory, it will provide for counterconditioning. As a not-unfamiliar example, consider the father who is distressed that his young son cries when he is hurt since that is not "manly." To eliminate that behavior, the father decides to spank the boy when he catches him crying for getting hurt. But note that this punishment does not suit the crime; instead, spanking elicits crying that is, in fact, the same response as that being punished. The father is most sure to find that, at least initially, the boy's tendency to cry is increased now not only because he has been hurt but as an anticipatory response to the spanking he will receive for crying.

It is not always easy to find a punishment that perfectly suits the crime. If, for example, a child has stolen a toy from a neighbor, there is no simple stimulus that will reflexively elicit returning the toy. This fact makes the escape response (eR in the figure) an important part of the story of effective punishment. Even when the uR to punishment is not incompatible with the punished response, the agent controlling punishment can require that the organism perform an escape response that is incompatible. This, too, will tend to become anticipatory and provide for counterconditioning as shown by the heavy arrow (2) in the figure. For example, the parent might use as punishment the withholding of attention until the child returns the toy thus insuring that an incompatible response is made.

Another, and in the long run more important, way in which punishment affects behavior involves the third response elicited by an aversive event, namely fear. To understand this effect, recall first that all responses produce feedback stimuli telling the organism what he is doing; these are indicated in the figure by $s_{iR}$ to refer to the feedback stimuli resulting from the performance of the instrumental response. Note that these stimuli regularly precede in time $r_{fear}$ and should thus become conditioned to it. This is shown by the heavy arrow (3) in the figure. In short, an organism becomes afraid whenever he feels himself beginning to make a response that has been punished.

Once fear has thus been conditioned, the organism is in a potential learning situation: if he makes the response of stopping-responding, his fears are reduced. This is simply because he is no longer producing the feedback stimuli that were eliciting the fear. And fear-reduction is secondary negative reinforcement which will strengthen the response of stopping-responding. This procedure may work even with a punishment that does not suit the crime although, in such a case, the principle of the anticipatory response is working against the principle of punishment and reduces its effectiveness. The organism then has to learn how to behave in order to avoid punishment.

This discussion of the way in which punishment works, together with earlier principles, enables us to state some basic rules to guide an agent in administering punishments. Doing so does not advocate the use of punishment, but since it is probably an inescapable technique in the control of behavior, an understanding of how to use it effectively is essential.

1. Avoid inadequate punishments. If a response is not eliminated by punishment, it will not only persist while it is rewarded but will become fixated and persist even after it is no longer rewarded. States that impose too small a fine to prevent speeding may be teaching their drivers speeding habits that they perform even when there is no reason to do so.

2. If possible, punishment should suit the crime. This means that the punishment should reflexively elicit a response incompatible with the punished response. Time in a penitentiary cell may elicit only the planning of better crimes rather than socially acceptable behavior.

3. At least, require an incompatible escape response. This means that the person must engage in incompatible behavior to terminate the aversive state. A fixed number of days in jail for vandalism is no proper treatment; the person should have to repair the damage, and punishment lasts until he has done so.

4. If possible, punish immediately. Note that both from the point of view of the anticipatory response and the learning of fear, we are dealing with classical conditioning. And such conditioning is maximally effective if the response is elicited very shortly after the conditioned stimulus. Waiting until a "more appropriate" time to correct behavior provides little or no correction at all.

5. Otherwise, reinstate the stimuli and the response. Perhaps this can be done verbally by reminding the person of the behavior being punished; if possible, reinstate the cues in reality. When relying on counterconditioning, for example, replay the scene. A child who drops

his clothes on the floor on entering the house should not be made simply to pick them up; he should put them back on, return outside, and re-enter to hang up the clothes. And when relying on conditioning of fear, feedback stimuli from the response must be present when the punishment is applied. The big brother who has hit his little sister that afternoon might be required to hit her now and then be punished.

6. Avoid rewards after punishments. We have noted that stimuli preceding rewarding events acquire secondary reinforcing value; even if the stimulus is initially aversive, it can become emotionally positive if it leads to pleasant consequences. Parents who employ punishment should therefore avoid letting any feelings of guilt lead them to lavish love and affection upon the child immediately after punishing him. Otherwise, fear of punishment is reduced because it is a means to love and affection; in extreme form, this results in what is called masochism; a person who enjoys enduring pain.

7. Finally, always provide acceptable alternatives to the punished response. Punishment, even if it eliminates a response, leads to conflict. We have previously described conflict between habit and inhibition; the potential problem is only intensified by punishment. If the motivation for making a response is left unresolved, the person cannot completely escape his temptation; if performing that response is punished, the person cannot fully engage in the activity. He is left in a state of continual conflict leading to the misery that often culminates in neurotic behaviors, inadequate solutions and general maladjustment. Only if the person is given an alternative way of reducing the drive motivating the tendency to make an undesired response can it be reduced sufficiently that he can leave the situation and engage in normal behavior.

That this outcome is more than a remote possibility is amply illustrated in the clinical literature. In western society, most neuroses implicate sex precisely because of the strong prohibitions surrounding most manifestations of this basic motivation. If the young person is denied any form of sexual expression, he is inevitably left in conflict because of the persisting drive. Other cultures have been found where, for example, guilt, shame and secrecy surround hunger rather than sex; their neuroses implicate hunger precisely because of the strong prohibitions surrounding what they consider the private activities involved in eating! In sum, never punish a person for desiring attention, love, affection, comfort, success, or the physical manifestations of sex. If his way of achieving those are socially undersirable, they can be reduced or eliminated by punishment but, for his personal well-being, a socially acceptable alternative must be provided.

## True-False Items:  Response Persistence

1. In a learning context, "resistance to extinction" is a technical term for the drive for self-preservation.

(It would probably be better to use the term, "resistance to experimental extinction," since the referent is the number of times the response will occur during nonreinforcement. False.)

2. The worse the conditions for learning, the greater the persistence.

(Learning is fastest if the organism can make the same response to the same stimulus and receive regular reinforcement for doing so. Persistence, however, is fostered by variability in the stimulus, the response and the reinforcement. In addition, lots of training with large rewards promotes learning but little persistence. True.)

3. The "partial reinforcement effect" is the emotional consequence of not receiving reward every time.

(Partial reinforcement is, indeed, the condition in which some trials are not reinforced. The effect of this is to increase resistance to extinction. The emotional consequences of nonreinforcement have been used to help account for the partial reinforcement effect. False.)

4. A person can learn to behave according to the adage, "If at first you don't succeed, try, try again."

(If an organism encounters partial reinforcement in a variety of situations, the persistence in the face of failure can generalize to new situations in later life. True.)

5. A response may become fixated by punishment.

(If an organism persists in responding in spite of some amount of punishment, he may persist even when reward is removed and punishment is continued. This is called fixation. True.)

6. In extinguishing fears, shaping is a waste of time; it is best to face the problem squarely.

(The answer depends to some extent upon the strength of the fear; intense fears are rarely extinguished directly because they elicit such strong emotional responses. The art of shaping the extinction of fear is to induce enough fear so that some extinction can occur, but at a level with which the person can cope. False.)

7. Counterconditioning involves learning new responses to old stimuli.

(An "old" stimulus in this context is one to which the organism has already learned a response. Similarly, a "new" response is one that is incompatible with the original response. This is thus a short way to say that the original response is replaced by learning another response to that same stimulus. True.)

8. Negative punishment tends to weaken a response; positive punishment tends to strengthen a response.

(Punishment leads to weakening. As with reinforcement, "negative" refers to the removal of something and "positive" to the application of something, but now the reverse operations. Taking away something pleasant or giving something unpleasant are punishments. False.)

9. The principle of punishment is a special case of the principle of the anticipatory response.

(Understanding the effects of punishment requires the use of both principles, but they are not the same. Punishment tends to weaken a response, but the responses produced by punishment also tend to become anticipatory. It is the net effect of these two tendencies that determines the outcome. False.)

10. A punishment that "suits the crime" is one that is properly gauged in intensity according to the severity of the crime.

(The expression, "suit the crime" has been used with respect to the nature of the punishment and not its intensity. A punishment should elicit responses incompatible with those being punished. Perhaps its intensity should correspond to the severity of the crime, in order to compete successfully with it, but that is a separate issue. False.)

11. Punishment makes the organism afraid to make the response.

(Punishment associates fear with the feedback stimuli produced when that response is made. The organism may thus not respond in order to avoid this fear, or may stop the response if it begins in order to escape this fear. True.)

12. It is best to "count to ten" and calm down before punishing a response.

(Punishment is most effective if given immediately after an undesirable response. When that is not practicable, it is advisable to replay the scene, at least verbally, so that those cues are present at the time punishment is administered. False.)

# 9

## Generalization, Discrimination and Differentiation

We have previously indicated that learning is somewhat specific to the particular stimuli and responses involved during practice. Learning is partly restricted to the environment in which practice occurs, such as the room in which a student studies, and is partly restricted to the behaviors in which he engages, such as the specific examples given in a text. But learning is not completely restricted to the original stimuli and responses. If, for example, you find a particular piece of fish distasteful, you are likely to generalize your reaction to other fish of the same species and even to other fish which look somewhat similar to it. The person who "eats with his eyes" is indeed one who generalizes his expectations about the taste of foods to their appearance in relation to his past experiences. Thus, other stimuli can elicit a learned response. And in acquiring table manners, we learn to use a knife and fork in a particular way but we are not incapable of somewhat different techniques if necessary. The American who normally scoops potatoes and vegetables onto his fork with his preferred hand may feel embarrassed in a British home where they press food upon the back of the fork with the knife, but he can use his utensils that way if required to do so, although not so adeptly as if he had practiced that mode of responding. Thus, we can make responses other than those we practiced.

Accordingly, one of the most basic principles of learned behavior is that of generalization: WHENEVER A RESPONSE HAS BEEN LEARNED IN ONE STIMULUS SITUATION, SIMILAR STIMULUS SITUATIONS WILL ALSO TEND TO ELICIT THAT RESPONSE IN PROPORTION TO THEIR SIMILARITY, AND THAT STIMULUS SITUATION WILL ALSO TEND TO ELICIT SIMILAR RESPONSES IN PROPORTION TO THEIR SIMILARITY. There are, in effect, two

128

aspects to this principle. The one is that of *stimulus generalization*, the greater the similarity any situation is to that in which practice occurred, the greater the likelihood that the learned response will occur. The other is that of *response generalization*, that when the learned response itself is for some reason blocked, the organism will tend to make responses that are similar to that which he practiced. Both aspects of this principle apply to all learned habits whether they be acquired through the process of classical, operant or instrumental conditioning.

It should be recognized that this is an exceedingly adaptive principle. As a rule, similar situations require similar responses. Indeed, one could argue that no stimulus situation is exactly identical to another, so that generalization is necessary in order to learn. In general, the response most likely to be appropriate in a new situation is one that is most similar to one practiced in a similar situation. Consider, for example, the behavior of ballroom dancing. Having learned to dance with one partner, it is probably best to make those same responses when confronted with a new partner. And having learned one particular type of dance, it is likely that many of those learned responses will be appropriate in learning a new type of dance. These generalizations are, of course, not perfect, which is why this chapter will also consider the related processes of discrimination and differentiation.

The principle of generalization is also of considerable practical importance in understanding behavior. Racial prejudice, for example, be it positive or negative, is a familiar illustration of stimulus generalization. Experiences with one person which involve emotional responses will generalize to other people who present a similar appearance. One obvious source of similarity is racial features, including color of the skin, shape of the nose, slant of the eyes, or whatever. Furthermore, within these are still finer details upon which generalization may be based. To most people, the eyes are the principal feature by which they distinguish people, but some attend more to the mouth, the nose and to some extent the chin and forehead. Disagreements as to whether two people look alike result from concentrating on different features. And when you meet a person to whom you take an instant like or dislike, it is because his features, including the sound of his voice and certain of his mannerisms, are similar to someone you have known or perhaps even encountered as a movie actor and for whom you developed emotional responses which now generalize to the new person. The most fundamental principles involved in understanding interpersonal relations are classical conditioning and generalization; emotional responses become conditioned to people as stimuli and generalize to similar people.

## The Concept of Similarity

As with other basic principles whose initial statement can be made with remarkable simplicity, there are complexities that are implicit in the principle of generalization. The most important concerns the concept of *similarity*: how does one measure or estimate the extent to which two stimuli or two responses are similar to each other? There are three aspects to the answer to this question.

### Continuous Dimensions

Many events vary along natural, physical dimensions for which there is a measure available. On the stimulus side, for example, tones vary in pitch and loudness; lights vary in color and brightness; objects vary in size including height, length and volume as well as shape. And on the response side, behaviors vary in force, speed and direction. For each of these, a physical measure exists and similarity can be measured along that continuous dimension. Thus, the closer two tones are in pitch, the more similar they are and the greater the generalization we expect between them. Particularly when dealing with simple stimuli, the most useful index of similarity involves a measure of its physical attributes.

### Common Elements

When events are complex and contain a number of elements, the approach to measuring similarity is by counting the number of elements two events have in common. For example, the game of tennis is quite complex, containing elements such as a racquet, a ball, a court with a net, and the responses of hitting the ball over the net into designated areas and keeping score in a particular way. Many of the elements of this game are similar to those in ping pong although the size of the racquet, ball and court are different. Tennis is also similar to squash at least in that both involve hitting a ball with a racquet and taking turns doing so. Tennis is less similar to baseball and still less similar to football as the number of players, the nature of the ball and the object of the game change. One way of measuring the similarity of complex events is to count the number of common elements or features which they share.

### Learned Similarity

Not only may events be similar because of their inherent appearance, nature or structure, which can be measured along continuous dimensions or counted as common elements, events may acquire similarity.

This fact can be seen most clearly in the effects of language. All words have associated meanings, and insofar as the meanings of different words are similar, they tend to elicit similar responses. The words "couch" and "sofa," for example, have no sounds in common and do not sound alike but because they mean very much the same thing, they have acquired similarity. Similarly, the words "rocket" and "missile" may have acquired similarity for those who have not learned the distinction. Evidence for this assertion comes from the study of *semantic generalization;* if a human is conditioned to respond with an eyeblink to a word as a stimulus, greater generalization will occur to words with similar meanings than to words with similar sounds.

This process is not restricted to language although that is the most obvious source of evidence. More generally, *stimuli and responses may acquire similarity insofar as they become associated with similar responses.* If, for example, a rat is first trained to make one response to two rather different stimuli and then a second response is trained to one of them, that response will show greater generalization to the other stimulus as a result of the original training. Similarly, returning to language, we respond similarly to all dogs because we have learned to apply the same label to them.

## Summary

We can summarize these approaches to estimating similarity by again considering people as stimuli. In the first place, we differ from each other along a number of continuous dimensions: our physical size, the color of our skin, hair and eyes, the pitch of our voice and so on. In each of these dimensions, similarity can be measured along those dimensions according to physical units. In addition, people present a complex of elements and our similarity depends in part upon how many of these we share with another person. Even two people whose eyes look very much the same may readily be distinguished if they have different colored hair. And finally, we attach to people labels such as Russian, dean, doctor or whatever, and these labels tend to increase the similarity among people who share them. The generalization of our learned responses is based on all of these sources of similarity.

## Factors which INCREASE Generalization

As we have indicated, the amount of generalization is based primarily upon similarity. We often refer to the *gradient of generalization* to reflect the fact that the amount of generalization varies with similarity rather than being an all-or-none affair. Such a gradient was shown in Figure 9 in our discussion of classical conditioning: as similarity decreases, generalization decreases. There are, however, two factors involved in the acquisition of a habit which affect the amount of generalization between stimuli of some degree of similarity.

### Reinforcement Variability

It is perhaps obvious that variability in the stimulus and response during practice will increase the amount to which learning will generalize. The larger the number of stimuli to which the response has become associated, the wider the range of stimuli that will lead to that response; and the larger the number of responses practiced, the wider the range of behaviors that are learned. It is perhaps less obvious that the amount of generalization also depends on reinforcement variability. However, *responses acquired under conditions of variable reward generalize more extensively than responses acquired under conditions of constant reward.*

### Punishment

It is also a somewhat surprising fact that ineffective punishment, that is punishment that does not successfully eliminate the behavior, leads to greater generalization than if the response is not punished. In fact, punishment may lead to a *greater tendency* to respond to different stimuli than to the original stimulus itself. This is the phenomenon of *displacement,* the theoretical basis for which is the same as that for disinhibition described in Figure 12. A tendency to respond is built up on the basis of reinforcement; a tendency not to respond is built up on the basis of punishment. Because of the differential degree of generalization of these two tendencies, the net effect may be to respond more to a somewhat different stimulus. A woman may first develop affection for one man and then find some aspects of their relationship aversive; a somewhat similar man is then likely to elicit her strongest affectional responses. In general, *punishment of a response increases the amount of generalization.*

## Factors which DECREASE Generalization

Some aspects of the training conditions may also lead to less generalization than might otherwise be expected. Two of these, in particular, are worth noting.

### Amount of Reward

The larger the amount of reward given during the acquisition of a response, the *less* the amount of generalization that learning will exhibit if the stimulus is changed or a different response is required. Although large rewards lead to vigorous performance, learning is more specific as a result.

## Extended Training

Rewarded training beyond the point at which there is further improvement in performance also leads to *less* generalization. Extended training progressively increases the specificity of the learning to the particular stimuli and responses practiced. This fact can be shown most clearly in the context of compound stimuli. If a response is conditioned to a compound conditioned stimulus composed (say) of a light and a tone, after a moderate amount of training either element alone will elicit the conditioned response. After extensive training, however, only the compound itself will elicit the response; the elements, although a part of and hence similar to the compound, are no longer effective. The person who has "overtrained" may do worse in a test situation because it may involve somewhat different stimuli or require somewhat different responses from those practiced, and he will be less likely to perform appropriately.

## Summary of Generalization

At one and the same time, learning is somewhat specific to the particular stimuli and responses involved during practice and also generalizes to somewhat similar stimuli and responses in proportion to their similarity. The degree of similarity may be measured along continuous dimensions for which there are physical measures, it may be estimated from the number of elements that complex events have in common, and it may be affected by learning similar responses to somewhat different stimuli. The amount of generalization not only depends on similarity but also upon certain features of the training situation, being increased by variability in reinforcement and by the inclusion of ineffective punishment, and being decreased by experience with large rewards and with training extended beyond the point of improvement in performance. These latter factors, it should be noted, are the same ones that affect the persistence of learning. That is to say, those training conditions that increase persistence also increase generalization and those that decrease persistence also decrease generalization.

## Discrimination and Differentiation

We have already anticipated the fact that generalization is not always adaptive. Two people may appear to be quite similar even though they are, in fact, markedly different individuals who are properly responded to differently. Even identical twins are individuals. The rattlesnake and the western bull snake look very much alike although one is a menace to mankind and the other is beneficial. And although activities such as tennis and squash have many elements in common, they also require somewhat different skills. In short, although generalization is often adaptive and perhaps a necessary principle for survival, organisms also need to be able to overcome the effects of generalization in those situations where it is inappropriate.

In order to do so, we distinguish between two types of processes. The process of *discrimination* arises when somewhat similar stimuli encounter differential reinforcement so that responding to them identically is not adaptive. The process of *differentiation* arises when somewhat similar responses encounter differential reinforcement so that the performance of one is more adaptive than performance of the other. In effect, these are the processes by which an organism learns to offset the basic tendency to generalize and to respond only to those stimuli that are appropriate and to make only those responses that are appropriate.

In the following treatment, we shall confine ourselves to the process of discrimination. This is done primarily because considerably more experimental evidence is available simply because one can more readily present and control the stimuli to which an organism is exposed than he can the responses which he makes. However, insofar as comparable research has been done, the evidence suggests that the two processes are fundamentally the same and that the principles of the one are matched by comparable principles of the other. In most instances, the reader can properly substitute the word "response" for the word "stimulus" in the following presentation and arrive at an appropriate conclusion.

There is probably good reason for this identity of principles. We have previously noted that all responses produce feedback stimuli indicating to the organism what he is doing. Differentiating between responses may thus be thought of as discriminating between the feedback stimuli produced by somewhat similar responses. That is to say, responses are different because they feel different, and selecting which response to make is fundamentally the same as selecting which stimulus to respond to. The difference is only on the basis of whether the stimuli are external or response-produced and while, at a molecular level, there are theoretical reasons for distinguishing between the processes, for most purposes they may be treated as comparable.

## Types of Discrimination Situations

Discrimination learning is the process resulting from the differential reinforcement of somewhat similar stimuli. By *differential reinforcement*, we mean simply that the consequences associated with these stimuli are not the same so that responding the same to them is not appropriate. In effect, the organism must learn to distinguish between the stimuli and respond differently depending on which stimulus is present. There are four basic contexts in which this process can be studied.

### Differential (Multiple)[2] Classical Conditioning

We have already described this process in our development of a theory of classical conditioning, but for completeness, it should be reviewed here. *Differential classical conditioning* occurs when there are two conditioned stimuli which occur in an irregular and unpredictable order, and when one of these is followed by the unconditioned stimulus and the other is not. For example, in the Pavlovian context, a 1000 cycle tone might be followed by food while a 2000 cycle tone is not followed by food. Differential conditioning is demonstrated when the organism comes to salivate only to the former tone.

Differential classical conditioning is very important in everyday life. Continuing the examples from interpersonal relationships, we learn to like one person but dislike another person who is somewhat similar to the first. The treatment of racial prejudice is, in fact, to arrange for differential conditioning so that the person learns that emotional responses generalized from one member of a race to another are not appropriate.

### Differential (Multiple) Operant Conditioning

We briefly introduced the idea of differential operant conditioning as one of the more complex schedules of reinforcement. *Differential operant conditioning* occurs when on some occasions one stimulus is present and one schedule is in force while on other occasions, a similar stimulus is present but a different schedule is in force. For example, a

---

[2]The basic operation performed in the first three types of discrimination situations is the same: two different but somewhat similar stimuli occur in an irregular and unpredictable order followed by different consequences. They differ as to which type of conditioning procedure is employed. Those working in classical conditioning have used the word "differential," those working in operant conditioning have used the word "multiple," and those working in instrumental conditioning have often used the word "successive." None of these words appear to be logically superior to the others; the word "differential" appears to be the one students can most readily associate with the fundamental operation. The reader should, however, be aware of and be able to recognize the others.

pigeon might encounter a fixed-interval schedule when the key that he is pecking is red, while the schedule is a fixed-ratio when that key is green. Differential operant conditioning is demonstrated when the organism responds differentially to the two stimuli, responding appropriate to the schedule which the stimulus indicates is in force.

As an example from interpersonal relations, consider the response of swearing. This is, of course, a freely available response which may occur as a part of verbal behavior at any time. It is well known that a high frequency of this response is not only permitted but is actually expected and approved in most military contexts; however, it is disapproved in most homes. The soldier, then, is confronted with the necessity to discriminate between these two contexts, coloring his language with four-letter words while he is on base, but avoiding their use when he is on leave at home. With greater or less success, soldiers display differential operant conditioning.

### Differential (Multiple) Instrumental Conditioning

Recall that the principal variable of interest in instrumental conditioning is the condition of reinforcement. When the performance of a response is enabled for discrete trials, the speed or vigor of that response depends upon such variables as the amount and delay of reinforcement. *Differential instrumental conditioning* refers to the situation in which the consequences of making the response in one situation are different from those in another situation. For example, a rat might sometimes be placed in a black alley and rewarded for running to the goal box with food; on other occasions he is placed in a white alley where the goal box is empty. Differential instrumental conditioning is demonstrated when his performance in the two situations is different and appropriate to the reward or nonreward experienced there.

As an everyday example in an interpersonal context, consider a girl's response of accepting a date. This is an instumental situation since she cannot accept dates unless they are offered to her, but when they arise, she can accept or decline. Although two boys may, in many ways, appear to be quite similar, she may find that she enjoys going out with one of them but not with the other. She displays differential instrumental conditioning by learning to accept the one and decline the other.

### Simultaneous Discrimination

In each of the above three types of differential conditioning, the to-be-discriminated stimuli are never presented simultaneously. Instead, sometimes one is present and sometimes the other is present and, when only one is reinforced, the problem may be thought of as a "go-no-go" decision. In *simultaneous discrimination learning,* the two stimuli are presented at the same time, and the consequences of responding to one are different from the consequences of responding to the other. This procedure may be thought of as "stimulus selection," and is illustrated when a rat confronts two doors, one black and the other white, with food reward behind only one. Learning to choose the correct color door regardless of its position illustrates simultaneous discrimination learning.

This is the type of problem which voters confront during an election. Not infrequently, the candidates are in many ways similar. Each may appear to promise pretty much the same things yet the voter must choose between them. He is thus confronted with a simultaneous discrimination problem.

### Summary of Types of Discrimination Situations

Each of the four types of discrimination situations have one feature in common: two stimuli which are sufficiently similar that generalization between them occurs are treated differently so that the organism must learn to distinguish between them and respond differently. At this point, several more general features should be noted. In the first place, one need not be restricted to only two stimuli. Any number of somewhat similar stimuli might be embedded within any of the types of discrimination situations and in a variety of complex combinations. Restricting to two stimuli provides the simplest illustration of the basic processes involved. Secondly, the situation need not be as simple as that one stimulus is reinforced while the second stimulus is not. In the classical case, for example, one CS might be followed by one US while a second CS is followed by another US. Again, it is simpler first to study the limiting case of differential reinforcement of something versus nothing. The basic process uncovered as a result of experimental analysis of these situations is that organisms can learn to respond differentially even to highly similar stimuli when the consequences make such discrimination appropriate. There are certainly limitations to this conclusion, some of which are indicated in the next section.

## Factors which Affect Discrimination Learning

In describing the types of discrimination situations, we have actually described the operations that may be performed by an experimenter or the environment. That is to say, differential reinforcement is associated with similar stimuli, but it is an empirical question as to whether and how rapidly an organism may learn to respond differently. There are a number of factors which affect how readily performance adjusts appropriately.

### Similarity

The most obvious but also most important factors affecting the ease of discrimination learning concern the similarity of the stimuli and the reinforcement conditions. The more similar the stimuli are, the greater the amount of generalization that will occur between them and hence the more difficult it will be for the organism to respond differentially. Similarly, the more similar the reinforcement conditions associated with each stimulus, the less basis there is for differential responding and the less likely it is to occur. This is apparent in the limiting case: if the stimulus or reward conditions are actually not different to the organism in question, then there is no basis for him to learn to respond differentially. As these differences increase, the ease of discrimination also increases. At the other extreme, if the stimuli become so different that there is no generalization in the first place, there is no occasion for discrimination *learning*. The process is of interest when the stimuli are discriminably different to the organism but are sufficiently similar that generalization would normally occur.

### Nondifferential Reinforcement

Discrimination learning may be preceded by a stage during which the two stimuli are presented but are not differentially reinforced. In the classical case, for example, both CSs might first be followed by the US after which the US is omitted for one of them and continued for the other. The evidence shows that such *prior nondifferential reinforcement retards subsequent discrimination learning*. Having first learned to make the same response to two similar stimuli, their similarity is effectively increased and subsequently overcoming the generalization between them is more difficult.

Indeed, if nondifferential reinforcement is coupled with punishment for errors during early trials, a subsequent discrimination may not be learned at all. For example, consider a rat that is first forced to choose between two stimuli, one of which is black and the other white, under conditions in which reward is half the time behind one stimulus and half the time behind the other *and* if he happens to choose the wrong stimulus, he experiences an aversive consequence. During this stage, he is likely to adopt a stereotyped solution, such as always going in the same direction since there is no better alternative available. More importantly, however, if the conditions are subsequently changed so that reward is always behind (say) the black door, he may never learn this discrimination! His earlier solution, although no longer adaptive, persists not only because it received partial reinforcement initially but also because it was fixated by partial punishment. Here is another situation in which organisms may learn not to learn.

## Transposition

Once a discrimination has been formed between one pair of stimuli, we may inquire as to how the organism will respond if a new, but similar pair is presented. We might, for example, first train a monkey to select the larger of two relatively small stimuli; then we can present him with two relatively large stimuli but also differing in size from each other. *Transposition* refers to the fact that organisms, in many situations, tend to choose from between the two new stimuli on the basis of the same relationship as was appropriate during the original discrimination. In this example, the monkey is likely to select the larger of the new stimuli although their absolute sizes are different. This observation is true even in the special case where the smaller of the two new stimuli is actually the same size as the larger of the original pair, so that he selects not the stimulus that he was trained to choose but rather a totally new stimulus.

One cannot say in advance whether the phenomenon of transposition will be beneficial or harmful to later discrimination learning. It depends upon which response is correct in the new context. If the same relative choice is correct, then he will perform correctly from the beginning. If the opposite relative choice is correct, however, then the tendency to transpose on the basis of the relationship between the stimuli will be detrimental.

The term "transposition" was borrowed from music where the same piece can be played in different keys and still sound very much the same. It is one of the bases for our earlier assertion that relationships among stimuli themselves qualify as stimuli. Organisms can learn to select the larger, the brighter, the heavier, etc., of two stimuli even if he is never confronted with the same pair of stimuli but if he is consistently rewarded for responding on the basis of such a relationship. It is also interesting to note that adult humans display a greater tendency to transpose a learned discrimination than infants or lower animals. Learning words for relationships requires attending to them and facilitates subsequent learning based upon them.

## Transfer

When the organism is confronted with a very difficult discrimination because the stimuli involved are highly similar, learning may be facilitated by first learning an easier discrimination involving the same dimension. For example, if a rat is to be trained to select between two very similar grey stimuli, he can learn this most readily if he is first trained to select between a black and a white stimulus and if these are then gradually made more similar as they approach the ultimate difficult discrimination. This transfer effect may be beneficial including all of the training trials given; an organism learns a difficult discrimination faster by first starting on an easy one than by being given the same amount of training all on the difficult problem. Indeed, in some cases a difficult discrimination can be learned only if preceded by pretraining on easier tasks along the same dimension.

The optimal procedures for using the transfer of discrimination to facilitate learning have not yet been worked out experimentally. However, the student can profit from reviewing our discussion of shaping a response and noting that the present procedure is essentially the shaping of a discrimination. Because of the similarity between differentiating responses and discriminating stimuli, it will not be surprising if very much the same rules apply. Specifically, for example, it is probably not advisable to spend too much time on the easier problems; once the discrimination process begins on those, it is best to move on rapidly toward the more difficult ones.

### Learning to Learn

The rate at which discrimination learning proceeds depends importantly upon the amount of experience the organism has had with discrimination problems even though they involve different stimulus dimensions than the problem now involved. A monkey, for example, might first be required to learn to select the larger of two blocks of wood, and require forty or fifty trials to do so consistently. He might then be required to learn to select the green ball instead of the red one, and he will probably require fewer trials to learn this problem. As this is continued with new stimuli, each discrimination problem becomes progressively easier until, in the limiting case, he will make at most one error. This is called *learning to learn* or a *discrimination learning set*. Having solved a number of simple discrimination problems, he is now able to solve comparable problems readily. His first choice must be made by chance, but whether he is correct or not on that trial, he thereafter knows which stimulus is correct and will select it consistently.

It is this fact of learning to learn that helps account for some of the quantitative differences between the learning by adult humans and that by other animals. During the years of childhood, a person is taught a great many discriminations. In effect, we have learned to learn a wide variety of types of material as a result of being exposed to a graduated series of problems of those types. Your ability to read and understand this book is heavily dependent upon years of prior training, both in reading and in assimilating information of this type presented in this manner. Probably as more is discovered about the learning process, better programs will be devised to take advantage of not only our capacity to learn, but also our capacity to learn how to learn.

### Summary of Factors which Affect Discrimination Learning

It is intuitively obvious and is experimentally demonstrable that organisms can tell the difference between stimuli even when they are sufficiently similar that generalization between them occurs. How fine a discrimination an organism can learn and how rapidly he learns it, however, depend only partly upon factors in the situation itself such as the similarity of the stimuli and reward conditions. They also depend importantly upon the past experiences of the organism in question. Let us review the effects of these experiences in the context of racial prejudice against the Negro.

In this case, generalization is based on the color of the skin. The occurrence of such generalization is normal, natural and inevitable. At the same time, the generalization is inappropriate, since skin color is known not to be a perfect predictor of behavioral traits and each person should be evaluated individually. We first noted that prior non-differential reinforcement retards subsequent discrimination learning. In this context, then, an individual who is early exposed to various Negroes whose behavioral traits are, in fact, quite similar and undesirable to him, will have more difficulty later learning to discriminate between Negroes on the basis of characteristics other than skin color than the person who has early learned such discriminations. We have noted that learned discriminations transpose to new situations on the basis of the relative relationship between the early stimuli. Thus, a person who has first learned that a somewhat darker person is less acceptable or more unacceptable than a somewhat lighter person will later transpose this relationship so that the darker the skin, the worse he will assume the person to be. We have observed that difficult discriminations are most readily formed by first learning easier discriminations involving the same dimensions. Hence, to facilitate learning to discriminate among Negroes whose skin color make them inevitably highly similar, exposure to people whose other physical traits are highly dissimilar would lead to transfer to more difficult discriminations among more similar people. And we have seen that organisms can learn to learn discriminations as a result simply of learning a large number of problems of that type. Accordingly, explicit training in discriminating people on the basis of traits and features other than skin color should facilitate later discrimination among members of the same race.

## Errorless Discrimination Learning

Discrimination learning is demonstrated when an organism responds differently to stimuli which are sufficiently similar that generalization occurs between them. In each of the procedures we have discussed, the organism first learns to respond to one stimulus because doing so is reinforced. This tendency to respond then generalizes to the second stimulus so that he also responds to it. However, that response is not reinforced and in time the discrimination is learned. The reader might do well to review the theoretical description of differential classical conditioning in which this process was described in detail.

Of considerable interest would be a procedure in which appropriate differential responding could be achieved without the necessity for the organism to encounter the frustration resulting from responding and not being rewarded. One can build up enough inhibition as a result of nonreinforcement so that the erroneous responses are eventually eliminated but the aversive aspects of frustration and inhibition could lead one to favor a procedure in which errors never occur in the first place.

There is preliminary evidence that such procedures may, in fact, be possible. Working within the context of operant conditioning, we can first train a pigeon to peck a key that is (say) green in order to obtain food. Then carefully watching the bird, we can present very dim and brief exposures of a red stimulus at times when the bird is otherwise engaged and unlikely to peck the key, returning it immediately to green. We can then increase the brightness of the red stimulus and then progressively increase its duration, all the while taking care that key-pecking is not likely to occur during its presence. By such a procedure, we may arrive at a stage in which the bird's behavior looks very much like that of another bird trained in differential operant conditioning by standard procedures: he pecks when the key is green and doesn't peck when the key is red, with both now exposed equally often and at equal brightnesses.

Such an "errorless" bird is quite different with respect to the underlying basis for his differential behavior. Specifically, phenomena indicative of inhibition in a bird trained by usual procedures are not revealed by birds trained in this gradual shaping fashion. The potential practical significance of this demonstration is by no means yet understood, but it strongly suggests that we should add to the methods we have already described, namely, those of positive control and aversive control, the concept of *neutral control of behavior*.

The position implied by this concept is that habits may be developed simply by responding; they do not need to be rewarded explicitly nor is anything else necessary save that they occur. Conversely, habits are "broken" simply by not making the response; they don't have to be punished explicitly. In effect, there is a habit of "not-responding" which ideally is learned in the first place but which may also be learned as a form of counterconditioning for undesirable habits. And this latter is quite different from a habit that is inhibited as a result of nonreinforcement or punishment.

It would be premature to generalize upon this notion too extensively until a firmer experimental base has been laid. But it would suggest that scenes such as toilet training can be accomplished without the use of obvious rewards for acceptable behavior or obvious punishment for unacceptable behavior; if the parent simply arranges that the child uses the toilet by diligent observation of his biological schedule for a while, that response will become associated with that stimulus without further ado. For such a child, there is nothing particularly good about using the toilet nor particularly bad about not doing so—it is simply the way it is done. The person who is addicted to biting his nails may eliminate this behavior without the trauma of shame and aversive control: if, probably with the help of others, he simply pays conscious attention to not making that response for a while, the habit of not doing so will supplant the original habit and it is gone simply because he doesn't do it any more. The possibility of controlling behavior without the use of emotional consequences is one of the exciting possibilities that is only beginning to be revealed.

### True-False Items: Generalization, Discrimination and Differentiation

1. A single situation cannot reflect stimulus generalization and response generalization at the same time.

(If a new situation is encountered, the tendency will be to make the response learned in a similar situation; if, however, that response is not possible, the tendency will be to make a somewhat similar response. False.)

2. Stimuli cannot be similar on the basis of continuous dimensions, common elements, and learned similarity at the same time.

(Two pizza pies may differ in the continuous dimension of the amount of an ingredient they contain, the number of common ingredients they contain, and the name attached to them. Especially among complex stimuli, all bases for measuring similarity may be involved. False.)

3. Learning different responses to somewhat similar stimuli may increase their distinctiveness.

(Although we have concentrated on the fact that learning similar responses to different stimuli increases their similarity, the reverse process also occurs. Stimuli become more different as an organism learns to respond differently to them. True.)

4. A daughter is likely to choose as a husband a man who is somewhat similar to her father because of displacement.

(If a daughter loves her father, similar men will be attractive because of generalization. However, the incest taboo leads to an avoidance of her father and, also by generalization, men very similar to him. Her strongest attraction will thus be a man who is similar but nevertheless, distinctively different. This is an illustration of displacement. True.)

5. Responses which generalize very broadly do not persist very long.

(Quite the reverse; factors which increase generalization also increase persistence. This is fortunate since we typically want to learn responses that will persist and generalize to new situations. It may be unfortunate, however, since we likely learn undesirable responses under conditions that promote both persistence and generalization. False.)

6. Discrimination is responding the same way to similar stimuli while differentiation is responding differently to them.

(In everyday language, we may say racial "discrimination" for the behavior of treating members of a race alike. However, as used here, discrimination is distinguishing between somewhat similar stimuli and differentiation is distinguishing the distinctive feedback from somewhat similar responses. False.)

7. What the organism learns about the difference between the stimuli depends upon the type of discrimination situation employed.

(The different situations require somewhat different behaviors for an organism to indicate that he is discriminating between the stimuli. But what he is learning is very much the same as indicated by the fact that one can change the type of situation and still see some evidence of stimulus control. False.)

8. In teaching a child the distinction between "good" and "bad," it is best to treat his behavior indiscriminately until he is old enough to understand.

(This approach would constitute prior nondifferential reinforcement which would make the discrimination more difficult to learn. False.)

9. In teaching a child the distinction between "good" and "bad," it is best to begin with examples that are extreme.

(Fine distinctions can be learned more readily if preceded by easier, but similar, ones. The converse may also be true: starting with a difficult problem may make an easier one more difficult. In any event, the process of shaping applies equally to discrimination and differentiation learning. True.)

10. The rate of learning, typically, at first increases but then eventually decreases with age, largely as a result of prior learning.

(There may be important constitutional changes that occur during childhood and old age which affect the rate of learning. But one important fact is that we learn to learn and can solve new problems more quickly as a result. However, as we accumulate habits, these may begin to interfere with learning incompatible ones. Hence, our prior learning history does greatly affect how rapidly we can learn a new task. True.)

11. A child's expectations when opening a Christmas package depends upon its size largely as a result of transposition.

(If, historically, larger packages have contained better presents, this relationship will be learned so that his future expectations will reflect transposition on the basis of this relationship. True.)

12. Stimulus control over behavior requires that errors occur so that they can be nonreinforced or perhaps punished.

(Undesirable or inappropriate responses can be eliminated by nonreinforcement and punishment. However, it may also be possible to arrange conditions so that they never occur in the first place and hence never get learned. False.)

# 10

# An Overview of Learning

We have now completed a survey of the fundamental principles of learning. In doing so, we have necessarily been submerged in a large number of technical terms and details which may have interfered with seeing the overall organization of these materials. Hence, let us now try to regain a general overview of the topic.

At the most general level, we can say that organisms learn one thing: that stimuli occur regularly in the environment. Learning means to come to anticipate or expect the occurrence of stimuli and to respond appropriately. Learning is what in logic is called an "if-then" relationship—if something happens, something else happens. Regularity may occur simply over time; the sun rises and sets each day. More commonly, a stimulus is more-or-less regularly preceded by another stimulus which occurs irregularly over time. The adage, "where there's smoke, there's fire," captures one such regularity among stimuli. Similarly, thunder regularly follows lightning. We called the learning that results from pairing two stimuli in temporal order *classical conditioning*. The response occasioned by the second stimulus tends to become anticipatory and to antedate its initial time of occurrence.

The second regularity is when a stimulus follows a response—if you do something, then something happens. If you throw a stone in the air, you will see it first rise and then fall. If you brush at a fly that has landed on your neck, he will fly away. We distinguished between two types of situations in which this learning process is studied experimentally: operant conditioning and instrumental conditioning. In *operant conditioning*, the response is freely available and can be made repeatedly at least for some period of time. Throwing stones into the air is such a freely available behavior. In *instrumental conditioning*, a single response can be made during discrete trials or opportunities. Brushing a fly is such a response because it can only be made when a fly lands on your neck.

The reason for distinguishing between operant and instrumental conditioning is *not* because fundamentally different principles are involved. In each case, the organism learns that a stimulus follows a response. The distinction is necessary because somewhat different methods and procedures apply. When a response is freely available, the behavior of interest is the rate at which it occurs over time. We saw that this behavior depends importantly on the schedule of reinforcement. How frequently a boy asks a girl for a date depends in part upon how frequently she accepts the invitation. When a response is periodically enabled by circumstances, the behavior of interest is how rapidly or vigorously the response is made. We saw that this behavior depends importantly on the condition of reinforcement. How rapidly a girl accepts a date depends in part upon how pleasurable previous dates have been.

At a more complex level, adjustment to the environment may require that the organism distinguish between (respond differently to) similar stimuli. We called this *discrimination learning* and saw that it could be studied in each of the conditioning situations; classical, operant or instrumental. A dark cloud may signify impending rain, a lighter cloud may provide only brief shade. The visitor to a foreign country may find that drinking tap water is safe in some hotels but not in others. The appropriate response to a cutting remark may depend on whether it was made in jest or whether it was serious.

Discrimination learning can be viewed as a "conditional if-then" relationship. That is to say, if something happens, then something else happens—provided the conditions are right. When an organism has learned this conditional relationship, we say that his behavior has been brought under stimulus control. What he does depends upon which stimulus is present.

We also described a closely related process in which the regularity depends on how a response is made. *Differentiation learning* occurs when responding in one way leads to one outcome, and responding in another way leads to another outcome. All of our skills reflect learning not just what to do, but how to do it in order to get the most reward.

Certainly, there are still more complex situations in which learning occurs. The next obvious extension is to combine discrimination learning and differentiation learning, so that the organism learns how to respond one way in one environment and in a different way in another environment. More complex patterns of stimuli may be involved in the learning of abstract concepts. More complex patterns of responses may be involved in the solving of problems. An understanding of such situations will probably require the introduction of new principles of learning. But these fundamental ones that we have described will still apply.

The goal of psychology is to understand behavior as evidenced by the ability to predict and control behavior. In a similar sense, learning enables us to predict and control our environment. We learn to predict our environment when stimuli follow stimuli, and we may also control our environment when stimuli follow responses. We may learn fine stimulus discriminations and response differentiations in order better to predict and control the environment. It is for this reason that the topic of learning is of intimate, personal importance to everyone. And the better you understand the learning process itself, the better you can learn, the better you can help others learn, and the better off we will all be as a result.

# 11

# Introduction to Motivation

*Motivational factors are ones that refer to states of the organism that are relatively temporary and reversible and which tend to energize or activate the behavior of organisms.* Primary motivation refers to those factors that have these properties without any special learning experiences and which are thus characteristic of all normal members of the species.

It is perhaps simpler and more appropriate to think of primary motivation as unlearned motivational dispositions. That is to say, the organism is predisposed to become motivated upon the occasion of specific environmental circumstances. A baby gets hungry without training and becomes frightened by the loss of physical support, but these motives are aroused only if the appropriate conditions occur. Furthermore, even the motivated organism does not display vigorous random activity, but rather responds to stimuli in his environment when appropriate. A food-deprived rat, for example, becomes aroused into activity only when signals appear that feeding time is approaching.

This basic conception of motivation bears repeating. In the first place, you are not now actively motivated by the fear of loss of physical support, but were an earthquake to begin, your disposition to be motivated by that fear would become apparent. This drive would then probably be evident in vigorous activity aimed at self-preservation. In less violent circumstances, such as a fear of personal inferiority, our initial efforts to reduce the drive may be ineffectual and we lapse into inactivity. But the drive remains as a disposition to respond to any signal offering relief. Charlatans, quacks and "con men" prey upon such unresolved motives. One of the homey ways to illustrate this two stage image of motivation—the disposition to become motivated if something happens, and then the disposition to respond to potential stimuli—is to observe a group of people facing each other at a cocktail party when there is an occasional lapse in the conversation. Silence is a very powerful motivator in a social setting, and the increasing anxiety as silence continues is readily apparent in the mannerisms and postures of the people. Everyone is desperately trying to think of something to say. And this motivation is also apparent when someone finally does start a new train of conversation, since the others act eager to listen and may even blurt out interruptions once a new stimulus is provided.

## Biological Needs and Psychological Drives

It is necessary to distinguish the concept of "biological need" from "psychological drive." All organisms require certain conditions in order to survive, and these may be thought of as *biological needs*. A human, for example, must eat food, drink fluid, eliminate wastes, breathe air, and if the species is to survive, copulate. Other biological needs give fewer outward signs of their necessity, such as the requirement for an adequate supply of vitamins and minerals. The biological needs differ for different species, but each has some specific requirements for survival.

*Psychological drives* impel the organism to respond. Most biological needs give rise to psychological drives; for example, the need for food produces the primary drive of hunger that activates the organism to seek food. Were this not the case, of course, then the organism would not respond in such a way as to obtain the commodities necessary for survival.

The reason for distinguishing between biological needs and psychological drives is that they are not perfectly related to each other. In the first place, there are biological needs that do not give rise to psychological drives, and this helps clarify the nature of the distinction. One example is the need for oxygen (as distinct from breathing). It is a somewhat surprising fact to many that the human is not motivated by deprivation of oxygen provided that breathing of non-toxic gas is not restrained. This fact became apparent only when airplanes were designed that permitted the pilot to reach altitudes where the normal oxygen supply was inadequate for human survival, and the pilots did not become aware of their distress until they began to "black out" and from that inferred that something must be wrong. A psychological drive impels the organism to do something to correct the deficiency, and deprivation of oxygen as well as some specific vitamins, although vital for survival and hence comprising biological needs, simply do not motivate the organism.

Furthermore, there appear to be psychological drives for which no obvious biological need can be defined. Perhaps the most important of these are "curiosity" or "exploratory" tendencies. A person's biological needs may be completely satisfied, and yet he may explore his environment and undertake tasks simply out of curiosity. The evidence is becoming clear that many organisms, including rats, are motivated by curiosity.

These failures of correspondence between biological needs and psychological drives can be understood by consideration of the natural environment of our ancestors. Following familiar principles of evolution, it is likely that only those psychological drives would be selectively bred into the species that favored the survival of those possessing such drives. Suppose, then, that a mutant organism were born that *was* motivated by deprivation of oxygen. Since the air supply near the surface of the earth contains a sufficient supply of oxygen for everyone, such a mutant would not be at any particular advantage in the fight for survival. An organism that was not motivated to breathe, however, would of course not consume the air containing the oxygen and hence would not survive.

Curiosity may be considered similarly. When an early mutant was born with motivation produced by curiosity, it is reasonable to expect that he would discover facts about his environment which, while of no special value at the moment, might favor his survival subsequently in time of distress. Curiosity might also, however, "kill the cat" as the saying goes, but tendencies to explore the environment tempered with a reasonable degree of caution, could on balance favor survival.

Accordingly, it is useful to consider biological needs and their probable significance in evolution, but it is important not to confuse them with psychological drives. The latter are states that impel the organism into action, that activate behavior, that provide the energy converting dormant habits into actual behavior. As such, motivation is a hypothetical construct just as learning is—we cannot look directly at motivation. When an organism responds, we know that he is motivated, but it requires a special type of experimental analysis to determine the nature of this motivation.

## An Experimental Distinction of Learning and Motivation

Let us train two groups of rats in an operant conditioning situation to obtain food by pressing a bar. During this training phase, both groups are treated identically, given a small amount of training each day until their rate of responding is high and equal.

Then one day let us treat the two groups differently. For one group we will disconnect the feeder so that bar pressing no longer produces food. We have seen in an earlier chapter that the result of this operation is experimental extinction—the rate of responding decreases gradually until the rat stops pressing the bar altogether. For the other group, let us continue to give reward for responding. If we leave the subjects in this group in the apparatus for a while, we will observe that their rate of bar pressing also begins to decrease and eventually stops altogether. The reason is simple: the rat is getting full of food.

The reason we believe the former to be an operation that affects learning and the latter to be an operation that affects motivation results from waiting a day and returning both groups of rats to the apparatus. For the animals that were extinguished, only a little responding will be observed (that resulting from spontaneous recovery). For the animals that were rewarded, responding will return completely to the high level that obtained before the satiation session. The learning effects have persisted in the one group; the motivational effects have dissipated in the other group.

This illustration shows that we cannot tell just from a change in behavior whether it resulted from a change in learning or a change in motivation. Learning is inferred only when a relatively permanent change results from practice in the situation. Motivation, on the other hand, can be increased or decreased rapidly, and these changes do not necessarily require practice in the situation. We could as well have reduced the rats' rate of bar pressing by stuffing them with food in their home cages before putting them in the apparatus. Motives may change from moment to moment; learning changes are gradual, cumulative and persistent.

## How do Learning and Motivation Combine?

The logic of the distinction between learning and motivation concerns their conceptual status. Learning is viewed as a potential for behavior—as habits (or knowledge) available for execution. Motivation is the activator or energizer of these habits into actual performance. This conceptualization is captured mathematically by saying that learning and motivation combine multiplicatively to determine performance.

A multiplicative combination rule has one significant property: if either term is zero, the combination is zero. This property is presumed to apply to behavior. An organism will not perform if habit is missing (loosely: he doesn't know what to do) or if motivation is missing (loosely: he doesn't want to do it). Performance occurs only when some degree of both learning and motivation are present, and the more of each, the greater the performance.

The importance of recognizing this combination rule is that the same level of performance may result from different combinations of the two factors, and the way to deal with or to understand behavior depends on the strength of these underlying factors. Suppose, for example, that I observe that you are turning the pages of a textbook quite infrequently over time. This poor performance could result from either of two problems. On the one hand, the difficulty may reflect your learning since you may have gone through the typical educational system in which slow reading is inadvertently taught. If this is indeed the difficulty, then proper treatment must be of a learning nature such as a remedial speed reading course. On the other hand, the difficulty may be in your motivational state, since you may be disinterested in the task and are dividing your attention between the reading assignment and more appealing day dreams. If this is the difficulty, then perhaps a reminder that the reading covers material over which you will be examined the next day may suffice to increase your rate of page-turning noticeably. Observe that a learning factor requires time and practice to correct while a motivational factor can be changed rapidly. This is the essence of the distinction and is the basic reason for trying to separate learning from motivation.

## How Does Motivation Affect Learning?

Although we have taken some pains to separate the two factors of learning and motivation, they are not entirely independent of each other. One question reflecting this relationship is the way in which motivation affects learning. A categorical answer to this question is simple: *motivation has no direct effect upon learning.* The word "direct" in that statement is critical, since we shall shortly discuss two ways in which motivation *in*directly affects learning, but the initial proposition remains. Learning does not depend upon motivation.

Some older psychologies, and some quite common popular beliefs about learning, ascribe to motivation a kind of "stamping in" role for learning. According to such views, information may be passing through the individual's system, but it is not stored for permanent retrieval unless the individual is intent upon learning, is motivated to learn and is rewarded for learning. This is in error and a much simpler principle obtains: *organisms learn everything to which they are exposed.* In short, some learning occurs whenever a response is made.

The implications of that statement are widespread and of great practical importance. To give one familiar example, consider the person who is so anguished over a personal problem one evening that he is unable to study or concentrate on anything else, so he goes to bed. Being emotionally upset prevents sleeping, of course, so he lies in bed fitfully worrying about his problem. Since it is unlikely that he will have solved it that night, and since he may have produced other problems by neither working nor sleeping well, the next evening he is still wrought up upon retiring and again worries himself ultimately to sleep. The basic principle of learning says that such experiences will lead to learning to worry about problems in bed! Once well learned, he may be sitting at his desk or in front of a television so sleepy that he cannot keep his eyes open, so he stumbles to the bathroom, dons his pajamas, climbs into bed where his eyes pop open and his mind comes alert to worry about problems. Insomnia is largely self-taught.

Indeed, becoming sleepy when confronted with a textbook or other work is equally self-taught by students who try to force themselves to study when overly tired. With practice, the wide awake student can spread his work out before him intent upon a productive study session, and then almost immediately put his head on the desk and go to sleep. The significance of the principle should not be overlooked because of its simplicity; whatever you do, you learn to do—whether you want to or not.

### Motivation Affects the Responses Learned

But motivation is important in understanding learning because of its indirect effects. The principle that responses that are made are learned implies that responses must be made to be learned. Motivation is necessary for performance and affects the nature of the performance. Motivation is therefore indirectly necessary for learning.

Recalling that what is learned depends on what is practiced is also meaningful in this context. If motivation is poor, so that practice is done in a sloppy and inaccurate manner, then the response learned is sloppy and inaccurate! Again, realize that motivation is *not* functioning to impress the experience so that it will be learned—whatever is experienced is learned. But motivation is partly responsible for what is experienced and in this way is indirectly responsible for what is learned.

There is a somewhat curious fact: motivation can be too high for efficient learning. There appears to be an optimal level of motivation for the learning of any task, the optimum depending on the difficulty of the task. In general, *the more difficult the task, the lower the level of motivation that will promote efficient learning*. The reason for this is not yet completely clear, but it is presumably related to the energizing effects of motivation. Under lower motivation, performance is slower; the person is thus more likely to observe small distinctions, relationships and fine details that might be obscured if he dashes pell mell through the material.

Students often complain to the teacher of a difficult subject such as psychology: "I really tried! I attended every class, took lots of notes, read and reread the text. My roommate cut half the classes and only read the book the night before the examination. Why did he do better than I did?" Perhaps, of course, the roommate is brighter or has a better background for the subject. But it is also possible that the complaining student is too highly motivated; he memorizes and rehearses the facts but fails to think about them. And recall that extended practice on the same stereotyped responses reduces the extent to which these will generalize to the somewhat different problems encountered in an examination. Motivation affects the way you practice, what you observe and what you do. And these are what you learn.

### Motivation Affects the Stimuli that Are Learned

Although the primary role of motivation is to energize habits into performance, *drives also have stimulus properties.* You know when you are hungry, or when you are thirsty, or when you are afraid. This is because internal stimuli are produced whenever a motive is aroused and these are somewhat distinctive for the different drives. These internal events are called *drive stimuli.*

The importance of recognizing the existence of drive stimuli is that they are present at the time learning takes place, which means that part of the stimulus complex in which learning occurs is the drive present at the time. The importance of this fact will be discussed later in this chapter in the context of irrelevant motivation. For the present, suffice it to say that your behavior is not only energized but is also partly guided by your state of motivation. You may respond to the same external stimulus differently depending upon what drives are present at the time. An evening creak in the house as it cools from the heat of the day is treated with indifference unless you are anxious as a result of a newspaper story reporting burglaries in your neighborhood.

## Drive Motivation and Incentive Motivation

It is important to distinguish between two sources of motivation even though both are necessary for performance. *Drive motivation* refers to the internal source of energy driving the organism to do something. As we have seen, many of these are based upon biological needs; organisms are impelled to reduce drives. *Incentive motivation* refers to the organism's expectation of reward for making a particular response. Incentive motivation may be thought of as a pull toward a goal but it should be carefully distinguished from the goal itself. In everyday language, we often speak of the goal as the "incentive." Here we are not talking about the goal but rather about the motivation to respond resulting from the fact that the response is rewarded.

These two sources of motivation are relatively easily separated in the animal laboratory. Consider, for example, a rat running down an alley. His drive motivation is based upon the need for food resulting from being deprived of food for some period of time. His incentive motivation is based on his prior experiences of finding food at the end of the alley. Each can be manipulated independently: the longer he has been deprived of food, the higher his hunger drive; the larger the reward he has previously received in the goal, the higher his incentive motivation. And for the rat to run, both must be present. If he is not hungry, no amount of food in the goal will induce him to run; if there is no food in the goal, no amount of hunger will induce him to run there. Drive motivation pushes the animal out of the start box while incentive motivation pulls him toward the goal box.

A simple physical analogy may help make this conception clear. Consider the way a flashlight bulb is illuminated by a battery. The battery has two poles, positive and negative; electric energy flows from the positive pole toward the negative pole. If these are connected through the light bulb, energy flows and the lamp is lit. Learning is like the light bulb in this analogy, drive motivation corresponding to the positive pole of the battery and incentive motivation corresponding to the negative pole. Performance will occur (the light bulb will light) only if the circuit is complete to both sources of motivation. And we know that the stronger the battery or the bigger the light bulb, the brighter the light. So too, the better the learning and the stronger both sources of motivation, the greater the performance.

It is not always easy to make the distinction between drive and incentive in everyday contexts, but it is nevertheless important to do so. For example, we not infrequently say that an individual knows perfectly well what he is supposed to do, but simply lacks motivation to do it. When that is true, it is necessary further to determine which source of motivation is weak. Suppose, for example, that a student appears to be unmotivated to study his lessons. The typical interpretation is that he does not want to learn, that he is not interested in the subject. That interpretation assumes that the deficit is in drive motivation, and indeed it may well be. But it is at least equally likely that the student really wants very much to learn but that the program to which he is being exposed is not one from which he can learn. In such a case, which is probably much more common than realized, the deficit is in incentive motivation: the student simply has no expectation that he will learn if he pays attention or studies. The appropriate treatment depends on the source of the motivational deficit. In the case of low drive, offering inducements or even making threats may improve the student's performance. But in the case of low incentive, such approaches may only aggravate the situation; the student needs a better program!

Specifically, you may not want to read the assigned pages in this book. This says that your motivation is weak but fails to distinguish between the drive and incentive sources of motivation. If you fully understand this material from this style of writing, and still don't want to read this book, your drive motivation is weak. In effect, you do not believe that this approach to psychology has any value to you. Alternatively, if you are convinced from the examples that there is value, but you can't understand this manner of presentation, your incentive motivation is weak. In effect, your efforts to learn are frustrated. In a sense, if you have either or both of these problems this book has failed since its objective is to make the technical content understandable to the average reader and, at the same time, to convince him of the importance of learning that content. Hopefully, you have neither of these problems here, but it is still informative to make the distinction. As another example, if you don't "like" mathematics, is it because you see no purpose for your goals to study numbers or is it because no one has presented mathematics to you in a manner that was understandable with a reasonable amount of effort? In everyday language, organisms have to want something and also expect to get it in order to be motivated. These two sides of the coin are drive and incentive motivation, respectively.

## Irrelevant Drive

In the view that we wish to develop, drive motivation acts indiscriminately on habits; drive may be thought of as a general energizer. That is to say, *any source of drive is capable of potentiating any habit* regardless of the drive condition under which that habit was acquired.

The area of research concerning this assertion is that dealing with irrelevant drive. An *irrelevant drive* is one that is not appropriate to the nature of the reward that has been experienced for making a response. Note that we are not saying that the drive is irrelevant to the organism; presumably, all motives are important to him. We are saying only that the drive is not reduced by the goal event. If you are working at a job for money and are at the same time anxious about an upcoming examination, anxiety is an irrelevant drive with respect to your performance on the job. Money does not (hopefully) help you pass the examination. Nevertheless, your anxiety may affect your work.

The simplest context in which to summarize the results of experimental analysis of irrelevant drives is the hungry rat trained to run down a short alley to obtain food. In this situation, hunger is a relevant drive because the goal object is food which reduces hunger. But suppose, after training the rat under these conditions, we add some degree of thirst to his prevailing level of hunger. Now he is both hungry and thirsty, thirst being an irrelevant drive because the dry food as the reward does not reduce it. The question is what effect the addition of thirst to his motivational complex will have upon his performance of a response learned simply for food.

The answer to that question is shown graphically in Figure 25. What is found is that adding moderate degrees of thirst to his prevailing hunger increases his performance of a response rewarded with food. If the degree of thirst is increased still further, however, performance

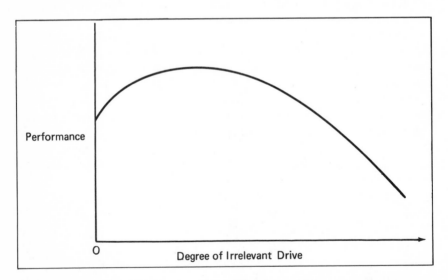

**Figure 25.** The effect of adding an irrelevant drive on performance. Above zero is the performance with only the relevant drive, say, a hungry rat's speed of running toward food. Moderate amounts of an irrelevant drive, e.g., thirst, will increase performance; more intense irrelevant drive will decrease performance.

gets weaker eventually reaching a level below that which would be expected had there been no irrelevant thirst drive at all. Clearly, the performance of a response depends importantly upon the presence of drives that are not related to the goal of that response.

There are two principles necessary to understand this phenomenon. The first is that drives serve as general energizers; thirst must be able to help potentiate a response based on hunger-food else performance would never have shown an increase as a result of adding thirst. How much effect this will have depends on the strength of the original drive. Were drive motivation already maximal on the basis of hunger alone, adding more drive from thirst could not be expected to increase performance. But this type of study does show that a learned habit can be potentiated by an irrelevant drive.

To understand the eventual decrease when thirst is very strong requires the use of the concept of the drive stimulus. Recall that drives not only serve to potentiate behavior, they also provide internal stimuli that may help also to direct behavior. We learn what to do in the presence of particular drive stimuli. The stronger the irrelevant thirst drive, the stronger the thirst drive stimulus and the more it changes the total stimulus situation from the conditions that were present during training. We know that a change in the stimulus situation leads to lower performance because of a stimulus generalization decrement. In effect, then, adding an irrelevant drive does two things: it increases the total drive which alone would lead to increased performance; at the same time, it adds a new drive stimulus which, by changing the situation, tends to lead to lower performance. The combination of these produces the observed results. As long as the increased drive can offset the decreased habit, performance is increased by adding an irrelevant drive. Beyond that point, however, the further change in the situation leads to progressively lower performance. In short, the irrelevant drive stimuli may begin to elicit responses appropriate to that drive and hence interfere with the observed behavior.

From this analysis, we would not expect the decrease in performance when an added drive is very strong if the responses that had been learned to its drive stimuli were the same as the one being observed. For example, a group of adolescent girls may have learned to giggle at the antics of a nearby group of boys as a result of the social motives thus aroused. They may also have learned to giggle to help conceal anxieties when their conversation takes on sexual overtones. If both occur at the same time, their giggling will be doubly potentiated.

With this background, return to the situation in which you are working at a job while simultaneously anxious about a forthcoming examination. So long as that anxiety is reasonably moderate, you will actually work faster and harder than usual. If, however, your anxiety is very strong, you will work more slowly and less effectively because, although under very high drive, the anxiety is producing responses of thinking about the test, trying to think over that material, worrying about the outcome and what may happen—all of which may interfere with attending to your job.

Fear or anxiety is probably the most common irrelevant drive in human behavior, and understanding its effects and how they operate is important in controlling behavior. How will anxiety affect a student's performance on an examination, an actor's performance, or behaviors such as driving, playing tennis, or thinking? In many cases, a small amount of anxiety is beneficial; these are times when the relevant drive is not terribly strong and the added drive will help potentiate practiced habits. In other cases, they interfere with performance—and the reason they do so is that they bring in the responses associated with them to compete with the appropriate behavior. In many of these latter cases, however, the detrimental effects can be reduced or even reversed by learning adaptive responses to fear and anxiety.

And this knowledge can be applied with drives other than fear. Suppose you are going to attend a lecture, sermon, show or date that you expect to be dull and boring, but you feel it your duty to attend and appear to be attentive. You can carry this off more effectively if you will arrange to be mildly hungry at the time. Suppose you are going to a party at which you expect to be rather anxious so that you might drink too much and hence talk too much; you can reduce this likelihood by insuring that there are no irrelevant drives of hunger and thirst (the latter by drinking water!) to potentiate your drinking and talking behaviors. Indeed, you can discover for yourself that such a trivial matter as wearing moderately uncomfortable shoes may be beneficial or detrimental depending upon the strength of your other drives motivating your behavior in various situations.

### Summary

Let us try to summarize this approach to an understanding of motivation by describing how to apply it to a motivational problem. As a specific illustration, consider the student who professes to be really motivated to study and learn psychology but who finds his mind wandering into daydreams whenever he tries. There are a variety of similar illustrations, such as the man who really wants to be a success but finds himself frequently goofing off, the woman who really wants to love her husband but finds herself frequently creating arguments, and so on. The way to tackle the problem is the same.

First, be sure it is indeed a motivational problem; have the desired habits really been learned? In the case of psychology, the student may have learned to learn other types of subject matters: he may know how to memorize a foreign-language vocabulary, to read a story for its impact, to solve algebra problems. But he may not know how to play the science game of looking at empirical phenomena, inferring from those what the underlying principles are, and then deducing from those principles new predictions. Don't start attacking motivation unless the habits are there.

Then, analyze the motivational conditions for the desired behavior; are they really what they appear to be? Perhaps the student really wants psychology to be the study of the mind and to deal with ESP, clairvoyance, magic and mysticism. *In trying to increase the tendency for desired behavior, concentrate on incentive motivation*: be sure something rewarding results from the response. Increasing drive may further arouse the person but will not lead to better responding without incentive. The topics of learning and motivation may not be as exciting as the supernatural, but they are of real value. Find realistic incentive motivation for the desired responses.

Finally, analyze the motivational conditions for the competing behavior; what drive is it servicing? And don't be afraid to accept that drive as real and natural. For example, I would say that everyone needs to daydream. Certainly daydreams shouldn't compete with important activities of the moment, and it is probably wise to maintain some contact with reality. But a reasonable amount of realistic daydreaming is a normal part of healthy mental life. *In trying to decrease the tendency for an undesired response, concentrate on drive motivation*: be sure the drive is somehow adequately satisfied. Removing the incentive leaves the person still motivated with no way to reduce it. Accordingly, the student might schedule some time each day consciously and freely to daydream. Provide acceptable outlets for the drive that is motivating competing responses.

Our most general view of behavior, then, is this: performance requires learning and motivation; motivation in turn involves drive and incentive. If desired responses are not occurring, first be sure the habit is present and then provide incentive motivation. If undesired responses are occurring, identify the drive and let it otherwise be satisfied. (In some cases, this latter drive may itself be undesirable and require treatment.)

## True-False Items:   Introduction to Motivation

1. Motivation is a hypothetical process which combines multiplicatively with the hypothetical process of learning.

(Neither learning nor motivation can be observed directly; they are thus hypothetical constructs inferred from observations of performance. The assumptions that both are necessary to produce behavior leads to the assumption that they combine multiplicatively. True.)

2. The same level of performance can result from different combinations of learning and motivation.

(Both learning and motivation vary in strength, the former on the basis of practice, the latter on the basis of deprivation and prior reward. Hence, the combined value may reflect quite different underlying strengths of the two processes. True.)

3. Motivation has no direct effect upon learning.

(We have taken the position that learning results simply from practice so that habits are formed whenever responses occur. Motivation is necessary for responses to occur and hence indirectly affects what is practiced and learned, but learning itself does not require motivation. True.)

4. Motivation can be both too high and too low for efficient learning.

(Motivation tends to energize behavior. If motivation is low, the response may be practiced slowly and ineffectually leading to poor learning. On the other hand, high motivation may lead to fast and stereotyped practice that detracts from fine discriminations and differentiations. Hence, there is an optimal level of motivation depending on the difficulty of the task. True.)

5. The drive stimulus is the event that produces motivation.

(There is a drive stimulus associated with each drive enabling the organism to discriminate between and behave adaptively to his needs. The drive stimuli, however, do not produce the motivation; they are simply associated with it. Motivation is produced by deprivation or painful stimulation. False.)

6. A motivational disposition is a person that gets mad easily.

(We have not used the term "disposition" in the sense of a person's personality traits. Rather, we have said that organisms are disposed in the sense of readiness to become motivated upon the occasion of certain events. False.)

7. The biological need for food is equivalent to the psychological drive of hunger.

(It is important to distinguish between needs and drives, the former being conditions necessary for survival and the latter being a source of energy motivating behavior. Drives are often based on needs but the relationship is not perfect. False.)

8. The principal operational distinction between learning and motivation concerns their permanence.

(Habits are acquired gradually over repeated practice while motivation can be changed relatively rapidly; habit must be acquired in the situation while motivation may be changed outside the situation. Nevertheless, the principal basis for the distinction is one of permanence, habits being at least somewhat permanent while motivation is more transitory. True.)

9. Drive motivation is the internal push and incentive motivation is the external pull.

(Both motivational processes are internal. It is true that incentive motivation is based on prior experience and hence expectation of reward, but it is not the reward itself. Motivation is inside the organism even though it represents an attraction toward a goal. False.)

10. An irrelevant drive is one of little or no concern to the organism.

(The way we have used the term, the relevance of a drive is based on its relationship to the reward given for a particular response. A drive may be vital to an organism's survival, but still be irrelevant to a habit the reward for which is not appropriate to the drive. False.)

11. Any drive can energize any habit.

(Insofar as its energizing role is concerned, a drive is non-specific and acts on any habit. It does bring in drive stimuli with which competing habits may be associated thus leading to poorer performance. But its activating role is general. True.)

12. The author's practical advice is this: when trying to increase a response, increase incentive motivation; when trying to decrease a response, decrease drive motivation.

(Both drive and incentive are integral parts of motivation and a change in either changes performance accordingly. However, as a matter of practical fact, lack of performance is usually due to too little incentive motivation and adding drive motivation that cannot be reduced is of little value and may even intensify the person's conflict. Hence, it is better to increase the expected reward for responding. Conversely, undesirable responses are inevitably motivated and removing the reward leaves the organism's drive unresolved. Accordingly, it is better to provide an alternative, acceptable way of reducing that drive or, if it is itself undesirable, to remove it. True.)

# 12

# Primary Motivation

We have said that primary motivation refers to unlearned motivational dispositions—conditions which tend to arouse the organism without any special training or experience. The most important of these to the student of learning are pain, hunger, thirst and sex. There are, certainly other primary drives such as those based on the needs to breathe air and to eliminate wastes from the body. These are generally of less interest simply because the drive-reducing response is normally freely available to the organism so that little learning is motivated by these drives.

This is not to say that no learning occurs with respect to such other primary drives. Although breathing is instinctive, some people such as opera singers and deep sea divers must practice special techniques to control their breathing behavior. And, of course, all socialized humans have learned where the response of elimination should normally occur and where it should not occur. That such learned inhibitions can lead to very strong motivation is illustrated by the adult man who, upon being injured, is expected to urinate in bed with the use of a special container. The fact of the matter is that many men, although in agonizing need to urinate, have extreme difficulty in accomplishing this primitive biological response in that context. Presumably this results from early training experiences involving bed-wetting. This particular illustration, incidentally, provides an excellent example of the important role of feedback stimuli on controlling behavior; urination may be stimulated in such a man by the sound of running water splashing into the sink!

Accordingly, our focus on the primary drives of pain, hunger, thirst and sex should not lead to the inference that other primary drives are not important in understanding behavior. They simply provide the principal occasions for learning and hence are the ones that have received the most attention from experimental psychologists interested in that process.

## The Pain Drive

There is little to add to our previous discussions involving the pain drive. The descriptions of aversive control, especially escape and avoidance learning, suffice to demonstrate the motivating power of noxious stimuli. It may be useful, however, to review escape learning as a model of motivation.

A painful stimulus first arouses the organism into action; this conspicuously reveals the fact that pain is motivating and that drive energizes or activates the organism. The drive stimulus provided by pain is explicit and clearly leads to a variety of unlearned reflexes or instincts as ways of attempting to cope with the drive. If none of these is effective in terminating the drive state, a new response will be learned that is effective; this illustrates the fact that drive reduction is a rewarding event. Pain can be turned on and off rapidly, it can energize behavior, it can help guide behavior through the distinctiveness of the painful stimuli, and it can provide an opportunity to reward responses that terminate it, thus fostering the performance of those responses. This encapsulates one view of motivation.

It is worth noting that pain itself is mediated by a separate system in the body. That is to say, although some degree of discomfort may be experienced by over-stimulation of other receptors, such as touch, temperature, light or sound, pain proper is experienced only when special receptors located rather deep under the surface of the skin are stimulated. That these receptors are not evenly distributed around the body may easily be shown by pinching oneself in various places. The same pressure is noticeably more painful in some areas than in others; for example, the bottom of the elbow is essentially devoid of pain receptors. The eye is extremely sensitive to pain from even a minute particle, the genitalia are relatively insensitive, and many internal organs such as the kidney and liver do not respond painfully to injury. *Accordingly, the intensity of pain and hence the degree of drive motivation produced by an aversive stimulus depends upon the nature of that stimulus and where it is applied.*

## The Concept of a Dual-control System

There are, in general, two ways in which the energy controlling a system may be arranged. One is a single-control system in which there is a natural resting state of the system and one source of energy which tends to drive the system from that state. The kitchen oven is an example of such a means of control: its natural temperature is that of the kitchen, and there is a single heating coil by which the temperature may be raised.

In contrast, a dual-control system has two opposing sources of energy so that the state of the system depends on the relative action of these two sources. An oven could be made into a dual control system by the addition of refrigeration coils in which case the temperature would depend on the extent to which the heating and cooling coils were energized. The advantage of such a dual control system is perhaps obvious: it enables the system to be changed rapidly in either direction. Thus, an automobile is a dual-control system containing both an accelerator and a brake by which its speed can be controlled. A dual control system can attain the same state in a variety of ways as a reflection of the action of the opposing controls.

By-and-large, the body is constructed on a dual-control principle. This is familiar in the case of the muscles; there are both flexors and extensors at each joint enabling, by a fascinating process of reciprocal action, the movement of those joints. So, too, most bodily glands are controlled by two opposing nervous systems. In this context, you might recall our theory of classical conditioning and recognize it as assuming a dual-control process of learning: habit tends to activate a response and inhibition tends to reduce that activation.

Many motivational systems are also under dual control. In the case of the maintenance of body temperature, for example, one may exercise or simply shiver when cold as a way of burning up sugar to produce heat; alternatively, the body may be cooled by the evaporation of perspiration. It is now well known that sleep is also under dual neurological control; anatomically distinct centers in the brain tend to lead to sleep or wakefulness. Our state of being asleep or awake depends on the relative activity in these two centers. This is why original sleeping pills were unsatisfactory; although they activated the sleep center, they left the wakefulness center aroused so that sleep was less relaxing. Modern potions tend to inhibit the wakefulness center, enabling the sleep center to dominate more naturally.

## The Hunger and Thirst Drives

The evidence that both hunger and thirst are under dual control is now well established. The intricate details are not yet fully understood, but it is appropriate to review the evidence available as a background for describing some of the behavioral effects of hunger and thirst.

## Biological Bases

It is an obvious behavioral fact that deprivation of food produces the hunger drive and deprivation of water produces the thirst drive. Let us simply assert some of the known biological bases for these effects.

1. First to remove one common misconception: contractions of the stomach (hunger pangs) are not the principal basis of the hunger drive. These normally accompany hunger but eliminating them by distending the stomach with an inflated balloon does not reduce the hunger experienced by a deprived person. Similarly, dryness of the mouth and throat are not the principal bases of the thirst drive. Hunger and thirst are mediated more centrally than these familiar stimuli.

2. There is a "center" in the brain which, when stimulated electrically, produces hunger in a normally satiated organism. Stimulation of this hunger center not only induces the organism to eat, but will motivate him to learn and perform instrumental responses in order to obtain food. A similar center can induce drinking in a water-satiated organism.

3. Consistent with the notion that these constitute hunger and thirst centers is the effect of their surgical removal or destruction. Removing the hunger center produces an organism that never displays normal hunger, does not eat and must be fed intravenously. Removal of the thirst center removes evidence of normal thirst, and removal of both eliminates both eating and drinking.

4. That the normal control of these centers is biochemical can be demonstrated by injecting a small quantity of one hormone into certain brain structures. A fully satiated organism will display all the signs of a hungry organism when so stimulated chemically in the brain. That this description is oversimplified, however, can be shown by injecting another hormone into the same center. This chemical now produces evidence of thirst! In short, the same center may produce quite different effects depending on the way in which it is chemically stimulated.

5. Electrical stimulation of an anatomically different center eliminates hunger. Stimulation of the "satiety" center will cause a food-deprived organism to stop eating. Stimulation of a comparable center can eliminate thirst.

6. Consistent with the notion that these comprise satiety centers is the effect of their surgical removal or destruction. Such an organism is insatiable and stops eating only to the discomfort of an extremely

full stomach. Given unlimited food, such an organism will reach a weight several times larger than normal and, if sensory feedback from distention of the stomach is disrupted, the organism is likely literally to explode.

The pattern which thus emerges runs something as follows: deprivation of food or water causes a biochemical change in the blood through which the drives of hunger and thirst are mediated. That this is true has been shown by transfusing blood from a food-deprived animal into a satiated one, and vice versa. The deprived animal now behaves as if satiated and the satiated animal now behaves as if hungry. Hence, through the biochemical changes in the blood, hunger and thirst centers in the brain are aroused giving rise to these psychological drives. The exact mechanism of this activation is not yet known; for example, differences in the pressure around certain cells in the brain has been implicated in the case of thirst. But in any event, the drive is experienced as a result of appropriate activation of distinct brain structures.

These drives then energize behavior until consummatory responses are made. The occurrence of these responses then leads to stimulation of the appropriate satiety center terminating the psychological drive. In view of the drive-reduction hypothesis concerning reinforcement, it is interesting that the satiety centers are indeed locations where electrical stimulation of the brain is rewarding. Activation of these centers can turn off the drive long before the digestive processes that restore the biochemical balance of the blood and conclude the stimulation of the hunger and thirst centers are complete.

### Hunger and Thirst as Psychological Drives

Normally, hunger or thirst are induced simply by depriving an organism of food or water. The greater the length of deprivation, presumably the greater the drive. The effect of different degrees of deprivation on instrumental performance is shown graphically in Figure 26. Here we are comparing the response strength of different groups of subjects trained under different degrees of deprivation. The greater the deprivation (and hence presumably the greater the drive) the stronger the observed performance up to the point where physical weakness begins to occur. Short of that, however, *performance is an increasing function of drive*—a fact consistent with our interpretation that drives energize the performance of habits.

### Changes in Drive Level

After training has been accomplished under one level of drive, one may inquire as to the effects on performance of changing the drive level to either a higher or lower value. Attending only to the energizing role of drives, one would expect an immediate change in behavior to the level appropriate to the new drive level. But one must also consider the drive stimulus which is also changed when the drive level is changed. Since the organism learned to respond at one drive stimulus level, a change in that will produce some generalization decrement. Hence, *the observed effect of changing the drive level is to produce a level*

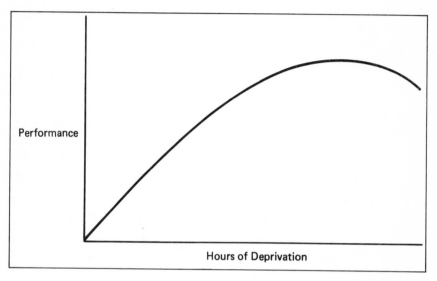

**Figure 26.** The effect of deprivation of food or water on performance. In general, the longer an organism has been without food or water, the higher his level of performance to obtain them, except after severe deprivation when physical weakness occurs.

*of performance that is somewhat below that observed with subjects trained under that drive level.* It may thus happen that an increase in drive does not lead to an increase in performance because the organism, although now more strongly motivated, is in a sufficiently different stimulus situation that more habit is lost than drive is gained. The student who is already very anxious will not be helped by being reminded of the importance of this examination.

## Specific Hungers

Thus far, we have talked about hunger as a general concept that is produced by deprivation of food and that is reduced by eating. Hunger may be more specific than thus implied.

## Food Preferences

Foods may be equally nutritious but not be equally palatable. As a result, there are demonstrable unlearned preferences for some foods over others. For example, rats prefer sweetened food and will eat more of it than an unsweetened food even if the sweetening is nonnutritive saccharine. Similarly, children may prefer their milk flavored with chocolate. Futhermore, most humans have acquired a preference for certain types of foods usually as a result of their early experiences with them. Many Americans do not like snails or fried ants although these are considered delicacies in other cultures. Accordingly, to say that a person is hungry is incomplete because his eating habits may have become directed into learned preferences for particular kinds of foods.

## Specific Deprivations

It is also demonstrable that specific hungers may be based on deprivation of specific substances. For example, a rat that is fed a salt-free food diet will drink salty water even though normally rats prefer plain tap water. This is comparable to the pregnant woman who occasionally expresses a craving for a particular type of food. However, it should be noted that the "wisdom of the body" with respect to such specific hungers is not perfect and some important substances do not give rise to drives motivating their consumption. But the experiences you may have had in which salty popcorn tastes especially good on some occasions reflects the fact that one may not simply be hungry but rather, hungry for particular commodities.

## The Sex Drive

Contrary to the impression of many adolescents, *the sex drive is the weakest of the primary drives.* That is to say, hunger, thirst and pain can readily achieve compelling proportions far exceeding that produced by even complete sexual abstinence. Nevertheless, the sex drive is a very important one in American life for reasons reflected in the British characterization of the Yank soldier during the Second World War as being "overpaid, overfed and oversexed." Preoccupation with sex only occurs after the other primary drives are satisfied. Furthermore, the cultural prohibitions surrounding sexual expression prior to marriage virtually insure an emphasis upon this source of motivation among young people.

The other primary drives, as noted earlier, may be based upon the biological survival needs of the individual organism. This is not true of the sex drive since an individual could presumably go through an entire lifetime without ever knowing overt satisfaction of the sex drive. The principle of natural selection still applies, however: were a species ever produced for which sex did not provide a compelling psychological drive, the resulting lack of offspring would obviously mean that that species would quickly become extinct. In a larger sense than the individual, the sex drive is indeed based on a survival need.

## Biological Bases

The biochemical control of behavior is clearly illustrated in the case of sex. Hormones produced in the testes, the ovaries, and the pituitary gland have profound effects upon our masculinity/femininity. This has been shown to the extreme by Frank Beach. He has injected pregnant female dogs with male hormones, removed the ovaries from the "female" pups at birth and injected them with male hormones. Such dogs become truly bisexual and develop a rudimentary penis and prostate gland. Both males and females produce both male and female hormones; it is the relative balance of these that not only determines our physical sexual characteristics but also affects the extent to which our everyday behavior conforms to what are considered characteristics of the masculine male or the feminine female. The removal of the testes or ovaries has less pronounced effects the older the person is at the time of surgery; sexually experienced adult males, for example, continue to behave in a masculine manner, sexually and otherwise, for years although, if not treated with male hormones, they gradually develop increasingly feminine features and traits. The story of hormones and behavior is a fascinating one that is only now beginning to unfold to experimental analysis.

In order to describe the neurological control of sexual behavior, it is necessary first to review some highlights of neuroanatomy. Mammals contain two distinct nervous systems: the central and the autonomic. The brain and spinal column with its extensions to the muscles of the body comprise the central nervous system. Anatomically separate is the autonomic nervous system which controls the more biological, internal processes and organs. This latter system, in turn, has two distinct branches: the sympathetic and the parasympathetic which oppose each other in the control of these biological processes. When the parasympathetic is dominant, as in times of rest and relaxation, breathing is regular, the heart rate is slow and steady, and digestive processes such as conversion of starches into sugar by the liver take place. When the sympathetic is dominant, as in times of stress or arousal, breathing becomes more rapid, heart rate increases the blood supply to the muscles, and digestive processes are reversed such as the release of sugar from the liver to provide extra energy for action. The autonomic nervous system is thus under dual control.

Sexual arousal refers to erection by the male, tumescence by the female, and secretion of pre-coital fluids by both. These behaviors are mediated by the parasympathetic branch of the autonomic nervous system. You are probably familiar with awakening of an early morning in a state of apparent sexual arousal without any accompanying sexual thoughts or desires. This is because the parasympathetic system acts diffusely over its entire course, and when it is in complete control of the body as in some stages of sleep, sexual arousal is a normal and natural component of the scene.

Sexual climax refers to ejaculation by the male and orgasm by both male and female. This event is mediated by the sympathetic branch of the autonomic nervous system. You may be familiar with some degree of orgastic experience occurring in a nonsexual context but when the sympathetic is aroused by anxiety. This is also a normal and natural reaction of the diffuse action of the sympathetic system.

The inner events accompanying sexual behavior thus run the following course. Erotic stimulation first activates the parasympathetic leading to sexual arousal. Continued stimulation increases the activation of this system but also begins to activate the sympathetic. In time, the parasympathetic reaches its limit of activation and then the sympathetic becomes dominant, leading to orgasm and return to inactivity as the parasympathetic is subdued. The antagonism within the autonomic nervous system is nowhere better revealed than in the sexual arena.

There is one important additional part of the story. The time course of these events is not necessarily the same in male and female. One can only speculate about the evolutionary basis for this difference. Presumably, the original purpose was to enable the female to accommodate a number of different males during the period of her maximal fertility, thus increasing the probability of her becoming pregnant and perpetuating the species. However, the rate at which these processes occur is not invariant, depending in part on learning and concurrent emotions. This will be illustrated later in our discussion of drive incompatibility.

## Sex and Early Experience

Freud at first startled the world by asserting that people do not wait until puberty to initiate a sex life. It is not necessary here to debate the correctness of his descriptions of infantile sexuality and the persisting effects of early conflicts. It is, however, appropriate to note that the picture of childhood innocence is somewhat misleading. Even babies derive pleasure from erotic stimulation. Children are certainly interested in and curious about their genitalia, and various kinds of sex-related contacts do occur during the years before puberty. The importance of these should not be underestimated.

One source of evidence on this topic has come from the work of Harry Harlow. He first developed successful procedures for breeding monkeys in captivity and separating the infant from its mother at birth and raising it on a "surrogate mother." It was, indeed, this line of research that led to the important discovery that contact comfort is a very powerful source of primary reward and promotes the development of emotional security. But more relevant to the present topic are the results of raising such monkeys in an environment in which they are not permitted to play with other infant monkeys during the first six months of life. Total isolation during this period has profound effects upon their behavior as adults; specifically, they are incapable of indulging in mature sexual behavior. Comparable isolation at a later age has no such deleterious effects. Six-month old monkeys certainly do not engage in actual sexual activity, but they do enter into miniature forms of social interaction and rough-and-tumble play which are apparently essential to normal development.

A second source of evidence concerning the importance of early experiences comes from rats. If a thirty-day old male rat (who is still prepubescent) is placed in the context of a receptive female rat, he will engage in some investigatory behaviors even though he is incapable of copulation. During this exposure, a series of electric shocks is applied after which he is returned to his home cage to reach maturity. When he is later placed in the context of a receptive female, he will not even attempt to copulate. Aversive events given early in association with sex-related stimuli, even though overt sexual behavior is not yet involved, are sufficient to modify the natural sexual responses of the adult!

Although these may appear to be rather cruel things to do to animals, it is probable that many parents are guilty of comparable approaches in dealing with their own children. A human infant may be essentially isolated during his first few years as if to protect him from danger. And virtually all children play "doctor" or "nurse" or some such activity in order to discover that about half of the people look pretty much like they do and the other half look interestingly different. Catching the child in such a scene, the parent may conspicuously reveal his own anxieties about sex and describe the behavior as naughty or something nice boys and girls don't do. Little do such parents realize the lasting effects that such treatment may have.

### Sex and Learning

Mating behavior provides the most convincing evidence of instincts, by which is meant unlearned tendencies to perform a complex behavior chain. Examples are familiar to all. It is, however, also a general principle that experience is of increasing importance the higher the order of species being studied. Insects, fish, birds and many mammals perform intricate series of activities culminating in reproduction. For example, the adult, sexually-naive male rat will likely copulate successfully the first time he is exposed to a receptive female rat. Certainly unlearned tendencies exist, but the question remains as to the extent to which such behaviors are learnable. And even with the rat, there are three ways in which the learnability of sexual behavior can be observed.

First, sexual arousal is learnable. If a male rat is repeatedly placed into an arena into which a receptive female is subsequently introduced, the arena will become associated with sexual activity. The male will learn to orient toward the location where the female will be introduced and then to initiate sexual approaches more rapidly. Second, sexual behavior is itself learnable. The experienced male rat is more adept at achieving intromission than his naive counterpart. Finally, the orgastic response itself is to some extent learnable. If the male rat is allowed only a limited amount of time with the female, he will learn to reach sexual climax more quickly than normal.

There are, of course, no comparable experimental data concerning the sexual behavior of humans, but there is every reason to believe that learning plays an even more important role. Arousal and orgasm are, indeed, reflexive responses to erotic stimulation. But arousal is also learnable and may become associated with particular places, times or scenes. And the great variety of sexual practices observed cross-culturally clearly attests to the fact that man is not committed to an instinctive mating pattern.

## Drive Incompatibility

It appears that drives interact with each other in such a way that the presence of one tends to override the presence of another. In a sense, this is highly adaptive since it forces the organism's attention toward one or another type of activity in order to satisfy the dominant drive without being distracted by competing responses relevant to other drives. There are many instances of drive incompatibility.

### Hunger and Thirst

There is now clear evidence that hunger and thirst are biologically incompatible; one cannot be intensely hungry and intensely thirsty at the same time even if deprived of both food and water. That this is a central process can be seen by returning to the procedure of inducing hunger or thirst by chemical injections into the brain. If a food-deprived organism is eating and is injected with a hormone to make him thirsty, he will stop eating. Similarly, if a thirsty organism is drinking and is injected with another hormone, he will stop drinking. Note that these observations help further to rule out the notion that hunger depends on stomach contractions and thirst on dryness of the mouth. The water-deprived animal's mouth is still dry, but he will not drink if made hungry by a chemical in his brain. In effect, arousing the hunger center tends to inhibit the thirst center, and vice versa.

### Hunger and Fear

There is also a neurological incompatibility between the processes involved in digestion and those involved in fear or anxiety. Each may interfere with the other depending on their relative strengths. A person who is mildly anxious, for example, may find it satisfying to nibble more-or-less constantly; keeping the digestive system functioning inhibits his anxieties to some extent. Alternatively, however, intense fear essentially eliminates hunger and precludes proper digestion. If bad news arrives just before your regular dinner time, you probably don't want to eat.

This incompatibility can be demonstrated experimentally. Two monkeys are placed side by side in restraining chairs and confronted with the threat of occasional electric shocks. One of the monkeys, which is sometimes called the "executive," is given a bar which, if depressed, will postpone shock for (say) a minute. Regular depression of the bar will prevent both monkeys from ever getting shocked. This executive monkey quickly learns the task and needs only an occasional shock (accompanied by a noisy reminder from his colleague) to maintain bar pressing. The usual schedule is for this condition to remain in force for a six-hour period, followed by a six-hour break for eating, drinking and sleeping, then another six-hour danger period, and so on around the clock day after day. Within several weeks, the executive monkey but not his colleague may develop ulcers! Although both receive the same number of shocks, the anxiety of an upcoming session in which avoidance responding will be motivated by fear prevents proper digestion. It is clearly undesirable for a person to carry his anxieties to the dinner table.

### Sex and Fear

Fear may also have important effects upon sexual behavior. This is especially true when the fears concern sex itself. This fact can be illustrated with the two most common fears that people may take to bed with them. One is the fear of failing to become sexually aroused. In the case of the male, this is called impotence and completely precludes sexual intercourse. In the case of the female, for whom this fear is more common, it is called frigidity and reduces the likelihood of sexual satisfaction. The second fear is of premature orgasm, which is more common in the male but certainly of concern to both.

These fears may involve positive feedback and eventuate in self-fulfilling prophecies. To understand this, it is only necessary to know that fear reflects activity in the sympathetic branch of the autonomic nervous system. Sexual arousal requires dominance by the parasympathetic, which is more difficult to achieve if the sympathetic is aroused by fear. Sexual climax reflects eventual dominance of the sympathetic, which is more readily achieved if erotic stimulation is played upon a background of arousal by fear.

## Consummatory Behavior as Learnable Responses

We normally think of eating, drinking and indulging in sexual behavior as consummatory responses motivated by hunger, thirst and sex and hence performed in their service. While this is certainly true, it is important to note that these are also learnable responses in their own right. This conclusion has already been implied in our earlier discussion, but it is worth repeating.

A new illustration is provided by placing a hungry rat in an operant situation in which he is working for food on a schedule in which periodically a signal appears indicating that pressing a bar will now be rewarded. If a water bottle is also available, he may learn to drink as well as bar press. This can be understood as a superstition. If the dry food eventually leads the rat to become thirsty, he may be drinking water at the time a signal for food occurs. This reinforces the drinking response so that it is likely to occur during the next interval between signals. And so on progressively until the rat may consume three or four times his normal daily consumption of water during an hour or so in an operant conditioning situation where he is working for food.

The general point is this: although consummatory responses are intrinsically rewarded by the reduction in their relevant drives, *the frequency of occurrence of consummatory behavior may also depend on extrinsic rewards.* That is to say, we may eat for reasons other than hunger, we may drink for reasons other than thirst, and we may engage in sex for reasons other than sexual deprivation. Chefs, wine-tasters and prostitutes do their "thing" for money. But we all may learn to eat, to drink, and to engage in sex to help reduce our anxieties. We may develop superstitions about the effects of these behaviors. And like all habits, learning involving consummatory responses is permanent. Many middle-aged people get fat simply because they have carried their adolescent eating habits into adulthood where the need for food is less— they eat to be eating and not because they are hungry. Early preoccupations with sex may persist. In short, all of the principles of learning apply to consummatory behaviors.

## True-False Items: Primary Motivation

1. All primary drives can be reduced to four: hunger, thirst, sex and pain.

(These are the four primary drives that are most often considered in relation to learning because the drive-reducing response may not be freely available. However, there are other primary drives about which some learning may occur. False.)

2. Pain is produced by overstimulation of the basic senses of touch, sight, sound, taste and smell.

(Overstimulation of these sensory systems produces discomfort which is indeed aversive. Pain, itself, however, is mediated by a separate sensory system. False.)

3. Stomach contractions and dryness of the mouth are actually unrelated to hunger and thirst.

(Under normal conditions, these experiences do arise as a result of deprivation of food or water and hence are related to these drives. They are not, however, the principal basis for our experience of the hunger and thirst drives. False.)

4. Our state of hunger depends on the activity in a single, specific center in the brain.

(There is a hunger center in the brain which partly determines our state of hunger. However, there is also a satiety center and the experience of the hunger drive depends on the relative activity in these two centers. False.)

5. One sure way to increase performance is to increase drive.

(Increasing drive does lead to increased activation of the organism. However, it may also change the stimulus situation because of a change in the drive stimulus sufficiently that the loss in habit offsets the increase in motivation. False.)

6. The concept "hunger" is an aggregation of our desires for a variety of specific commodities.

(We do develop specific hungers for some specific commodities over and above a general state of hunger, but the latter is a general state. False.)

7. Sex is the weakest primary drive and yet may be relatively important to an understanding of behavior.

(Sex is the weakest primary drive; organisms will tolerate more pain and do more work to eat or drink than to copulate. However, when the other primary drives are reasonably satisfied, sex may become the dominant drive motivating behavior. Preoccupation with sex may also result from anxiety. Hence, the topic may be extremely important to an understanding of behavior. True.)

8. Adult sexual behavior is importantly affected by nonsexual activities that occur before puberty.

(Infants engage in social interactions and exploratory activities involving their bodies that are important in maturing toward adult sexuality. True.)

9. One reason for distinguishing between sexual arousal and sexual climax is that arousal is learnable and climax is not.

(Both of these are reflexive responses to adequate erotic stimulation; however, not only can arousal become associated with initially ineffective stimulus situations, but climax may also be affected by learning. False.)

10. Sex is really not a psychological drive because indulgence in sex is not necessary for survival.

(Although sex is not a survival need of the individual organism, it does give rise to a psychological drive motivating behavior. Perhaps its relative weakness is understandable in that only individuals that were capable of reducing their other primary drives would experience the sex drive at sufficient intensity to motivate reproduction. False.)

11. Hunger and thirst combine together because they are both consummatory responses made with the mouth.

(Although eating and drinking are done with the mouth, and may even overlap as in eating moist foods, the psychological drives of hunger and thirst are biologically incompatible. False.)

12. Eating, drinking, and engaging in sex are instinctive responses to the hunger, thirst and sex drives and hence are not learnable.

(These consummatory responses do provide intrinsic rewards for these drives. However, they are also learnable in the sense of being associated with other drives or desires, and may occur habitually in the absence of the relevant drive. False.)

# 13 ————————————————————

# Secondary Motivation

*Secondary motivation refers to drives that have been learned or ac-quired by the organism rather than ones that arise from biological needs without prior experience.* Secondary motivation is not secondary in the sense of being of lesser strength or significance than the primary drives; indeed, in a successful culture, secondary motivation provides the pre-dominant source of energy for our behavior. "Secondary" means only that these drives are dependent for strength on learning, on an his-torical relationship with the primary, unlearned drives.

The basic paradigm for the acquisition of motivating properties by an initially neutral stimulus is the familiar one of classical conditioning. ANY STIMULUS WHICH, MORE-OR-LESS REGULARLY, PRE-CEDES IN TIME THE OCCURRENCE OF AN AVERSIVE EVENT WILL ITSELF COME TO FUNCTION AS A MOTIVATING EVENT IN ITS OWN RIGHT. The presumed mechanism for this learning is the response of "fear," which is part of the response initially made to any primarily aversive event and which becomes associated with the neutral stimulus.

A familiar illustration would be the motivating power of a parental threat. Assuming the parents at least occasionally follow through if their child continues to misbehave after being scolded, the words "or else" acquire strong motivating value. Depending on the relative strength of the adversary, such threats come to be as effective as the subsequent whipping would be. There are three basic laboratory demonstrations of the fact that stimuli which precede aversive events themselves acquire motivating properties.

## Drives Energize

In our discussion of drive motivation, we presented the argument that drives serve as general energizers, i.e., they activate or potentiate any habits associated with the existing stimuli. We have also noted that adding irrelevant drives may reduce performance because of the incompatible responses produced by their drive stimuli. However, when the responses to the irrelevant drive are not incompatible with the habit being studied, the energizing value of an irrelevant drive can be readily observed.

To illustrate this in the context of secondary motivation, consider the following study. Rats are placed individually in a small enclosure often called a "jiggle cage" because it is suspended on a spring so that the motions of the rat jiggle the cage permitting the experimenter to measure the vigor of any gross responses that occur. The observed behavior is the startle response to a sharp noise—specifically the "pop" of a cap pistol. Rats show a distinct startle to an occasional noise.

The second stage of the study consists of pairing a tone with an electric shock according to the basic classical conditioning paradigm. That is to say, a tone is sounded, followed shortly by an unavoidable electric shock, and this sequence is repeated a number of times. The tone should thereby acquire motivating value. This is demonstrated by the energizing properties of drives during the third stage of the study. The tone is sounded, but instead of the shock, the cap pistol is fired. The vigor of the startle response to the cap pistol is significantly greater than it was prior to the pairing of the tone and the shock. The tone, in effect, energizes a more vigorous response as would be expected if it were motivating.

Illustrations of comparable experiences in everyday life are easy to find. For example, all houses have occasional creaks, sounds and noises which are typically unnoticed by the occupants. If, however, you are reading a murder mystery, your response to these noises may be noticeably greater. The story produces some degree of anxiety which then potentiates your reactivity to the noises. In a similar vein, if you are tense or otherwise frustrated, you will react more violently to criticism than when these learned drives are not present. In general, then, stimuli paired with aversive events will increase responsiveness in situations where the responses are not incompatible.

## Drive Reduction is Reinforcing

Although we have left some question as to whether all reinforcing events entail drive reduction, the weaker proposition is certainly true: reduction of a drive is reinforcing. Accordingly, if a stimulus can acquire motivating properties, its termination should be capable of reinforcing a learned response. We encountered this notion earlier in the context of secondary negative reinforcement, but we can now consider a more direct demonstration.

For the purpose of illustrating this feature of secondary motivation, we will examine a study by Neal Miller. He first observed rats explore a two-compartment apparatus, and noted that there was no particular preference for one or the other compartment. Rats were then locked in one compartment and given occasional electric shocks. Following this experience, Miller observed not only that the rats, if given a chance, would quickly scamper out of that compartment into the other one, but would if necessary learn a new response such as pressing a bar in order to get out of the compartment in which they were shocked. Since this learning took place without any shock being given, the rats must have been reinforced simply by getting out of the compartment that had earlier contained shock. This observation is consistent with the argument that the stimulus situation of that compartment had acquired motivating properties on the basis of the conditioning procedure, and that termination of those stimuli would serve as a (secondary negative) reinforcement.

Again there are countless everyday illustrations of comparable phenomena. The boy who has been bitten by a dog will run away in the future at the very sight of the dog. The girl who has had unpleasant experiences on a date with a particular boy may learn a variety of devious methods to avoid him. In general, stimuli that have been classically paired with aversive events not only motivate behavior in general, but lead to learning of responses to terminate them.

### Some Drives Are Biologically Incompatible

The pain-fear drive is inherently incompatible with the vegetative drives such as hunger, thirst and sex. This can be demonstrated in the laboratory. We first observe the quantity of water that rats drink during a timed exposure period each day. Subsequently, we pair a tone with an electric shock a number of times while the rats are not permitted to drink and then observe the effect of presenting the tone while the rats are drinking. As expected from the incompatibility of fear with thirst, the rats quit drinking during the tone presentation.

### Summary of Procedure and Experimental Results

The procedure whereby a stimulus acquires motivational properties is classical conditioning: any stimulus, even a previously positive one, that is regularly followed by an aversive event will become a secondary motivator. This can be demonstrated in the ability of such a stimulus to potentiate compatible responses such as startle; it can be demon-

strated in the ability of such a stimulus to be used as a negative reinforcer for escape learning; and it can be demonstrated in the suppression such a stimulus exerts over incompatible drives such as hunger,
thirst and sex. All of these occur in everyday life and reflect the
learned motivating property of stimuli.

It should be noted at this point that the paradigm does not appear
to work if the primary motivation is hunger or thirst. That is to say,
stimuli regularly preceding increases in these drives do not acquire
motivating properties in the same sense that stimuli preceding aversive events do. That this failure is not due simply to an inability to
turn these vegetative drives on quickly the way pain-fear can be in-
stantly aroused is revealed in a recent study by Neal Miller.

We have seen that electrical stimulation applied to an appropriate
region of the brain produces all of the behaviors commonly associated
with the hunger drive. In this way, hunger can be turned on essentially as quickly as pain-fear can be turned on by externally applied
electric shock. Miller found that a stimulus that regularly precedes
brain stimulation which in turn produces hunger does not acquire
secondary motivating properties. The rats do not avoid or attempt to
terminate stimuli signalling the onset of hunger. Indeed, satiated rats
will even learn to go to that arm of a maze where such a stimulus is
turned on so that they eat! For a stimulus to acquire motivating power,
it must be paired with an aversive stimulus.

## Frustration

There is a second type of aversive event other than pain that appears
to give rise to a learnable drive. This is the frustration induced when
an organism fails to receive an expected reward. Everyone is familiar
with frustration as a personal experience and there are various references to it in the experimental literature. Rats which sit placidly on
the experimenter's shoulder while being carried back from the goal of
a maze to the start may begin to bite his ear once extinction begins.

A more formal demonstration of the effects of frustration is to run
rats in a "double runway," so called because it consists of two runways
in sequence. That is to say, the rat leaves the start box and runs to
a first goal box where he is detained briefly and then he is released
to run on to a second goal box. In one demonstration procedure, food
reward is initially placed in both goal boxes. After a number of such
experiences, food is omitted from the first goal box and interest centers on the speed at which the rats run from there toward the second
goal box. The finding of interest is that they now run significantly

faster; the frustration produced by failing to find the customary food in the first goal box persists as a drive further to potentiate running in the second portion of the maze.

With this demonstration that frustration has the energizing function of a drive, we can return to a phenomenon that we earlier introduced. Recall that partial reinforcement (reward given on only part of the trials) leads to more vigorous performance at least during the early portions of a behavior chain. It is this finding that most clearly suggests that the frustration drive is learnable. Since the frustration produced by occasional nonreinforcement becomes anticipatory, it begins to occur earlier in a behavior chain and helps potentiate the response. We also noted that occasional nonreinforcement during training makes the behavior more persistent. This is, in part, because it provides experience with continuing to respond in spite of frustration.

Accordingly, our understanding of frustration is essentially identical to our understanding of fear and indeed, they are quite similar responses. Both are produced by aversive events, the one by pain and the other by nonreinforcement. Both are drives serving to potentiate behavior. Both provide drive stimuli that help guide behavior depending on what the organism has learned to do in the presence of these drives. And both drives are learnable in the sense that they can become associated with originally neutral events. And, because of their similarity, they transfer to each other. Training to tolerate frustration facilitates tolerating fear and training to perform in the face of fear facilitates performance in the face of frustration.

## Other Sources of Secondary Motivation?

There are some who argue that this account of secondary motivation, while true, is incomplete—at least for humans. Their contention is that man is not so base a creature that his motives are based entirely on fear and frustration. Rather there are positive learned drives such as honesty and courage which evolve in the socialized human and motivate much of his behavior. It should first be noted that this position is arguing for a source of learned motivation based on secondary reinforcement. That is to say, the assumption is that, once events acquire secondary reinforcing value, they become intrinsically valuable so that the person desires them in their own right. Specifically, for example, we first learn that social approval is secondarily reinforcing because it is paired with pleasant events. Thereafter, we are presumed to develop a desire for social approval in its own right and work for it even when subsequent rewards are not given.

The argument against this position is that of parsimony, the preference for simplicity. We all agree that fear is a source of secondary motivation and hence that fear of social disapproval will be learned because it is often followed by undersirable consequences. Our apparent desire for social approval can thus be understood simply as a reduction in our continuing fear of social disapproval without appealing to any new principle.

Secondly, what little evidence there is runs counter to a positive source of secondary motivation. Recall the study in which chimps worked for poker chips which had acquired secondary reinforcing value because of their association with grapes. The important observation is that the chips were perfectly good reinforcers when the chimps were hungry, but had no value in their own right; the chimps would not work for them when satiated.

Finally, in most if not all cases, the fear analysis provides a better understanding of the behavior, even if not a picture of goodness and light. Are people really motivated by a drive for honesty, or are they honest as a rule because of a fear of dishonesty? Are people really courageous in the face of danger, or are they instead afraid of being thought a coward? Are people moral because it is good, or are they moral because immorality is bad? Do people achieve because they need to achieve, or do they achieve because they need to prove that they are not inferior? Perhaps there is no single answer to all of these questions, but the extent to which these behaviors are motivated by fear must first be recognized before proposing additional sources of secondary motivation.

In doing so, it is important to add that the rules and customs of society may become internalized and the person may punish himself for the failure to comply with them. For example, a student may know perfectly well that he can get away with cheating on an examination, but not do so because the resulting grade would be a deception that he would feel guilty about.

## How to Deal with Fear

One of the most common types of questions asked by young people is how they can deal with their fears. The typical approach is something like: "How can I get over my fear of . . .?" where the feared scene may be examinations, dates, other people, animals, and on and on and on. The golfer may make a hundred two-foot putts in a row on the practice green and then feel his stomach clutch when he has such a putt in a match. The student may know the material forward and backward, but become so anxious during an examination that his mind goes blank. While we cannot yet give a completely adequate solution to such problems, there are several potentially useful things that can be said.

First, however, it should be noted that the very fact that these questions arise is perhaps the most dramatic proof that the basic principles of learning that we have been discussing apply to the everyday behavior of people. Were learning not automatic, were performance always under voluntary control, were behavior always rational, no one would have a problem with fear. The fact is that your body learns to secrete adrenalin to stimuli such as social rejection in the same way that dogs learn to salivate to tones. The principles are inescapable.

## Fear is Not Always Bad

Let us begin by recognizing that fear is not inherently bad from a behavioral point of view. Fears provide motivation and, as such, can both energize and guide behavior. Fears are useful when they inhibit socially undesirable behavior; dishonest behavior is largely prevented by fear of being caught and punished. Fears are also useful when they facilitate performance of socially desirable behavior; fear of being thought a coward may motivate us to perform tasks that risk well-being. Fears provide an important mechanism through which society controls the behavior of its members.

Even in many situations in which fear may appear to be detrimental, the difficulty is not with fear itself but in the way we have learned to respond to fear. Since fear is a drive, it can help motivate behavior and arouse us to our best possible performance. But it can do so only if the response we have learned to the drive stimulus of fear feeds into the required response. Specifically, if one knows that he is going to be anxious in a test situation, then one adaptive approach is not to try to overcome those fears but rather to practice the response under conditions of anxiety. In this way, one learns to respond with fear present and available to help motivate performance. Stage performers, for example, have generally not overcome their stagefright; instead they have taught themselves to respond in spite of it and, in fact, may not be able to perform as perfectly unless they are somewhat anxious. So too with training soldiers for combat, for teaching students for examinations, and practicing skills for an athletic contest. Even were it possible completely to eliminate the fear of those situations, it is more useful to learn to respond with some fear present.

## When is Fear Harmful?

There are occasions, however, in which fear is clearly detrimental to well-being. If you are afraid concerning properties of yourself as a person, there is no way to avoid or escape from them. Fear then becomes chronic and leads to continual misery. Fearing dishonesty is adaptive: you can avoid it by behaving honestly. But fearing inferiority is maladaptive because you cannot get away from yourself. So too, fears concerning your physical appearance or inescapable motives for pleasure lead to persisting anxiety, shame or guilt which almost inevitably interfere with good adjustment.

In like fashion, fearing unavoidable and actually harmless events in the environment is undesirable. Being afraid of the dark, of small enclosures like elevators, of heights like tall buildings, and the like, precludes behaving normally. Although you can successfully avoid some common scenes, such as flying in an airplane, other situations are an inevitable part of modern life and fear of them is maladaptive.

Perhaps the worst effect of fear is when it becomes involved in a vicious positive feedback circle. Many people, for example, are afraid of being sick; for them, sickness is a sign of personal weakness or threatens the possibility of death. Such a person may have a minor pain in his abdomen and although he is afraid that it is an ulcer, he is also afraid to admit it. So he worries about it, a response which interferes with digestion and leads to secretions of acids that produce ulcers. The effect of his fear is thus to increase his abdominal pain which further increases his fear that he has an ulcer. In time, he may indeed develop an ulcer and be forced to see a doctor when an early examination could have prevented the entire affair.

One of the most famous lines of President Franklin D. Roosevelt was in his inaugural address: "The only thing we have to fear is fear itself." The reader should now be able to understand the full meaning of such an expression. We are indeed in trouble if we are afraid that we will behave badly if we get afraid. Things can be going quite well so long as we are relaxed; but a little anxiety with the least thing that goes wrong leads to an increased fear that we are indeed getting afraid, which progressively feeds upon itself to the point of panic. The major importance of learning to deal with fear is so that one will not be afraid that fear will inevitably ruin his performance.

## How to Control Fear

There are several things a person can do about his fears. The first that should not be dismissed too lightly is simply to avoid the situation of which you are afraid. Although many feared situations, such as examinations and social contacts must be faced, surprisingly many people continue to expose themselves to properly avoidable situations about which they are anxious. The girl concerned about her appearance can consult an expert for advice on hair styling, make-up techniques, and selecting a wardrobe that will almost certainly eliminate her imagined problem. The boy who is having difficulty in one school because he is fighting the superior exploits of his father there can simply change schools. Before embarking on the job of eliminating a fear, first explore the possibility of realistically avoiding the stimuli which elicit the fear.

It is, however, maladaptive to avoid all situations of which people become afraid. Marriage, social gatherings, public appearances are important to social life. In dealing with these, the first thing to recall is that fears are learned by the principles of classical conditioning; they can thus be extinguished. This is not easy because of repeated spontaneous recovery and the possibility of disinhibition. Nevertheless, exposure to a feared stimulus without aversive experiences leads to extinction of fear. In following this procedure, gradual exposure may be much more effective than "sink or swim" techniques.

Punishment, however, does not suit the crime and hence does not eliminate fear. Indeed, we can demonstrate that it may make matters worse. We first train rats to run from a start box down a short alley to a goal box by shocking them in the alley if they fail to get to the goal in time. They readily learn to run rapidly. We then attempt to extinguish this fear-motivated avoidance response. For some of the animals the shock is simply disconnected and, over repeated trials, they will gradually slow down and stop running. For other animals, shock punishment is given in the last foot of the alley if they get there, but they can now avoid the shock by simply staying in the start box. These animals who are punished for responding to their learned fear require considerably more trials before they stop running. Since they do not know at first that shock will not be given if they stay put, they run; this puts them into the alley where they now get shock inducing them to run on to the goal box. Things are pretty much as they had been, only worse. Punishing fears produces more fear and confirms the expectation of aversive experiences in the situation.

The third technique of eliminating undesirable responses, namely counterconditioning, may be important in overcoming fears. If one can insure not only that nothing aversive happens in the situation but also that something pleasant does happen, then emotionally-positive responses will become conditioned to help override the fear.

Despite your probable belief to the contrary, fears can be brought under at least some degree of voluntary control. The reason that this is not easily taught is that we are dealing with private experiences that cannot be readily exposed for training by others. But relaxation is a learnable response. Few know how even to relax physically. If, however, you clench your fist tightly and then relax it, and do this repeatedly, you will learn what it feels like to relax your muscles. And if you say to yourself, "relax" as you do so, you can teach yourself to relax to verbal command. A similar process can be done with fear. First, think of a fearful situation sufficient to arouse your anxieties; then think of a pleasant situation and, at the same time, attend to what it feels like to relax from fear while telling yourself to "settle down." Deliberate practice of this kind can enable you to gain control over responses which you might think to be completely involuntary.

Finally, alcohol appears to work selectively to suppress the sympathetic system and hence reduce fear. This is not to recommend the use of alcohol for this purpose; indeed, it poses many dangers. But it is important to understand its effects. Alcohol is often thought of as a behavioral stimulant, but it does so not by arousing the nervous system but instead by inhibiting inhibitory systems. That it is a general depressant is also clear: one's reaction time is increased, vision is blurred, and in sufficient quantity, alcohol causes the person to pass out. By depressing the sympathetic system, alcohol leads to a direct reduction in fear. The difficulty is that the response of drinking is a learnable response. The person who begins to drink as a way of dealing with personal fears may thus be beginning a vicious positive feedback circle leading to alcoholism. For example, the student who is afraid of a forthcoming examination might visit a nearby bar. This indeed reduces his fear and reinforces his drinking behavior. But it also interferes with his effective performance which may last even into the next day since it requires about two hours for the liver to process a single ounce of alcohol. Accordingly, his fears of failure are increased leading to a need for more alcohol to reduce them. In short, drinking alcohol may be learned as a simple expression of the principle of reinforcement.

### True-False Items: Secondary Motivation

1. Originally neutral stimuli acquire motivating power by a process of classical conditioning.

(The process of classical conditioning is the pairing of two stimuli in temporal order. Secondary motivation is established by following an initially neutral stimulus with an aversive one. True.)

2. That stimuli can acquire motivating power is attested to by the ability of such stimuli to energize behavior and their termination to reinforce behavior.

(These are two basic properties of all drives that must be demonstrated to prove that an originally neutral stimulus has acquired motivational properties. True.)

3. Secondary motivation cannot be based on the primary drives of hunger, thirst and sex.

(This is apparently true with respect to thirst and hunger since experimental data are available. It is possible that sexual arousal leads to an increase in motivation, and arousal is learnable. However, there are no experimental data establishing this source of learned motivation. True.)

4. Frustration is similar to fear.

(Frustration is based on nonreinforcement, fear on painful events. Both are aversive and involve similar processes; this is demonstrated by the transfer of training with one to performance with the other. True.)

5. The author contends that all learned drives are based on aversive events.

(That aversive events can be used to establish secondary motivation is experimentally established. Other learned drives have been proposed, but their proponents have failed to demonstrate that a fear/frustration analysis is inadequate. Unless this is done, there is no reason to favor them. True.)

6. One way to improve society would be to eliminate all fears.

(Fears are not always harmful. They may facilitate desirable responses or help deter undesirable responses. Hence, it would not be appropriate to try to design a society in which there is no fear. False.)

7. Fears inevitably give rise to a vicious positive feedback situation.

(When fear produces responses which lead to a further increase in fear, a positive feedback circle is initiated. This is a not uncommon result but adaptive responses leading to a reduction in fear are also possible. False.)

8. The author's advice is never to try to control fear by avoiding feared situations.

(There are many situations of which people can be afraid which it would be maladaptive to attempt to avoid—even though people sometimes do. Hence, avoidance is not a general solution. The author's advice, rather, was not to neglect this possibility when it may be appropriate. False.)

9. Of the ways to eliminate undesirable fears, counterconditioning is the most effective, extinction is less effective, and punishment is ineffective.

(Fears are learned by classical conditioning and those principles apply. Hence, extinction is possible and counterconditioning is still more effective. Of special importance is the ineffectiveness of punishment since it can never suit the crime of becoming fearful and only intensifies the fear. True.)

10. One of the difficulties with dealing with fears is that they are completely involuntary.

(Although the principle of the anticipatory response is inevitable, some degree of voluntary control can be exerted over conditioned responses, including the internal ones associated with fear. False.)

11. One danger of alcohol is that it stimulates the nervous system.

(Alcohol is a neural depressant. It may appear to be a behavioral stimulant by depressing the sympathetic branch of the autonomic nervous system where inhibitions and fears reside. False.)

12. One danger of alcohol is that drinking is self-reinforcing.

(Assuming that any degree of fear or anxiety is present, alcohol inhibits that neural system and directly reduces those drives. Hence, the response is directly reinforced by its neurological action. True.)

# Incentive Motivation

To this point, we have tolerated what may appear to be an am-biguity. On the one hand, we have maintained that motivation is not necessary for learning: that learning results simply from practice. On the other hand, however, we have made repeated reference to the principle of reinforcement: that the tendency for responses to occur depends importantly upon the schedule and condition of reward. Reso-lution of this apparent ambiguity comes with understanding that *the principle of reinforcement is a performance principle, not a learning principle.* It correctly asserts that the vigor, speed, rate, or simple like-lihood of a response depends upon reward. But reward does not effect learning itself; rather, organisms come to expect or anticipate rewards which follow selected responses and this expectation is a source of motivation to make those responses.

## Evidence that Reward Affects Motivation

In reviewing the evidence that leads to this conception of the role of reward, it is important to keep in mind the fundamental distinction between learning and motivation. For a variable to affect learning, it must require repeated practice and lead to a relatively permanent change in behavior. Motivation, in contrast, is more transitory and can be increased or decreased rapidly. We shall see that the effects of reward on performance conform to a motivational interpretation of its role.

### Latent Learning

Suppose a hungry rat is allowed to wander through a maze that does not contain food. When he ultimately gets to the goal box, he is removed and given a number of such experiences. During such trials, there is very little improvement in his performance; he persists in entering as many blind alleys as correct paths and hence would not appear to be learning the maze. Recall that learning can only be inferred from a change in performance, and hence the expression "latent" learning. For we can show that the rat is indeed learning something about the route to the goal even though his performance does not indicate it.

This is done by now introducing reward in the form of food in the goal box. The rat's performance then shows a very rapid improvement, much more rapid than could be attributed to new learning. Within a very few trials, the rat is performing as well as other rats that had been receiving reward in the goal box from the very beginning. We thus conclude that reward is not necessary for learning, that the non-rewarded rat was learning the maze equally as well as his rewarded counterpart but that his learning was not evident in performance until incentive motivation was added by the introduction of reward for following the correct path.

### Changes in Reward

Latent learning is a special case of changing the reward, the case of going from no reward to some reward. But one can also observe the effects of other changes such as increasing or decreasing the amount of reward. We have already noted in our discussion of instrumental conditioning that the speed of a response depends upon the amount of reward that is received, and that changes in the reward lead to changes in performance appropriate to the direction of change in reward. Here we need only to note how these findings indicate that reward functions as a motivational variable.

Although larger rewards lead to better performance, they do not lead to better learning. This is clear from the fact that decreasing the amount of reward leads to a decrease in performance; since learning is permanent, it would not be lost from a decrease in the reward. Furthermore, the changes in performance following a change in the reward are very rapid, much more rapid than could reasonably result from learning. Instead, it appears that the amount of reward affects performance in a motivational manner since the change can occur so rapidly in either direction.

### Direct Placement

Finally, there is some evidence that the effects of reward on performance can occur without the actual response occurring. Clearly, if one can change performance without practice, the manipulation cannot involve learning. There are two variants of this procedure. In one, rats are first permitted to explore a maze without reward; they are then placed directly in the goal box and given food there. Following this, they are released from the start box and show an immediate improvement in their speed of running and the number of correct turns they make.

The other variant is simply the reverse and is sometimes called *latent extinction*. Rats are first trained to run through a maze with reward; after they are making few if any errors and are running rapidly to the goal box, they are placed directly in the goal box now without food. Following such placement in the empty goal box, they are run again from the start and now run more slowly and make more errors. Since performance can be changed by direct placements in which the reward is changed without being preceded by making the response of running through the maze, and since these effects are rapid and in either direction, the motivational role of reward is again evident.

## Summary

The conclusion is that reward affects performance not as a learning variable but as a motivational variable, that reward provides incentive motivating the performance of habits. This conclusion is supported by the observations that organisms can learn from exposure to a situation without reward, that their performance can be changed rapidly, for better or worse, by a change in the reward, and that some such changes can be produced without the response itself occurring. In short, rewards motivate behavior.

## Review of Positive Reinforcement

This understanding of the role of rewards applies to all of the situations discussed in previous chapters. We cannot review all of these here, but let us return to the operant conditioning situation in which a hungry rat is working for food by pressing a bar. We know that his rate of responding depends importantly upon the schedule of reinforcement. We are now in a better position to see why that is true. The rat presses the bar at a rate depending on his expectation that doing so will be rewarded, that is, on the momentary level of his incentive motivation.

If, for example, the schedule is a variable-interval one, so that responding may be rewarded at any time, there is no basis for his incentive motivation to vary over time. Responding is not always rewarded, but it is as likely to be now as later. This steady level of incentive leads to a steady rate of responding; the more frequent the reward, the higher this incentive and the higher this rate. This is a circumstance of maximum uncertainty about when to respond.

If, alternatively, the schedule is a fixed-interval one, then responding again immediately after one reward is never rewarded, so his incentive to respond then should be low. As time passes and the scheduled reward approaches, incentive to respond should increase leading to an increasing rate of responding. Thus, the scallop generated by a fixed-interval schedule reflects the rat's changing expectation of reward over time. And if an external stimulus, such as a light, is added to the situation to signal when responding will be rewarded, incentive motivation will come to be high in the presence of the stimulus and low in its absence. As a result, the discriminative behavior characteristic of differential operant conditioning occurs.

Thus, incentive motivation determines *when* a freely available operant response will occur. The student sitting in a lecture may find that the lecturer makes important points at irregular and unpredictable times during the period; he must then maintain a steady but low level of attention in order not to miss anything. Alternatively, the lecturer may rarely make two important points one right after the other since he builds up to each one over a reasonably constant period of time; the student can then let his mind wander after noting an important point, and gradually increase his attending as time passes. Or perhaps the lecturer always precedes his main points by a conspicuous sign such as moving to the front of the stage; if so, the student can concentrate his attention during those distinct occasions. Preferably, a student will listen with undivided attention throughout a lecture, but if getting the major points down in his notes is what he considers the important reason for his attending the lecture, then his behavior will reflect his changing incentive motivation to listen.

Incentive motivation also helps determine *how* a response is made. To understand this, let us return to the instrumental conditioning situation in which a hungry rat is running down an alley for food. We know that his speed of running depends importantly upon the condition of reinforcement, generally being faster the larger, more immediate and better the quality of the reward. These conditions lead to a high level of incentive and hence a high level of performance.

This interpretation can be made most clearly when the condition involves correlated reinforcement. Typically, reward is simply at the end of the alley and the sooner the rat gets there, the sooner he gets it. In *correlated reinforcement,* some quantitative dimension of the reward, such as its amount, depends upon some quantitative dimension of the response, such as its speed. Specifically, for example, the rat might get a larger reward if he runs slowly than if he runs fast. Under such a condition, the rat learns to run slowly, more slowly than the amount of reward he is receiving would produce under the typical condition. In effect, if the incentive motivation for a slow response is greater than that for a fast response, the former will be the one performed.

Conditions of correlated reinforcement are very prevalent in everyday life and account for all skilled performances. Not only the speed, but the vigor and rate of responding can be precisely controlled if reward is correlated with them. Thus, the skilled lecturer has learned not only how fast to talk but also how loudly to talk and how often to repeat his points depending on the size and background of his audience. This same principle has equally important implications for the design of optimal training programs. Where, for example, fast responses are desirable, they can be encouraged by explicitly giving greater rewards for faster responses. More generally, in controlling the behavior of ourselves and that of others, excellence is most likely to result from correlating reward with the degree of excellence observed.

Hopefully, it is by now clear that our interpretation that rewards affect behavior by determining the level of incentive motivation is *not* incompatible with the principle of positive reinforcement. That principle and the more specific facts describing its applications are empirically sound. The concept of incentive motivation is a way of conceptualizing the way in which rewards work to produce their observed results. As with learning and drive motivation, incentive motivation is hypothetical; none can be directly observed. But they are the presumed underlying processes determining behavior.

## Decision-Making

The concept of incentive motivation can be further enriched by consideration of decision making. In a sense, our earlier descriptions of discrimination and differentiation could have been described as decisions. A rat at a choice point where food is in one arm and not in the other certainly has to decide which way to go, just as does one confronting two stimuli behind only one of which is the reward. But these are not thought of as decision problems because the outcome is obvious in advance: the rat that knows where the food is will certainly go there. It becomes a *decision-making situation* when there are at least two aspects of the reward arranged so that one aspect favors one alternative and the other aspect favors the other alternative.

Decision-making is typically studied with humans, but animals have been shown to be consistent decision-makers. For example, if a rat receives a larger reward in one alley than in another, but has to wait longer for it there, his choice depends on the difference between the amounts relative to the difference between the delays. In similar fashion, if a rat must choose between a small, certain reward and a larger but uncertain reward, his choice depends on the difference in amount relative to the difference in probability. As a final illustration, if a rat has a choice between two alternatives, one of which contains a larger reward but also entails a mild shock punishment, his choice depends on the difference in reward relative to the strength of the shock. In effect, the rat weighs the two alternatives and behaves accordingly.

The important implication of such researches is the concept of *net incentive motivation*. That is to say, if a response is followed by several events, these combine into a single value upon which decisions are made. Suppose, for example, that you are given a choice between a sure one dollar or a one-in-five chance at five dollars. Clearly these alternatives would be equivalent over the long run, but given a single choice, you might prefer one over the other. What you do is to judge the difference in subjective (incentive) value between one and five dollars to you against your subjective estimate of the chances that a five-to-one shot will pay off. Interestingly enough the human's subjective estimate of probabilities does not perfectly match the objective probability; they tend to overestimate low-probability events and to underestimate high-probability events. (This is why novice gamblers usually lose to experts, the latter not betting the "long-shots" where the odds are actually longer than the wager would indicate.) But your choice will depend on the net incentive value of the two choices.

Most theories assume that decisions will display the property of *transitivity*. Specifically, if you indicate a preference for A over B, and also a preference for B over C, then you should indicate a preference for A over C. This property has obtained in all situations studied with animals and most of those studied with humans. However, a lack of transitivity has sometimes been found when humans are choosing among complex alternatives, such as a smoker stating preferences for different brands of cigarettes. It thus appears that attempts to measure the incentive value of outcomes by studying them in a decision-making situation may reveal important interactions.

## To Wit . . .

The only people with no drive motivation are dead. Under some conditions of deprivation, we are motivated to eat, to drink, or to engage in sex. We may be curious and even have a primary drive to learn about ourselves and our environment. In the absence of these, there are a host of socially acquired drives to fall back upon. We have learned the value of money, of social approval, of knowledge. And when we rest, it is not because we have done everything we would like to do, but because fatigue gives rise to a drive for sleep.

Thus motivated for self-preservation and self-actualization, we respond. And as we respond, we learn. The biblical saying, "As ye sow, so shall ye reap!" applies to our own behavior. We learn habits of overt action, from walking and talking through a countless number of everyday behaviors to the virtuoso performance of our special skills. We learn more covert habits of fear and other emotions. And we learn habits of thinking, attitudes toward ourselves and others, beliefs and dreams. If there is a limit to how much the human brain can learn, it is doubtful that anyone has ever tested that limit.

These habits are called into play by their consequences. If emotionally significant events follow upon one or another response in one or another situation, incentive motivation is generated which affects the future likelihood of those responses in those situations. These events service the drives with which the process began, leading on to new situations. Behavior is a continual progression of choice points, confronting us with stimuli among which we have learned to discriminate, requiring responses among which we have learned to differentiate, through which we run because of drive motivation, guided by incentive motivation.

Sometimes we are consciously aware of these processes. We know what we want, we canvas the alternatives one by one, and then deliberately select the one offering the greatest hope of success. But the same processes are taking place even when we are unaware of them and, indeed, even when we can't figure out why we do what we do. Understanding the fundamentals of learning and motivation is important precisely because behavior is inescapably controlled by them.

### True-False Items:  Incentive Motivation

1. The better the reward, the better the learning.

(Reward affects performance as a motivational factor. Indeed, as with drive motivation, incentive motivation may be too high for efficient learning of difficult material, although this fact has not been clearly established. In any event, better rewards do not insure better learning unless they lead to practicing better responses. False.)

2. Learning may occur and not be reflected in performance.

(We can correctly infer that learning has occurred only from a change in performance. However, the learning resulting from practice may be latent and not demonstrated unless motivated. True.)

3. Your tendency to make a response can be changed without your ever having made it.

(While there must be some habits upon which to base performance, your behavior can be radically altered by independent changes in incentive motivation. For example, a youth may never have stolen a woman's purse, but could be induced to do so if offered sufficient reward. True.)

4. Incentive motivation controls behavior only in special situations such as decision-making.

(The situations described in this chapter are the ones that have lead to the view that rewards affect motivation rather than learning. Once having adopted that view, however, it must apply to all situations involving reward or punishment. False.)

5. Your incentive motivation to make a response may change from moment to moment.

(If the likelihood that a response will be rewarded changes from moment to moment in a way you can discriminate, then your incentive motivation will mirror these changes so that you respond only when appropriate. True.)

6. Practice makes perfect.

(Whether practice makes perfect depends upon what is practiced. No amount of practice responding slowly will lead to an ability to respond fast. Indeed, extensive practice at a slow pace may interfere with later learning to respond fast. False.)

7. Racing is an instance of correlated reinforcement.

(In a race, whether you win, place or show depends on how fast you run. Reward is therefore correlated with excellence, and practice under such conditions tends to lead to learning excellence. True.)

8. Man is the only species capable of making real decisions.

(Decisions are required when several differences among the alternatives are pitted against each other. Others animals are capable of making consistent decisions, at least in simple situations. False.)

9. That people take gambles that must lose in the long run contradicts the notion of net incentive motivation.

(People will sometimes take bets even if they have proven mathematically that they are on the losing end of the odds. Nevertheless, we assume that there is sufficient net incentive to them, sometimes called the "utility of gambling." False.)

10. Transitivity is a necessary result of making decision.

(It would appear that a rational decision-maker would always display transitivity in his choices; each alternative has a value that determines his choice. However, lack of transitivity does sometimes occur in complex decisions. False.)

11. A lazy person has no drive motivation.

(His drive motivation may be weak, but a living person is always motivated by some drive or other. The chances, instead, are that he has low incentive motivation to work. False.)

12. Incentive motivation affects our decisions even when we are not consciously aware of evaluating the alternatives.

(Doing something may make us "feel better" even though we don't know why. It is the exception rather than the rule that we contemplate the alternatives; instead, we typically react automatically on the basis of past experiences of success and failure. True.)

# Concluding Remarks

To attempt a scientific understanding of human behavior is one of the most challenging undertakings in the history of man. This book was written in the belief that the fundamentals of learning and motivation, often revealed most simply in the animal laboratory, provide a useful foundation on which to build toward more complex aspects of behavior. The thesis is that these principles *do* apply regardless of the context in which behavior is observed. Certainly additional principles will be required adequately to describe man's behavior in his various personal, social and cultural settings. Nevertheless, a reasonable approach is to apply these fundamental principles to their limit and to incorporate new ideas with the same degree of experimental rigor.

There are many behavior scientists who do not find the approach taken in this book attractive. By-and-large, these are ones who have begun their study of human behavior in more complex contexts and who have found these principles wanting, at least at their present stage of development. And their response has been to devise other language systems which appear more amenable to the variety of emotions, interests, personalities and intellects encountered in such contexts. And this, too, is a reasonable approach since no one can confidently foretell what a comprehensive theory of behavior will look like.

Perhaps more important for the reader than the specific content of this book is the philosophy it reflects toward an understanding of behavior. It thus seems appropriate to end with a few remarks aimed in this direction.

Most important is the belief that behavior is *not* inherently mysterious, magical or mystical. Recall that primitive man was awed by an eclipse of the sun but the modern astronomer can predict one's occurrence years hence to the minute. Our understanding of behavior is

still primitive but we can be confident that there is an objective understanding to be had for everything that happens.

For example, there are the marvels of hypnotism, but this will be
seen as an extreme degree of susceptibility to suggestion and not so
radically different from the everyday influence others exert over us.
Those bewildering night dreams will be seen as meaningful by-products
of the brain's restorative processes. And when a husband and wife discover they are separately reminiscing about the same scene, we will
find that unnoticed stimuli in their environment have led to the same
associations. We may be tantalized by the unexplained, but this is not
to say they are inexplicable.

The explanation will come from a variety of sources. We are born
with an unknown number of behavioral capacities, tendencies and dispositions. We inherit our parents, our siblings and our social group
and are molded importantly by them. We live in an environment of
physical and chemical substances which affect our bodies and nervous
systems and hence our behavior. Not only do we develop specific
habits for specific situations but we tend to integrate these into a consistent style of life, a personality. We behave not only on the basis of
our own personal experiences, but also in concert with the behavior
of others around us whose experiences have been different. Learning
and motivation are but a part of psychology which, in turn, is but a
part of the total behavioral science enterprise.

These fundamental principles should have a sobering influence as
one moves on to other aspects of behavior. Whether one is dealing in
the home, the school, or the office, whether the behavior be economic,
political or social, whether one is performing routine functions, search-
ing for new solutions or contemplating creative ideas—in short, every-
where, all the time we are behaving in accord with our learning history
and the motives and expectations aroused in those situations. Psychology
is not a subject that should be packed away with one's notes and
textbook once the course is over. It is an attitude toward the understanding of behavior based on an uncompromising objectivity.

Science will never answer our questions about ultimate meaning and
purpose. It does not even aspire to do so. But scientific knowledge
should constrain our speculations and thus aim us closer to the Truth.
The first rule of science is to deny one's natural tendency to attend
selectively to those facts that tend to support his beliefs while ignoring
contradictory facts. Science continuously demands an "agonizing re-
appraisal."

For this reason, the fundamentals described in this book are dated.
Most of them have stood the test of sufficient time for experimental

analysis so that we can act on them with confidence. These are the facts and principles that have formed the content core of this book. Some, however, are now in a stage of rapid transition. These are the more theoretical propositions that have guided the organization of the relevant, contemporary knowledge. Unquestionably, these latter will respond to the endless parade of future research. Hopefully, however, they will provide a basis for a continuing evolution of our scientific understanding of behavior.

# Glossary

**Act:** A response defined by its consequences in physically altering the environment or the organism's relationship to it.

**Act, receptor-orienting:** The response of directing one's receptors toward a source of stimulation.

**Adaptation, sensory:** A physiological process whereby a receptor becomes less responsive during prolonged stimulation.

**Attention:** A psychological process of selecting from among the available stimuli those to which to respond.

**Aversive event:** A stimulus the termination of which leads to an increase in the probability of responses which precede that termination.

**Avoidance learning:** The acquisition of a response which prevents the occurrence of an aversive event.

**Avoidance, nondiscriminated:** Responding to prevent the occurrence of an aversive event which is not preceded by a warning signal but occurs regularly.

**Behavior chain:** A sequence of responses strung together in order to accomplish a goal.

**Condition of reinforcement:** The momentary, descriptive properties of a reward, such as its amount, delay and quality.

**Conditioning, classical:** A procedure in which a conditioned stimulus regularly precedes an unconditioned stimulus, the latter of which elicits a response that becomes conditioned to the former.

**Conditioning, differential classical:** A procedure in which two similar conditioned stimuli occur in an unpredictable order but only one is followed by the unconditioned stimulus.

**Conditioning, differential instrumental:** A procedure in which a response is periodically enabled, but is rewarded only in the presence of one stimulus and not in the presence of another similar stimulus.

**Conditioning, differential operant:** A procedure in which a freely available response is rewarded in the presence of one stimulus and not in the presence of another similar stimulus.

**Conditioning, higher-order:** A procedure in which a conditioned stimulus precedes a stimulus which elicits a response because of prior conditioning.

**205**

**Conditioning, instrumental:** A procedure in which a response is periodically enabled, its speed or vigor depending on the condition of reinforcement.

**Conditioning, operant:** A procedure in which a response is freely available, its rate of occurrence depending on the schedule of reinforcement.

**Conditioning, temporal:** A procedure in which an unconditioned stimulus occurs at regular intervals of time but is not preceded by a conditioned stimulus.

**Context:** The general environment in which learning occurs.

**Counterconditioning:** A procedure in which a new, incompatible response is learned to supplant a previously learned response.

**Decision-making situation:** A choice in which the reward is arranged so that one aspect favors one alternative and another aspect favors the other alternative.

**Decrement, stimulus generalization:** The loss in response strength resulting from a change in the stimulus situation.

**Differentiation learning:** Choosing a response or a way of responding based on prior differential reinforcement.

**Discrimination learning:** Choosing a stimulus to which to respond based on prior differential reinforcement.

**Disinhibition:** The reappearance of an extinguished response in the presence of an unusual context.

**Displacement:** The greater tendency to respond to different stimuli than to the original stimulus itself, based on both reward and punishment to the original stimulus.

**Drive, irrelevant:** A drive that is not appropriate to the nature of the reward that has been experienced for making a response.

**Drive motivation:** The internal source of energy driving the organism to do something, often based on biological needs.

**Drive, primary:** Conditions which tend to arouse the organism without any special training or experience.

**Drive, secondary:** Conditions which were originally neutral but arouse the organism as a result of prior association with aversive events.

**Drive stimulus:** The distinctive internal cues that arise in conjunction with the different drives.

**Escape learning:** The acquisition of a response that leads to termination of an aversive event.

**Extinction, experimental:** The procedure of consistently not reinforcing a learned response, leading to a gradual decrease in response strength.

**Extinction, resistance to:** A measure of the number of times that a learned response will persist after all reinforcement for the response is stopped.

**Feedback:** Stimuli produced by responses, both in terms of feeling the response occur and in terms of observing its effect on the environment.

**Feedback, positive:** Feedback which tends to increase the very response producing the feedback.

**Feedback, negative:** Feedback which tends to produce responding so as to remove the feedback.

**Fixation:** An increase in the persistence of a response produced by punishing it.

**Frustration:** The emotional response experienced when a previously rewarded response is not rewarded.

**Generalization, gradient of:** The fact that there is less tendency to make a learned response the more different a test stimulus is from the original one.

**Generalization, response:** The tendency to make responses similar to the one learned if that one is blocked.

**Generalization, semantic:** The tendency for humans to generalize responses to words with different sounds but similar meanings.

**Generalization, stimulus:** The tendency to make a learned response to stimuli that are similar to the original one.

**Goal gradient:** The tendency for response strength to change progressively as a goal is approached.

**Habit:** The theoretical term for the hypothesized internal process representing a learned association between a stimulus and response.

**Incentive motivation:** The internal source of energy based on the expectation of reward for making a particular response.

**Inhibition:** The theoretical term for the hypothesized internal process opposing habit.

**Inhibition, external:** The fact that a learned response is weaker in an unusual context.

**Instinct:** A complex chain of behaviors performed without the benefit of learning.

**Interval, interstimulus:** The interval of time between the conditioned and unconditioned stimuli in classical conditioning.

**Latent learning:** Learning resulting from practice without reward and hence not evident in performance unless incentive motivation is provided.

**Learning:** A relatively permanent process resulting from practice and reflected in a change in performance.

**Learning set:** The fact that organisms can learn a new problem faster if they have had experience with other problems of the same type.

**Movement:** Glandular secretions or muscular actions that have no direct, physical effect upon the external environment.

**Neurosis, experimental:** Maladjustive behavior in animals produced by strong conflict.

**Operant level:** The rate at which a freely-available response occurs if the consequences of that response are neutral (neither rewarding nor punishing).

**Punishment:** A procedure in which a response is followed by an aversive event.

**Punishment, negative:** Punishment accomplished by removing something emotionally-positive.

**Punishment, positive:** Punishment accomplished by applying something emotionally-negative.

**Redintegration:** The process of inferring a total complex stimulus from observing only a part of it.

**Reinforcement:** A procedure in which a response is followed by a rewarding event.

**Reinforcement, correlated:** A procedure in which some quantitative dimension of the reward, such as its amount, depends upon some quantitative dimension of the response, such as its speed.

**Reinforcement, differential:** A procedure in which the schedule or condition of reinforcement differs between stimuli or responses.

**Reinforcement, negative:** Reinforcement accomplished by the removal of an emotionally-negative event.

**Reinforcement, nondifferential:** The procedure of giving the same schedule or condition of reinforcement to different stimuli or responses.

**Reinforcement, partial:** The procedure of rewarding a response on only a portion of its occurrences.

**Reinforcement, positive:** Reinforcement accomplished by giving an emotionally-positive event.

**Reinforcement, primary:** An event that functions as a reward without any special training.

**Reinforcement, secondary:** An event that functions as a reward by virtue of having been associated with rewarding events.

**Response:** Any glandular secretion, muscular action, or other objectively identifiable aspect of the behavior of an organism.

**Response, anticipatory:** A response that antedates its original time of occurrence as a result of stimuli which precede it.

**Response, alternation:** The tendency not to repeat the same response right away even if it was rewarded.

**Response, avoidance:** A response which prevents the occurrence of an aversive event.

**Response, conditioned:** The learned response to the conditioned stimulus resulting from being paired with an unconditioned stimulus.

**Response, consummatory:** The act which reduces a deprivation drive, that is, eating, drinking, or copulating.

**Response, escape:** The response which terminates an aversive state of affairs.

**Response, incompatible:** A response which physically can not be performed at the same time as another response.

**Response, instrumental:** An act that is periodically enabled by the environment and which may produce reward or punishment.

**Response, latency:** The amount of time after the occurrence of a stimulus before the response occurs.

**Response, learnable:** A response which can become associated with originally ineffective stimuli or which can be modified by experience.

**Response, operant:** A response that is freely available to the organism and which may produce reward or punishment.

**Response, unconditioned:** The response elicited reflexively by the unconditioned stimulus.

**Satiation, response:** The reduced tendency to select a response as a result of repeated performance.

**Satiation, stimulus:** The tendency to avoid responding to the same stimulus right away even if it was rewarded.

**Schedule of reinforcement:** The occasions on which an operant response is reinforced, based either on the passage of time or the counting of responses.

**Schedule, continuous reinforcement:** A schedule in which every response is reinforced.

**Schedule, fixed interval:** A schedule in which the time between reinforcements is a constant, although one response must be made at the end of each interval to receive reward.

**Schedule, fixed ratio:** A schedule in which a constant number of responses is required in order to obtain reward.

**Schedule, mixed:** A schedule in which two (or more) simple schedules are combined so that sometimes one is in effect and sometimes another, without any external signal informing the organism which is which.

**Schedule, multiple:** A schedule in which two (or more) simple schedules are combined so that sometimes one is in effect and sometimes another, and where distinctive external stimuli signal which is which.

**Schedule, variable interval:** A schedule in which the time between reinforcements is variable, although one response must be made at the end of each interval to receive reward.

**Schedule, variable ratio:** A schedule in which a variable number of responses is required in order to obtain reward.

**Shaping:** The procedure of rewarding successive approximations to the desired response.

**Spontaneous recovery:** The fact that an extinguished response may reappear on a subsequent presentation of the CS after a lapse of time.

**Stimulus:** Formally, any adequate change in energy falling upon an appropriate sensory receptor. Functionally, any event that functions as such in the principles of behavior.

**Stimulus, conditioned:** A stimulus which initially does not elicit the response in question, but comes to do so as a result of being paired with an unconditioned stimulus.

**Stimulus, trace:** The hypothesized events in the nervous system resulting when an organism is stimulated, and which persist for some time after the stimulus is removed.

**Stimulus, unconditioned:** A stimulus which reflexively elicits a response.

**Superstition:** A response learned as a result of being adventitiously followed by a reward even though it did not actually produce the reward.

**Transposition:** The tendency to select from among new stimuli on the basis of the same relationship as previously reinforced.

# ————————— Suggested
# Readings for Further Study

Beecroft, R. S. *Classical conditioning.* Goleta, California: Psychonomic Press, 1966.

Brown, J. S. *The motivation of behavior.* New York: McGraw-Hill, 1961.

Bugelski, B. R. *The psychology of learning applied to teaching.* Indianapolis: Bobbs-Merrill, 1964.

Deese, J. *The psychology of learning.* New York: McGraw-Hill, 1958.

Dollard, J., & Miller, N. E. *Personality and psychotherapy.* New York: McGraw-Hill, 1950.

Hill, W. F. *Learning: A survey of psychological interpretations.* San Francisco: Chandler, 1963.

Kimble, G. A. *Hilgard and Marquis' conditioning and learning.* New York: Appleton-Century-Crofts, 1961.

Logan, F. A., & Wagner, A. R. *Reward and punishment.* Boston: Allyn & Bacon, 1965.

Osgood, C. E. *Method and theory in experimental psychology.* New York: Oxford University Press, 1953.

Reynolds, G. S. *A primer of operant conditioning.* New York: Scott-Foresman, 1968.

Riley, D. A. *Discrimination learning.* Boston: Allyn & Bacon, 1966.

Skinner, B. F. *Science and human behavior.* New York: Macmillan, 1953.

# References

*The following treatises represent the bases for various discussions within the text. They are listed here by subject for those who care to pursue a specific point.*

## Introduction to Learning

BEHAVIORIST APPROACH
Watson, J. B. *Behavior, An introduction to comparative psychology.* New York: Holt, Rinehart and Winston, 1914.

COGNITIVE APPROACH
Tolman, E. C. *Purposive behavior in animals and men.* New York: Appleton-Century-Crofts, 1932.

## The Stimulus

TIMING A RESPONSE
Logan, F. A. Variable DRL. *Psychonomic Science,* 1967, 9:393-394.

STIMULUS CHANGE
Logan, F. A., and Wagner, A. R. Direction of change in CS in eyelid conditioning. *Journal of Experimental Psychology,* 1962, 64:325-326.

ODDITY
Meyer, D. R., and Harlow, H. F. The development of transfer of response to patterning by monkeys. *Journal of Comparative and Physiological Psychology,* 1949, 42:454-462.

CONTEXT
Logan, F. A. Specificity of discrimination learning to the original context. *Science,* 1961, 133:1355-1356.

DELAYED FEEDBACK
Mowrer, O. H. *Learning theory and behavior.* New York: Wiley, 1960.

SENSORY ADAPTATION
Hecht, S. The influence of light adaptation on subsequent dark adaptation of
  the eye. *Journal of General Physiology*, 1937, 20:831-852.

RECEPTOR-ORIENTING ACTS
Tolman, E. C. The determiners of behavior at a choice point. *Psychological
  Review*, 1938, 45:1-41.

ATTENTION
Wagner, A. R., Logan, F. A., Haberlandt, K., and Price, T. Stimulus selection
  in animal discrimination learning. *Journal of Experimental Psychology*,
  1968, 76:171-180.

STIMULUS SATIATION
Glanzer, M. The role of stimulus satiation in spontaneous alternation. *Journal
  of Experimental Psychology*, 1953, 45:387-393.

## The Response

MOVEMENTS AND ACTS
Guthrie, E. R. *The psychology of learning*. New York: Harper and Row, 1952.

PUPILLARY CONTRACTION
Cason, H. The conditioned pupillary reaction. *Journal of Experimental Psychology*, 1922, 5:108-146.

SECRETION OF INTERNAL ORGANS
Miller, N. E. Learning of visceral and glandular responses. *Science*, 1969,
  163:434-445.

OPERANT LEVEL
Skinner, B. F. *The behavior of organisms*. New York: Appleton-Century-Crofts,
  1938.

QUANTITATIVE DIMENSIONS AS LEARNABLE RESPONSES
Notterman, J. M. Force emission during bar pressing. *Journal of Experimental
  Psychology*, 1959, 58:341-347.

RESPONSE ALTERNATION
Montgomery, K. C. "Spontaneous alternation" as a function of time between
  trials and amount of work. *Journal of Experimental Psychology*, 1951,
  42:82-93.

RESPONSE SATIATION VS. STIMULUS SATIATION
Montgomery, K. C. A test of two explanations of spontaneous alternation.
  *Journal of Comparative and Physiological Psychology*, 1952, 45:287-293.

## Classical Conditioning

CLASSICAL CONDITIONING
Pavlov, I. P. *Conditioned reflexes*. London: Oxford University Press, 1927.

NONAVOIDANCE
Logan, F. A. A comparison of avoidance and nonavoidance eyelid conditioning. *Journal of Experimental Psychology*, 1951, 42:390-392.

INSTRUCTIONS

Hilgard, E. R., and Humphreys, L. G. The effect of supporting and antagonistic voluntary instructions on conditioned discrimination. *Journal of Experimental Psychology*, 1938, 22:291-304.

ANTICIPATORY RESPONSE IN MAZE

Spragg, S. D. S. Anticipatory responses in serial learning by chimpanzees. *Comparative Psychology Monographs*, 1936, 13:No. 2.

COURSE OF CONDITIONING

Spence, K. W. *Behavior theory and conditioning*. New Haven: Yale University Press, 1956.

INTENSITY OF CS

Hovland, C. I. The generalization of conditioned Responses: III. Extinction, spontaneous recovery, and disinhibition of conditioned and generalized responses. *Journal of Experimental Psychology*, 1937, 21:47-62.

INTENSITY OF US

Passey, G. E. The influence of intensity of unconditioned stimulus upon acquisition of a conditioned response. *Journal of Experimental Psychology*, 1948, 38:420-428.

DISTRIBUTION OF CONDITIONING TRIALS

Humphreys, L. G. Distributed practice in the development of the conditioned eyelid reaction. *Journal of General Psychology*, 1940, 22:379-385.

STIMULUS INCONGRUITY

Grant, D. A. Adding communication to the signalling property of the CS in classical conditioning. *Journal of General Psychology*, 1968, 79:147-175.

INTERSTIMULUS INTERVAL

Reynolds, B. The acquisition of a trace conditioned response as a function of the magnitude of the stimulus trace. *Journal of Experimental Psychology*, 1945, 35:15-30.

BACKWARD CONDITIONING

White, C. T., and Schlosberg, H. Degree of conditioning of the GSR as a function of the period of delay. *Journal of Experimental Psychology*, 1952, 43:357-362.

LATENCY OF CR

Spooner, A., and Kellogg, W. N. The backward conditioning curve. *American Journal of Psychology*, 1947, 60:321-324.

GENERALIZATION OF CR

Bass, M. J., and Hull, C. L. The irradiation of a tactile conditioned reflex in man. *Journal of Comparative Psychology*, 1934, 17:47-65.

EXTERNAL INHIBITION

Pavlov, I. P. *Lectures on conditioned reflexes*. New York: International, 1928.

EXPERIMENTAL EXTINCTION

Prokasy, W. F. Extinction and spontaneous recovery of conditioned eyelid responses as a function of amount of acquisition and extinction training. *Journal of Experimental Psychology*, 1958, 56:319-324.

SPONTANEOUS RECOVERY

Ellson, D. G. Spontaneous recovery of the galvanic skin response as a function of the recovery interval. *Journal of Experimental Psychology*, 1939, 25:586-600.

TEMPORAL SEQUENCE OF STIMULI
Masserman, J. H. *Behavior and neurosis.* Chicago: University of Chicago Press, 1943.


## Theory of Classical Conditioning

THEORY
Hull, C. L. *Principles of behavior.* New York: Appleton-Century-Crofts, 1943.

PERMANENCE OF HABIT
Hilgard, E. R., and Marquis, D. G. Acquisition, extinction, and retention of conditioned lid responses to light in dogs. *Journal of Comparative Psychology,* 1935, 19:29-58.

DISINHIBITION
Mednick, S. A., and Wild, C. Reciprocal augmentation of generalization and anxiety. *Journal of Experimental Psychology,* 1962, 63:621-626.

EXPERIMENTAL NEUROSIS
Pavlov, I. P. *Conditioned reflexes and psychiatry.* New York: International Publishers, 1941.


## Positive Reinforcement

SUPERSTITION
Skinner, B. F. "Superstition" in the pigeon. *Journal of Experimental Psychology,* 1948, 38:168-172.

AWARENESS
Greenspoon, J. The reinforcing effect of two spoken sounds on the frequency of two responses. *American Journal of Psychology,* 1955, 68:409-416.

ELECTRICAL STIMULUS OF THE BRAIN
Olds, J., and Milner, P. Positive reinforcement produced by electrical stimulation of septal area and other region of rat brain. *Journal of Comparative and Physiological Psychology,* 1954, 47:419-427.

DRIVE-REDUCTION HYPOTHESIS
Hull, C. L. The conflicting psychologies of learning—a way out. *Psychological Review,* 1935, 42:491-516.

SACCHARINE
Sheffield, F. E., and Roby, T. B. Reward value of a non-nutritive sweet taste. *Journal of Comparative Physiological Psychology,* 1950, 43:471-481.

SEXUAL STIMULATION
Sheffield, F. D., Wulff, J. J., and Backer, R. Reward value of copulation without sex drive reduction. *Journal of Comparative and Physiological Psychology,* 1951, 44:3-8.

PUZZLES
Harlow, H. F. Learning and satiation of responses in intrinsically motivated complex puzzle performance by monkeys. *Journal of Comparative and Physiological Psychology,* 1950, 43:289-294.

Exploration

Butler, R. A. Discrimination learning by rhesus monkeys to visual-exploration motivation. *Journal of Comparative and Physiological Psychology,* 1953, 46:95-98.

Persistence with Secondary Reinforcer

Bugelski, R. Extinction with and without sub-goal reinforcement. *Journal of Comparative Psychology,* 1938, 26:121-134.

Learning for Secondary Reinforcement

Schoenfeld, W. N., Antonitis, J. J., Bersh, P. J. A preliminary study of the training conditions necessary for secondary reinforcement. *Journal of Experimental Psychology,* 1950, 40:40-45.

Token-Reward

Cowles, J. T. Food tokens as incentives for learning by chimpanzees. *Comparative Psychology Monographs,* 1937, 14:No. 5.

High-probability Behaviors

Premack, D. Toward empirical behavior laws. I. Positive reinforcement. *Psychological Review,* 1959, 66:219-233.

Operant Conditioning

Ferster, C. S., and Skinner, B. F. *Schedules of reinforcement.* New York: Appleton-Century-Crofts, 1957.

Amount of Reward in Instrumental Learning

Crespi, L. P. Quantitative variations of incentive and performance in the white rat. *American Journal of Psychology,* 1942, 55:467-517.

Amount of Reward in Free Behavior

Logan, F. A. The free behavior situation. In *Nebraska Symposium on Motivation.* Lincoln: University of Nebraska Press, 1964.

Changes in Amount of Reward

Zeaman, D. Response latency as a function of the amount of reinforcement. *Journal of Experimental Psychology,* 1949, 39:466-483.

Delay of Reward

Logan, F. A. The role of delay of reinforcement in determining reaction potential. *Journal of Experimental Psychology,* 1952, 43:393-399.

Goal Gradient

Hull, C. L. The goal gradient hypothesis and maze learning. *Psychological Review,* 1932, 39:25-43.

## Negative Reinforcement

Escape Learning

Bower, G. H. Partial and correlated reward in escape learning. *Journal of Experimental Psychology,* 1960, 59:126-130.

Avoidance Learning

Mowrer, O. H. A stimulus-response analysis of anxiety and its role as a reinforcing agent. *Psychological Review,* 1939, 46:553-565.

Nondiscriminated Avoidance

Sidman, M. The temporal parameters of the maintenance of avoidance behavior by the white rat. *Journal of Comparative and Physiological Psychology,* 1953, 46:253-261.

Persistance of Avoidance Response

Solomon, R. L., and Wynne, L. C. Traumatic avoidance learning: The principles of anxiety conservation and partial irreversibility. *Psychological Review*, 1954, 61:353-385.

Helplessness

Maier, S. F., Seligman, M. E. P., and Solomon, R. L. Pavlovian fear conditioning and learned helplessness. In B. A. Campbell and R. M. Church (Eds.), *Punishment and aversive control*. New York: Appleton-Century-Crofts, 1969.

Elicited Aggression

Ulrich, R. E., and Azrin, N. H. Reflexive fighting in response to aversive stimulation. *Journal of Experimental Analysis of Behavior*, 1962, 5:511-521.


Response Persistence

Stimulus Variability

Brown, J. S., and Bass, B. The acquisition and extinction of an instrumental response under constant and variable stimulus conditions. *Journal of Comparative and Physiological Psychology*, 1958, 51:499-504.

Response Variability

Ferraro, D. P., and Branch, K. M. Variability of response location during regular and partial reinforcement. *Psychological Reports*, 1968, 23:1023-1031.

Partial Reinforcement Effect

Lewis, D. J. Partial reinforcement: A selective review of the literature since 1950. *Psychological Bulletin*, 1960, 57:1-28.

Frustration

Amsel, A. The role of frustrative nonreward in noncontinuous reward situations. *Psychological Bulletin*, 1958, 55:102-119.

Generalized Partial Reinforcement Effect

Brown, R. T., and Logan, F. A. Generalized partial reinforcement effect. *Journal of Comparative and Physiological Psychology*, 1965, 60:64-69.

Fixation

Farber, I. E. Response fixation under anxiety and non-anxiety conditions. *Journal of Experimental Psychology*, 1948, 38:111-131.

Partial Reinforcement Effect on Resistance to Punishment

Brown, R. T., and Wagner, A. R. Resistance to punishment and extinction following training with shock or nonreinforcement. *Journal of Experimental Psychology*, 1964, 68:503-507.

Amount of Reward

Wagner, A. R. Effects of amount and percentage of reinforcement and number of acquisition trials on conditioning and extinction. *Journal of Experimental Psychology*, 1961, 62:234-242.

Distribution of Extinction Trials

Reynolds, B. Extinction of trace conditioned response as a function of the spacing of trials during the acquisition and extinction series. *Journal of Experimental Psychology*, 1945, 35:81-95.

EXTINCTION TO GENERALIZED STIMULI
Guttman, N., and Kalish, H. I. Discriminability and stimulus generalization. *Journal of Experimental Psychology*, 1956, 51:79-88.

FORGETTING
Underwood, B. J., and Postman, L. Extra-experimental sources of interference in forgetting. *Psychological Review*, 1960, 67:73-95.

SUPPRESSION BY PUNISHMENT
Estes, W. K. An experimental study of punishment. *Psychological Monographs*, 1944, 57:No. 263.

FACILITATION BY PUNISHMENT
Muenzinger, K. F. Motivation in learning. I. Electric shock for correct response in the visual discrimination habit. *Journal of Comparative Psychology*, 1935, 17:267-277.

## Generalization, Discrimination and Differentiation

STIMULUS GENERALIZATION
Mostofsky, D. I. (Ed.) *Stimulus generalization*. Stanford: Stanford University Press, 1965.

RESPONSE GENERALIZATION
Wickens, D. D. The transference of conditioned excitation and conditioned inhibition from one muscle group to the antagonistic muscle group. *Journal of Experimental Psychology*, 1938, 22:101-123.

SEMANTIC GENERALIZATION
Razran, G. A quantitative study of meaning by conditioned salivary technique (semantic conditioning). *Science*, 1939, 90:89-91.

GENERALIZATION AND REINFORCEMENT VARIABILITY
Hearst, E., Koresko, M. B., and Poppen, R. Stimulus generalization and the response-reinforcement contingency. *Journal of Experimental Analysis of behavior*, 1964, 7:369-380.

GENERALIZATION AND PUNISHMENT
Honig, W. K., and Slivka, R. M. Stimulus generalization of the effects of punishment. *Journal of Experimental Analysis of Behavior*, 1964, 7:21-25.

GENERALIZATION AND AMOUNT OF REWARD
Dickson, J. F., and Thomas, D. R. Operant discrimination learning and stimulus generalization as a function of reward exposure. *Journal of Comparative and Physiological Psychology*, 1963, 56:829-833.

GENERALIZATION AND EXTENDED TRAINING
Thompson, R. F. Primary stimulus generalization as a function of acquisition level in the cat. *Journal of Comparative and Physiological Psychology*, 1958, 51:601-606.

NONDIFFERENTIAL REINFORCEMENT WITH PUNISHMENT
Maier, N. R. F. *Frustration, the study of behavior without a goal*. New York: McGraw-Hill, 1949.

TRANSPOSITION
Spence, K. W. The differential response in animals to stimuli varying within a single dimension. *Psychological Review*, 1937, 44:430-444.

RELATIONAL LEARNING

Woodbury, C. B. The learning of stimulus patterns by dogs. *Journal of Comparative Psychology*, 1943, 35:29-40.

TRANSPOSITION IN CHILDREN

Kendler, H. H., and Kendler, T. S. Vertical and horizontal processes in problem solving. *Psychological Review*, 1962, 69:1-16.

TRANSFER OF DISCRIMINATION

Lawrence, D. H. The transfer of a discrimination along a continuum. *Journal of Comparative and Physiological Psychology*, 1952, 45:511-516.

LEARNING TO LEARN

Harlow, H. F. The formation of learning sets. *Psychological Review*, 1949, 56:51-65.

ERRORLESS DISCRIMINATION LEARNING

Terrace, H. S. Discrimination learning with and without errors. *Journal of Experimental Analysis of Behavior*, 1963, 6:1-27.

## Introduction to Motivation

CURIOSITY

Berlyne, D. E. *Conflict, arousal and curiosity.* New York: McGraw-Hill, 1960.

COMBINATION OF LEARNING AND MOTIVATION

Spence, K. W. Learning and performance in eyelid conditioning as a function of the intensity of the UCS. *Journal of Experimental Psychology*, 1953, 45:57-63.

MOTIVATION AND TASK DIFFICULTY

Yerkes, R. M., and Dodson, J. D. The relation of strength of stimulus to rapidity of habit formation. *Journal of Comparative Neurological Psychology*, 1908, 18:459-482.

DRIVE STIMULI

Hull, C. L. Differential habituation to internal stimuli in the albino rat. *Journal of Comparative Psychology*, 1933, 16:255-273.

IRRELEVANT DRIVE

Kendler, H. H. Drive interaction: II. Experimental analysis of the role of drive in learning theory. *Journal of Experimental Psychology*, 1945, 35:188-198.

"STAMPING IN" BY REWARD

Thorndike, E. L. The law of effect. *American Journal of Psychology*, 1927, 29:212-222.

## Primary Motivation

PAIN

Sanders, F. K. Special senses, cutaneous sensation. *Annual Review of Physiology*, 1947, 9:553-568.

RECIPROCAL ACTION OF NERVOUS SYSTEM

Sherrington, C. S. *The integrative action of the nervous system.* New Haven: Yale University Press, 1906.

BIOLOGICAL BASES OF HUNGER AND THIRST
Miller, N. E. Experiments on motivation: Studies combining psychological, physiological and pharmacological techniques. *Science,* 1957, 126:1271-1278.

DRIVE ON PERFORMANCE
Yamaguchi, H. G. Drive (D) as a function of hours of hunger (h). *Journal of Experimental Psychology,* 1951, 42:108-117.

CHANGES IN DRIVE
Perin, C. T. Behavior potentiality as a joint function of the amount of training and the degree of hunger at the time of extinction. *Journal of Experimental Psychology,* 1942, 30:93-113.

FOOD PREFERENCES
Young, P. T. Appetite, palatability and feeding habit: A critical review. *Psychological Bulletin,* 1948, 45:289-320.

SPECIFIC HUNGERS
Richter, C. P. Total self-regulatory functions in animals and human beings. *Harvey Lectures,* 1942-43, 38:63-103.

EFFECT OF CASTRATION
Beach, F. A. Copulatory behavior in prepuberally castrated male rats and its modification by estrogen administration. *Endocrinology,* 1942, 31:679-683.

SEX AND EARLY EXPERIENCE
Alexander, B. K., and Harlow, H. F. Social behavior of juvenile rhesus monkeys subjected to different rearing conditions during the first six months of life. *Zoologische Jahrbucher—Physiology,* 1965, 71:489-508.

SEX AND LEARNING
Beach, F. A. Instinctive behavior: Reproductive activities. In S. S. Stevens (Ed.), *Handbook of experimental psychology.* New York: Wiley, 1951.

INCOMPATIBILITY OF HUNGER AND THIRST
Grossman, S. P. Effects of adrenergic and cholinergic blocking agents on hypothalamic mechanisms. *American Journal of Physiology,* 1062, 202:1230-1236.

EXECUTIVE MONKEY
Brady, J., Porter, R., Conrad, D., and Mason, J. Avoidance behavior and the development of gastroduodenal ulcers. *Journal of Experimental Analysis of Behavior,* 1958, 1:69-72.

## Secondary Motivation

DRINKING WHILE WORKING FOR FOOD
Falk, J. L. The motivational properties of schedule-induced polydipsia. *Journal of Experimental Analysis of Behavior,* 1966, 9:19-25.

DRIVES ENERGIZE
Brown, J. S., Kalish, H. I., and Farber, I. E. Conditioned fear as revealed by magnitude of startle response to an auditory stimulus. *Journal of Experimental Psychology,* 1951, 41:317-328.

DRIVE REDUCTION IS REINFORCING

Miller, N. E. Studies of fear as an acquirable drive: I. Fear as motivation and fear-reduction as reinforcement in the learning of new responses. *Journal of Experimental Psychology,* 1948, 38:89-101.

FEAR AND THIRST

Miller, N. E. Some recent studies of conflict behavior and drugs. *American Psychologist,* 1961, 16:12-24.

HUNGER AND SECONDARY MOTIVATION

Myers, A. K., Miller, N. E. Failure to find a learned drive based on hunger; evidence for learning motivated by "exploration." *Journal of Comparative and Physiological Psychology,* 1954, 47:428-436.

FRUSTRATION

Amsel, A., and Roussel, J. Motivational properties of frustration: I. Effect on a running response of the addition of frustration to the motivational complex. *Journal of Experimental Psychology,* 1952, 43:363-368.

EFFECT OF PUNISHING FEAR

Brown, J. S., Martin, R. C., and Morrow, M. W. Self-punitive behavior in the rat; facilitative effects of punishment on resistance to extinction. *Journal of Comparative and Physiological Psychology,* 1964, 57:127-133.


## Incentive Motivation

LATENT LEARNING

Blodgett, H. D. The effect of the introduction of reward upon the maze performance of rats. *University of California Publications in Psychology,* 1929, 4:113-134.

LATENT EXTINCTION

Moltz, H. Latent extinction and the fractional anticipatory response mechanism. *Psychological Review,* 1957, 64:229-241.

CORRELATED REINFORCEMENT

Logan, F. A. *Incentive.* New Haven: Yale University Press, 1960.

DECISION-MAKING

Logan, F. A. Decision-making by rats. *Journal of Comparative and Physiological Psychology,* 1965, 59:1-12 and 246-251.

SUBJECTIVE PROBABILITY

Edwards, W. Utility, subjective probability, their interaction and variance preference. *Journal of Conflict Resolution,* 1962, 6:42-51.

TRANSITIVITY

Edwards, W. The theory of decision making. *Psychological Bulletin,* 1954, 51:380-417.